THE MINES & MINING MEN OF MENHENIOT

STEPHEN BARTLETT

TWELVEHEADS PRESS

TRURO • 1994

CONTENTS

TWELVEHEADS PRESS

First published 1994 by Twelveheads Press,
Chy Mengleth, Twelveheads, Truro, Cornwall TR4 8SN.

ISBN 0 906294 31 2
British Library Cataloguing-in-Publication Data.
A catalogue record for this book is available from the British Library.

Printed by The Amadeus Press Ltd.,
Huddersfield, Yorks.

Front cover illustration:
Wheal Hony and Trelawny United. Former mine offices and weighbridge alongside the surviving chimney of Smith's engine house. *A. Kittridge 1993*

FOREWORD

MINES AND MINING MEN OF MENHENIOT represents the fruits of a long and detailed journey back into the life of a small east Cornwall community in the nineteenth century. It was a community steeped in a farming background but which from 1843 became the centre of a lead mining boom which saw the population double and a potential powder keg of cultures and lifestyles intermix, as massive engine houses dominated the skyline and the noise of working mines hung in the air. The steady thump of the largest pumping engines, intermittent activity of racing winding engines or the distinctive sound of the working stamps are all difficult to imagine in the tranquil Menheniot of today, which has long since returned to its agricultural roots. Nature and time have conspired to cover up much of that past, with woods and lush undergrowth healing any scars of the past, as such ivy clad ruins and waste tips that remain blend easily with the picturesque Menheniot of today.

What follows is first and foremost a mining history and indeed is a detailed coverage of mining in the parish from that early start in 1843 through to the early years of this century, incorporating all mines large and small; the first such comprehensive history to be published. However, it is also very much a story about people and much of that long journey which the writer took involved establishing the stories behind those who opened up and worked the mines themselves - adventurers, managers, pursers, mine agents and the working miners and their families. A whole section in itself emerged around that expanding population, with migrations in the 1840s and 1850s from western Cornwall, St Austell and the Devon border, all at a time when many western Cornish miners were taking the more publicised emigration routes to Australia, America and other far flung lands. These previously less well documented movements form yet another part of the Menheniot mining story, whilst in the overall context of Cornish social history tell yet another part of the county's mining story. The social make-up of the village, the miners' personal stories traced from the past and the book's appendices setting out comprehensive data on age and occupation profiles within the parish, will together hopefully add something to our general knowledge of Cornish communities in the nineteenth century, building on the work of A. K. Hamilton Jenkin and others.

I cannot claim to be a Menheniot resident, but can claim a particular link with the community's past for my great, great grandfather William Bartlett (1831-1908) was of parish farm labouring stock. He became a Menheniot lead miner and it was mining again which shaped his later life, forcing him to leave Menheniot in the 1870s as the largest mines closed. We do not know at which mine he worked, but the knowledge that much of what follows was seen and experienced by him has added a personal aspect and impetus to what has by necessity become an all embracing project. I have dedicated the book to that same William Bartlett - for what he saw a later generation has rediscovered and recorded for posterity.

Finally a word of caution. Much of Menheniot's mining past is hidden in deep undergrowth. Such old shafts that remain whilst usually capped or walled are potentially dangerous. All lie on private land and certain mine sites are now within the gardens and grounds of private residences. Please respect their privacy, the wishes of their owners and only visit with permission and with extreme care.

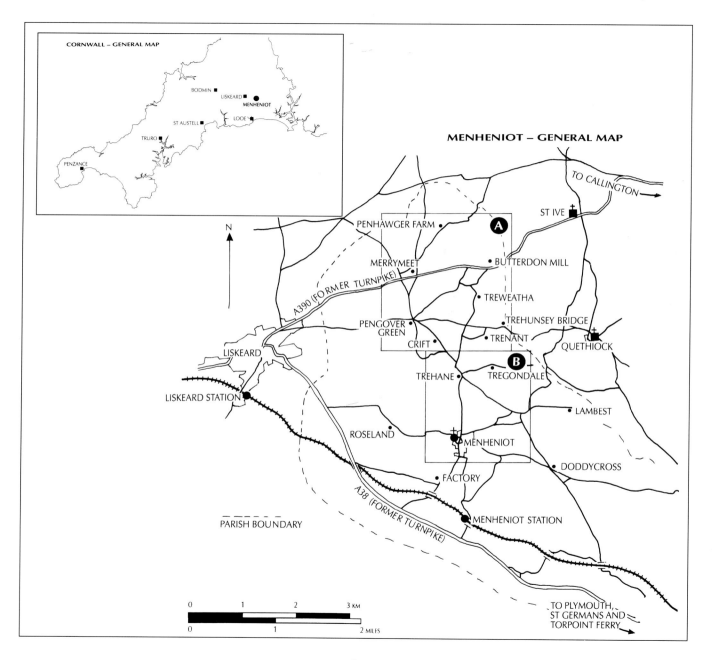

MENHENIOT – GENERAL MAP

CORNWALL – GENERAL MAP

BODMIN
LISKEARD
MENHENIOT
ST AUSTELL
LOOE
TRURO
PENZANCE

N

TO CALLINGTON

ST IVE

PENHAWGER FARM

Ⓐ

BUTTERDON MILL

MERRYMEET

A390 (FORMER TURNPIKE)

TREWEATHA

TREHUNSEY BRIDGE

PENGOVER GREEN

TRENANT

QUETHIOCK

CRIFT

Ⓑ

LISKEARD

TREHANE

TREGONDALE

LAMBEST

LISKEARD STATION

ROSELAND

MENHENIOT

DODDYCROSS

FACTORY

A38 (FORMER TURNPIKE)

MENHENIOT STATION

PARISH BOUNDARY

TO PLYMOUTH,
ST GERMANS AND
TORPOINT FERRY

0   1   2   3 KM

0   1   2 MILES

4

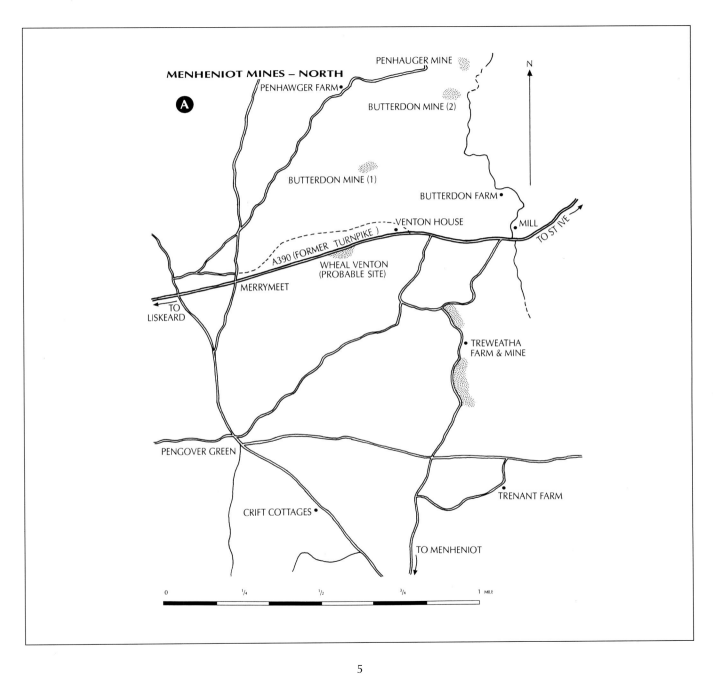

MENHENIOT MINES – NORTH

A

PENHAUGER MINE

PENHAWGER FARM •

BUTTERDON MINE (2)

N

BUTTERDON MINE (1)

BUTTERDON FARM •

VENTON HOUSE •

• MILL

TO ST IVE

A390 (FORMER TURNPIKE)

WHEAL VENTON
(PROBABLE SITE)

MERRYMEET

TO
LISKEARD

• TREWEATHA
FARM & MINE

PENGOVER GREEN

TRENANT FARM •

CRIFT COTTAGES •

TO MENHENIOT

0   ¼   ½   ¾   1   MILE

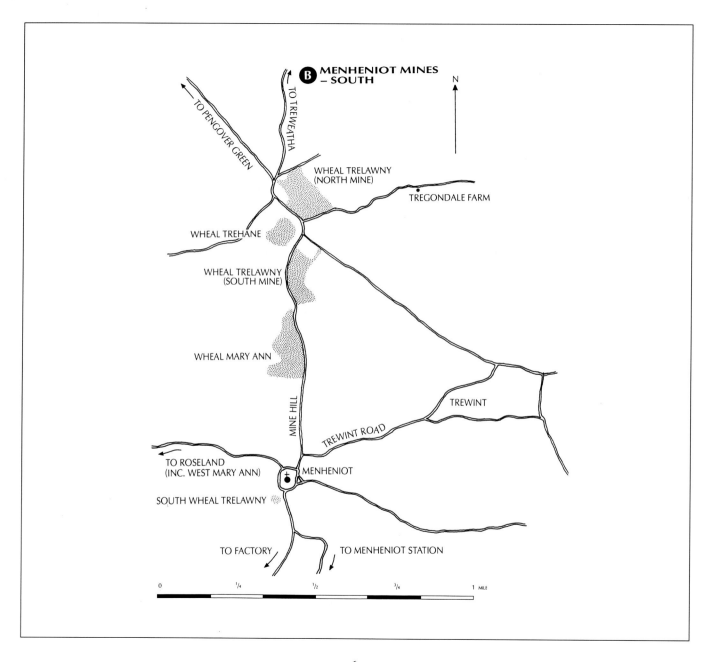

B MENHENIOT MINES – SOUTH

CHAPTER ONE
THE SCENE IS SET

The Mania for mining now pervaded the town and country...
and any little indication was seized and explored in confident anticipation of large returns.
JOHN ALLEN, LISKEARD 1856

WILLIAM BARTLETT WAS woken by a creaking sound from the simple rough beds close to his, followed by muffled coughs as his fellow farm servants stirred. A cold Spring dawn was breaking over Penhawger Farm, Menheniot and he shivered involuntarily, still lonely and a little frightened in his new surroundings. The year was 1841 and William was just nine years old, but as was the custom with farm labourers' large families in the area, he had already left home and was living and working with five teenage farm servants at Jacob and William Mutton's Penhawger Farm. A short distance away down high-banked leafy lanes, so typical of Cornwall, at Venton, Menheniot in three small cottages lived his parents William and Jane with three of their seven children, his grandparents John and Elizabeth Bartlett and his Uncle Francis Bartlett, with his wife Rebecca and two small children. Father, grandfather and uncle were all farm labourers and William was following in the time-honoured tradition at nine years of age as a farm servant. As young William Bartlett rose that morning, it would have been beyond his comprehension that within ten short years he would be descending to the bowels of the earth as a Menheniot lead miner, whilst his village sought to come to terms with a new and vibrant way of life.

Peter Clymo Jnr was forty-one years old and a wealthy, successful mine adventurer. The year was 1843 and as he strode purposefully along bustling Barras Street, Liskeard towards a pre-arranged meeting with his brother and fellow adventurer James Clymo, he hoped that something very special was about to break in their favour. The brothers were a powerful partnership, combining practical mining knowledge, an astute business mind and those vital elements in the fickle world of mining speculation, unwavering confidence in their own judgement and just a little luck. James Clymo was to report on the outcome of negotiations with Charles Trelawny of Coldrenick, land owner and mineral lord of key plots of land in Menheniot. The Clymos believed, in fact were convinced, that lead in commercially viable quantities lay beneath the soil of Menheniot, although the parish had no history of mining up to that time. Their task was to convince Charles Trelawny that it would be to their mutual benefit to grant a lease for the mineral rights. The brothers' strength in combining practical mining knowledge with financial astuteness meant that success with the lease would not only enable them to practically develop the mine, but also to market shares in the undertaking, at a commission or handsome premium, to other adventurers who may wish to join. But for the moment Menheniot was an untried speculation in virgin country, blissfully unaware of the events which were to follow.

A few years later, in 1849, William Bawden surveyed a very different scene, separated by some sixty miles, deep in western Cornwall in the parish of Breage. Yet he too was to become another piece of the jigsaw that was the story of Menheniot. William Bawden was an experienced tin miner of thirty years of age, supporting his wife Ann and

Penhawger Farm, Menheniot. Where future miner William Bartlett lodged as an 11 year old farm servant in 1841.

S. Bartlett 1991

five children in the well established, close-knit mining community of Breage. Times were changing however and he wondered how much longer the village, situated some four miles west of Helston and ten miles east of Penzance, overlooking the beautiful Mounts Bay, could continue to support his family. Great Wheal Vor Mine, since re-opening in 1836, had at one stage been producing one third of the tin output of all Cornwall and employed 1,174 persons. It had closed in 1847, hastened by legal disputes and poverty and unemployment was now rife in the parish, a story repeated in many west Cornish communities as mining fortunes followed a downward trend. Thoughts were turning to migration to distant corners of the world, where mining beckoned and Cornish Jacks were to become famous wherever men descended to the depths of the earth. Word was also about that the Menheniot area, near Liskeard, was looking for large numbers of miners to sustain its rapidly deepening and expanding lead mines and William and Ann would today make the important decision which would take them to a new life in eastern Cornwall. As William left for Menheniot, leaving his family to follow when he had found work and established a home for them, he was not alone - amongst the elite of Menheniot's lead miners, half of the western Cornish men who were to move there in this first surge came from just three parishes – Breage, Kenwyn and Kea.

Within this mixed community, which is central to our story, we find William Bartlett at nine years of age expecting to follow a little-changed farm labouring tradition, Peter Clymo Jnr, practical and dynamic mining adventurer, who more than any other man was to stamp his influence on Menheniot's mining fortunes and William Bawden, Breage tin miner who, with many like himself, crossed the country to herald the dawn of a new and vibrant era. All very different men, but each representing the three key social elements in Menheniot's future and all with a common destiny and a role to play in the emerging story of Menheniot. We shall return to William Bartlett and William Bawden and how Menheniot's mining fortunes effected their personal destiny under the heading 'Menheniot Family Life', meanwhile Peter Clymo Jnr remains to play a central role in much of the mining history that follows.

Turning to the parish itself, the population was to double in the twenty years between 1841 and 1861 and Menheniot's traditional farming community soon found itself facing traumatic change on an unheard of scale. Engine houses were erected on virgin ground and these were soon to contain massive engines which would drive the parish mines. Their hissing and clanking pistons soon became part of the sound of Menheniot, as water was pumped night and day from their dark depths. Tall grey stone chimneys flanked the engine houses, breaking the undulating skyline of this hilly, but lushly vegetated

Dean House, Liskeard. Built for Peter Clymo in 1855, at the height of Liskeard's mining prosperity. Later renamed Graylands.

S. Bartlett 1991

parish, whilst smoke from their coal-fired boilers rose high into the sky. At the same time rows of mining cottages sprung up, not in neat rows around the mine as in the industrial north of England, but in random dips and hollows all over the parish, as well as in the village of Menheniot itself.

The initially somewhat wild and hard-drinking mining vanguard gradually settled into a more traditional way of life as families joined their mining husbands and brought their own special influences to bear on life within the community. None of these changes were instantaneous, but it was the kaleidoscope of change, as the mines rose to prominence and then collapsed within thirty short years, which makes Menheniot's history special and worthy of a close and detailed inspection. Special too, along with the greater Liskeard and Caradon area, in the history of Cornish mining, booming as it did in the mid-nineteenth century at a time when mining fortunes were turning downwards in western Cornwall. It provided a late, spectacular, albeit unsustained, resurgence in the industry for in Menheniot's case a few decades, before mirroring the recession and social deprivation of its western neighbours. Such rapid change inevitably produced a tale of a resilient people who found housing shortages during the initial expansion and at the end of the period bitterness and resentment as the industry abandoned them. In between, Menheniot's two biggest mines, Wheal Trelawny and Wheal Mary Ann, provided steadiness of employment and a security which should not be underestimated in what were difficult times in Cornwall. It is therefore very much the long forgotten story of the mining community which share these pages alongside the history of the actual mines themselves.

At this point it is important to establish why, when the quest for metal in Cornwall had been actively pursued for hundreds of years, it was not until 1843 that the industry established itself in Menheniot. The answer lay quite simply in two coinciding factors, namely the expanding public demand for the metal lead in the buoyant Victorian building trade and also the newly established, but rapidly expanding, mining community centred on the market town of Liskeard, three and a half miles to the north west. Here, several fortunes having already been made in the copper mining ventures around Caradon Hill to the north of Liskeard, men were ready to speculate and organise speculation in any hopeful mining venture and once Menheniot was suspected of having mining potential, the confidence and expertise was there to drive the speculation forward.

Liskeard was indeed the springboard from which the Menheniot mining industry was first launched and it is to there we first turn our attention. In 1307 King Edward I granted a Charter appointing Helston, Truro, Bodmin, Lostwithiel and Liskeard as Coinage Towns and this was the foundation of the ancient Stannary Laws and Courts by which the industry continued to govern itself. The appointment of Liskeard is a clear indication of its eminence as a tin-producing district at that time. In 1569 Queen Elizabeth I granted a further Charter referring to Helston, Truro, Lostwithiel and Liskeard, but criticising the latter for failing to hold its coinage days regularly. Instructions were issued that these must be held at Liskeard on 21 and 22 June and on 5 and 6 October each year, and for many years tin continued to be brought for assaying or coining to the town. Eventually the practice died away, but was reintroduced in 1820, presumably marking an increase in tin mining activity again, and was maintained until the custom was abolished and substituted by simplified arrangements in 1838[1]. This demonstrates a steady, if unspectacular, association with tin mining, which is confirmed by references from the new Victorian mining fraternity to 'old mens' workings' on either side of Caradon Hill, as well as in certain other parishes but not, interestingly, in Menheniot

It was, however, the nineteenth century mining boom central to our story, which nurtured previously unheard of wealth and prosperity and transformed the market town into an important commercial centre. Copper was the metal that dramatically changed Liskeard's fortunes and the mine which was to be talked about throughout the mining fraternity was South Caradon. Modest development commenced in April 1836, by brothers James and Peter Clymo Jnr and fellow adventurer Tom Kittow, driving an exploratory adit into the side of Caradon Hill in St Cleer parish, north of Liskeard[2]. When favourable indications were met, further backers were sought, as finances were almost exhausted, but with little success and the group struggled on as best they could. James Clymo, determined to persevere, travelled to London with ore samples in an endeavour to dispose of shares on the London Market, the mine being divided into 64 equal shares. Returning disconsolately to Cornwall on the mail coach, having failed to attract any interest, he offered a half of the 64 shares to a travelling companion, who held large interests in Cornish mines.

Fortunately for the Clymos, the offer was refused, for soon afterwards a spectacular copper strike saw the value of each £5 share in South Caradon rise to £2,000 and by 1843, significantly the year that the Clymos turned their attention to the as yet unheard of Menheniot, dividends of around £10,000 per annum were being declared[3]. As a direct result of their earlier difficulties, South Caradon shares were tightly held by the original group and a few family and business associates, and those men continued to control and practically manage the mine for many years. Other successful ventures, notably West Caradon, blossomed and soon a bustling and prosperous mining community grew up within the market town of Liskeard. With it came the expansion of associated professions; accountants, solicitors and share dealers, as well as tradesmen of all descriptions to support and supply the ever-expanding mining industry and population. It was clear that James and Peter Clymo Jnr had more than demonstrated two necessary attributes of the mining adventurer, determination and just a little luck, as they stood poised and ready to launch themselves into Menheniot's mining future. We can only speculate how different Menheniot's mining saga may have been, had a certain Cornish adventurer accepted 32 of the 64 shares of the South Caradon Mine offered to him on that mail coach from London in 1837. At the time of that sensational strike, James and Peter Clymo Jnr were just 37 and 36 years old respectively.

WHEAL TRELAWNEY MINE.

At the general meeting, held on the 20th day of November 1862, a dividend of 10s. per share was declared.

FINANCIAL STATEMENT, THREE MONTHS ENDING WITH COST FOR AUGUST 1862.

Expenditure.

To labour cost for June, July, and August	...	...	...£3157 15 1
Merchants' bills for June, July, and August	...	...	...1407 12 4
Royalty account	...	...	...313 5 4
Income Tax	...	...	...86 11 9
Rent of Wharf at Looe	...	...	...12 0 0
Law charges	...	...	...23 4 6
Interest account	...	...	...21 10 9
Incidental expenses	...	...	...0 18 6
Balance carried to profit and loss account	...	...	...724 18 1
			£5747 16 4

Receipts.

By Sales of silver lead ore, viz.

Excess on estimate of sale included in last account	...	...£9 2 0
65 tons 14 cwt. 3 qrs. at 26l. 12s. 6d.	...	...1749 6 6
70 „ 2 „ 1 „ at 26l. 15s. 0d.	...	...1875 7 3
64 „ 18 „ 2 „ at 27l. 15s. 0d.	...	...1744 18 11
36 „ 6 „ 3 „ at 10l. 3s. 6d.	...	...369 1 8
		£5747 16 4

Profit and Loss.

To dividend of 10s. per share declared 14th August	...	...£520 0 0
Balance to next account	...	...2243 17 1
		£2763 17 1
By balance from last account	...	...£2038 19 0
Balance as above brought down	...	...724 18 1
		£2763 17 1

Liabilities.

To merchants	...	...£2363 14 7
Royalty	...	...454 3 11
Doctor	...	...61 2 1
Club	...	...42 9 1
Balance of profit and loss account	...	...2243 17 1
		£5165 7 2

Assets.

By cash at Bankers	...	...£1154 19 4
Arrears of calls	...	...22 10 0
Bills receivable	...	...3987 17 10
		£5165 7 2
By balance brought down	...	...£2243 17 1

AGENT'S REPORT.

The 182 south of Smith's is worth 4l. per fm. The 182 north is also worth 4l. per fm. The 172 south is worth 5l. per fm. The 172 north is also worth 4l. per fm. The 160 north of Chippendale's is worth 20l. per fm. This end has been driven 35 fms. over a good lode worth, on an average, 15l. per fm.

The 142 north of Chippendale's worth 4l. per fm., with good appearance. The 152 south of Trelawney's has an improved appearance, worth 4l. per fm.; at this point we expect an improvement. The 152 north of Trelawney's shaft is also improved, worth full 15l. per fm. Winze sinking below the 142, in advance of the end, 7 fms., worth 6l. per fm.

Our tribute department just the same.

On our obtaining a new lease from Charles Trelawney, Esq., which there is no doubt of, at a 20th dues, we shall resume the sinking of Trelawney's shaft, which is the only course with what we are doing for the permanent working of this mine.

Sold on Wednesday, Nov. 12, 60 tons of crop lead, at 27l. 17s. 6d.

The meetings are held three-monthly, and the next meeting will be held about the third week in February 1863.

Quarterly mine accounts presented to Wheal Trelawny's Adventurers' meeting in November 1862. These typically reflect the income and outgoings of a large Menheniot mine of the period.

CHAPTER TWO
MINING ORGANISATION AND PRACTICE

INEVITABLY AS OUR story unfolds detailed reference will be made to the organisation and practice involved in working Menheniot's mines, as well as the positions occupied by the principals concerned – manager, purser and mine agent. Many of the mining terms used can seem complicated and confusing when first encountered, as can the mysteries of the organisation of a nineteenth century Cornish mining company. A dictionary of Cornish mining Terms, edited from a list published in the *Mining Journal* in 1848, is reproduced as Appendix A to assist in clarifying detail. Mine depths were always expressed in fathoms, one fathom equal to six feet. Most mines were unlimited liability cost book concerns, with custom and practice evolving over several hundred years, whilst the leasing agreements from the landowners owning the mineral rights and the method for inviting bids from groups of miners to work sections of the mine, either by what was known as tutwork or tribute, all were steeped in history and tradition and worthy of being more deeply investigated as a subject in their own right. These practices continued to be refined and adapted throughout the nineteenth century and most held up surprisingly well to the increased scale of operations and finance necessary during this unprecedented period of change. Despite the availability from 1857 of limited liability legislation, with which we are more familiar today, some areas of Cornwall were slow to change and limited companies played little part in Menheniot's mining history until late in the century when its peak had long passed.

More than ten different lead mines were worked in Menheniot from 1843 onwards, two large Wheal Mary Ann and Wheal Trelawny, two of moderate size Wheal Trehane and Treweatha and the remainder of a speculative nature. All, both large and small, were basically structured in organisation and practice along similar lines. Despite being a new mining area, the expertise both in mining management and working miners was largely of western Cornish origin and the long established custom and practice brought with them from the west was adopted here in Menheniot. Initially a small group of people, possibly as few as three or four, would promote a mining venture, establish its boundaries, obtain a lease from the mineral lord, usually for 21 years and either be able to demonstrate the

worth of their venture on the basis of successful adjacent mines lying along what was considered to be a continuation of the mineral lode or, preferably, have some indication of the prospects by having sunk trial shafts or exposed promising mineralised ground at the surface. Additionally some outlay may have been made on materials and structures on site, but rarely more than a token provision.

The promoters of the Cost Book concern would then launch the company in the form of shares, typically Wheal Mary Ann in 256 shares in 1845, at a price fixed by themselves and usually immediately payable in full by the buyer, but occasionally by instalments. The payments made represented the initial working capital of the company, less a percentage for the original promoters' premium or expenses in launching the scheme. The initial promoters had first rights in investing themselves and here two very different types emerged. Men like Peter and James Clymo would have launched Wheal Trelawny and Wheal Mary Ann because they believed in their long term future and wished to be associated with success. They would have invested and retained a large percentage of shares themselves, although even they might have chosen to benefit from a percentage of their entitlement being sold on the open market, accruing a promoter's percentage from each share sold. Other partners, possibly share dealers or speculators, might waive their entitlement and launch as many shares as possible in the public arena, their role having been purely to package and launch the concern for short term profit from their promoter's premium. This ability to launch a mining concern and make money without actually taking any risks remained a temptation to less reputable developers to package and launch concerns with extremely doubtful prospects. Mining however was a high risk activity and deliberate misrepresentation was sometimes difficult to prove.

Cost Book companies worked on a remarkably simple system of accounting, the books being kept by the mine purser. Meetings of shareholders, known as adventurers, were called every two or three months, the latter becoming more common practice, when receipts for the previous period's ore sales and other income were balanced against expenditure and a loss or profit declared. All expenditure was normally accounted for currently and an exceptional expense such as a new engine house or boiler would be marked up, if paid for by single instalment, as a one-off expense that month, it not being normal practice to spread the expenditure over future quarters. This could cause otherwise profitable mines to move into debt for short periods, as happened at times with the otherwise solid profit making concerns of Wheal Trelawny and Wheal Mary Ann. Similarly, losses were the unlimited responsibility of the shareholders. If a loss had been made, the purser would recommend a 'call' of a prescribed amount per share, immediately payable, to cover the loss and the working expenses of the mine for the following period. If a profit on the previous period had been declared, the purser would again, having identified a suitable amount for the next month's working expenses, declare a dividend per share.

Fountain Hotel, Liskeard. A mid-19th century venue where Menheniot and Caradon mine adventurers gathered to hear their managers' reports.

S. Bartlett 1987

The Cost Book system, whilst lacking the sophistication of planning for the future, served its purpose well, concentrating adventurers' awareness in an industry that, by its very nature, bore heavy early losses in exploration in the hope of high returns on capital when ore was struck. Respected long term mining companies like Wheal Mary Ann and Wheal Trelawny, realising that investors preferred a regular dividend to spectacular declarations, learned how to control the system well to show a steady long term profit and Peter Clymo, for 24 years manager and purser of Wheal Mary Ann between 1846 and 1870, gained particular respect for his astute management of the mine's affairs. Such mines always pursued exploration and development, opening up new reserves well in advance of requirements and particularly easily mined reserves were deliberately left to bolster production during hard times. Astute control of production based on fluctuations in the metal market would contribute to steady dividends over a long period. A further manipulation of the system was to carry forward, following a good period, rather more than was

WEBB'S HOTEL LISKEARD.

Webbs Hotel, Liskeard pre-1906. Built in 1832 by R. Webb it was at the centre of 19th century commercial life and hosted many Menheniot mine meetings.

S. Bartlett collection

necessary for the next period's expenses, leaving a nicely balanced figure for the usual dividend to be declared. This could prove embarrassing if a further spectacular period followed, but in the uncertain world of fluctuating metal prices and changing mining fortunes, this often proved the means at the next declaration for offering a consistent dividend yet again.

At each three-monthly adventurers' meeting, having listened to the manager or mine agent's report on the practical workings of the mine, decisions would be taken on the future direction the mine should take or the need for investment in further equipment. Each adventurer was entitled to vote on such proposals, in proportion to his shareholding, although providing there was confidence in the local agent, they would normally follow the recommendations of their local professional mining team. However, if confidence had been lost, debts were rising or promises of finding the elusive mineral lode had failed to be met, impatient shareholders might more positively assert their views, particularly the distant non-Cornish element. Occasionally independent mining consultants might be brought in, a lucrative sideline for well established and respected mine captains, to produce an independent assessment of the mine's prospects. This was the drama of mining speculation in Cornwall and the walls of The White Hart Inn, Menheniot, and The Fountain Inn or Webbs Hotel, Liskeard, to name but a few regular locations for mine adventurers' meetings, held many secrets of accusation and counter-accusation as personalities clashed and less robust speculations staggered from crisis to crisis, hoping the well worn phrase '...your agent reports an encouraging change in the nature of the ground' really would this time prove to be the sign of better things to come. Menheniot shared in these less than successful ventures and long forgotten mines such at Butterdon, Penhauger, Wheal Venton and South Wheal Trelawny are today barely discernable, but once made local headlines in the heady 1840s and 1850s when confidence was supreme and speculation followed speculation.

Who were these Victorian men who invested heavily in Menheniot's mining industry, backing with their own money organisational ingenuity of Cornish mine captains and agents, who in turn might directly control the livelihoods of seven or eight hundred miners and their families dependent on the village's natural wealth? Cornish mining had progressively moved on from the romantic concept of three or four industrious local men combining limited funds to work small concerns. Mining investment was uncertain, required increasingly substantial outlay as the scale of nineteenth century operations increased which, after the Napoleonic Wars became beyond the ability of Cornish home-based finance to support. This situation had long been reached by the time first the Caradon mines north of Liskeard and later Menheniot burst onto the mining scene, the latter in the 1840s. Menheniot's adventurers fell into two distinct groups, local Cornish and London, or occasionally other provincial investors, the latter groups having been attracted by the mine's promoters seeking business support and launching the mine's shares on the London Market. Such mines maintained a London secretary, with an address in the City, who looked after the company's financial affairs there and formed the link between shareholders and the mine in distant Cornwall. He was not usually a full-time mine employee, but a professional agent administering the London interests of a large number of companies.

Cornish money which, owing to the success of Caradon mines, was reasonably available amongst Liskeard investors, came from a mixture of professional mining men, such as the Clymos, local professional men who were increasingly basing themselves in Liskeard such as solicitors, accountants, bankers, share dealers and most interestingly merchants dealing in mining supplies and equipment, particularly the staple diet of coal, candles and gunpowder. Relationships between the 'in-' (Cornish) and 'out-adventurers' (non-Cornish) were always somewhat strained with the out-adventurers jealous of the closer and better informed contacts which the locals had with the Cornish mine captains, upon which they all so much depended. Experience showed that less reputable captains soon learned that alternative sources of income were to be made from contracting for over-priced supplies and equipment, to the eternal gratitude of the local merchants, provided accounts were contained within limits which kept the shareholders paying their calls and covering the excesses. As merchants prospered, their holdings tended to increase and despite sensible managerial controls, with tendering being stipulated by more responsible mines, situations did occur where major shareholders were also major suppliers.

It would be wrong to suggest that the very fabric of the industry was rotten, but unquestionably by this time in Liskeard a great deal of money was swilling about in a somewhat uncontrolled manner, with fortunes being made and lost. Many of these, in the main, self-made men were tough, quick-witted and, like many pillars of Victorian society who had risen on the tide of industrial expansion, hid just the odd skeletons in otherwise impeccable pasts. The proportion of local and London money in Menheniot's mines varied significantly mine by mine and according to period. The major workings of Wheal Mary Ann and Wheal Trelawny always drew finance from a wide source, as did a surprising number of the speculative mines. However, some of the smaller concerns were launched almost exclusively on Liskeard money and as the nineteenth century wore on, with confidence in Cornish mining progressively being lost by London investors, the industry turned again to its own local resources as it fought to survive. West Mary Ann launched in 1875 in a desperate attempt to rediscover Menheniot's past glory, with Wheal Mary Ann, Wheal Trelawny and Treweatha lying desolate and abandoned, followed this trend and was reliant on the misplaced confidence of a by-then broken and severely shaken local economy.[1]

The first task in establishing a mining concern in Menheniot, as elsewhere in Cornwall, was to negotiate with the mineral lord for a lease. The mineral lord, who owned the rights to mine beneath the ground, was usually, but not always, what would more traditionally be known as the surface landlord. In Menheniot the situation was straightforward and both rights coincided. Menheniot's two largest mines, Wheal Trelawny and Wheal Mary Ann, obtained 21-year leases in 1843 and 1845 at 1-15th and 1-12th dues respectively. This signified that the mineral lord was entitled to that proportion of the sales of all ore raised and sold by the mines, which meant that even if costs exceeded ore sales, the mineral lord would still be entitled to his full dues, whilst the adventurers bore the full loss. It could, however, be said that when prices on the ore market fluctuated, as was common in this unpredictable trade, the mineral lord took the same reduction as the adventurers. Similarly his calls on the mine's finances during the early development years, when ore sales were smallest and financial outlay most stretched, were negligible. During bad times the mine might apply for the dues to be reduced or suspended, as were Wheal Trelawny's and Wheal Mary Ann's at various stages, but this was not always an easily negotiated option and success in these circumstances was decidedly mixed. However, it was not generally in the interests of a mineral lord for a mining concern to fail. Undoubtedly he had the easiest and most privileged position in the mining hierarchy, for at no financial outlay or risk, he stood to gain considerably from a successful concern. The linking of the dues to ore sales, with payments only rising when coincidental with success,

Charles Trelawny (1799–1883). Influential landowner and principal Mineral Lord of Wheal Trelawny Mine. He displayed consideration and understanding during hard times by waiving his rights to dues.

H. Sneyd collection

was seen as fairer than a fixed rental, which took no account of the long, lean period of mine development and generally the system was felt to work well.

In certain parishes where large estates dominated, notably Duchy of Cornwall lands, one large mineral lord tended to control all the rights, whereas in Menheniot land ownership was vested in somewhat smaller parcels, which led to complex deals having to be struck, sometimes involving two or three mineral lords to make a viable parcel of land for mineral development. The most influential of these in Menheniot were Charles Trelawny of Coldrenick, the principal of a group of mineral lords constituting Wheal Trelawny and Miss Mary Ann Pollard of Menheniot village, who farmed 41 acres at 81 years of age and in 1845 found herself astride what was to become the richest section of Menheniot's lead lode, over which several parties fought for the lease, by fair means and foul, as will later be related. She was to control the sole mineral rights to Wheal Mary Ann and she, with Charles Trelawny, unquestionably profited greatly from these two steadiest and greatest of Menheniot's mines. Other mineral lords, mostly gentlemen farmers who leased part of their land for mining, included George Rowe of Treweatha (later of Venton), J. Carthew, Thomas Kelly, R. S. Jago and George Roby of Pool Hall.

The practical management and detailed working of the mine was vested in the manager, purser and mine agents, the latter varying in numbers according to the scale of the operation. The manager and agents carried the courtesy title of Captain, a long-held Cornish tradition and in informal exchanges the mine manager might often be referred to as the mine Captain. The manager was responsible to the adventurers for the direct management of the mine, ensuring that costs were tightly controlled, both through competitive contract for materials and the economic and technically correct

Coldrenick House, family home of Charles Trelawny. This imposing Georgian House was demolished in 1862, to be replaced by a Victorian timber framed house in turn demolished in 1966. The present residence is converted from the original stable block.

H. Sneyd collection

sinking of shafts and driving of levels to pursue the elusive mineral lode. In following the chosen method to open up the mine, the manager was working to the direction of the adventurers through decisions taken at the mine meeting, but in practice, it was his professional guidance and recommendation which the adventurers were usually following. These were the men whose fame and fortune, or occasionally tarnished reputations, spread throughout Cornwall and became household names, the stories of their successes and triumphs growing on each re-telling and as the years

went by. They were also the men who, along with their trusted Senior agents, shared the accolades both upwards and downwards, their success being respected both within the professional and business communities of such mining centres as Liskeard, as well as being understood and looked up to by the working miners themselves.

The purser was responsible for maintaining the detailed accounts and ensuring that all financial matters were on a correct footing. He would keep the Cost Book, report the financial state of the mine to adventurers' meetings and both calculate and arrange collection or distribution of calls and dividends amongst the adventurers. Where a large proportion of up-country shareholders existed and there was a London market in a company's shares, a London secretary was appointed and he became an agent between the distant shareholders and the local management. Under these circumstances, some of the purser's duties were undertaken by the secretary. Historically in the early days of Cost Book mining, when small mines were a practical association of three or four working miners, then one of their number would be elected purser. By the mid-nineteenth century in the Menheniot era, this had evolved to either professional pursers, based in adjacent towns, handling the affairs of a collection of mines, much in the way a professional accountant does today, or, if the manager was financially, as well as practically, astute, it was not uncommon to combine the posts of manager and purser, as happened with Peter Clymo Jnr at Wheal Mary Ann. Indeed, it was a sign of strength and respect when such combined offices were bestowed.

The mine agent or agents were the practical link between the miners, the detailed daily working arrangements and the manager, best described as performing the roles of both Under-managers and foremen or supervisors. It was essential that they had practical mining experience underground and had proven technical ability to support the manager in his assessment of prospects and the changing nature of the mineral ground. This was needed to inspect and calculate the correct values for work to be set for tutwork contracts or tribute. The best mine agents shared the respect and trust of both manager and working men, becoming recognised leaders in the local communities both outside and within the mine. Many were to be found leading the spirited singing or preaching in the Methodist Chapels, already established in the Menheniot area but greatly increased in the mining era, often holding such key positions as Sunday School Superintendent. Whilst mine agents' posts were often held by older, deeply respected, former working miners of long service, this was not always the case. Mine agents in their twenties and thirties were not uncommon, Menheniot providing several examples, with John Pryor (aged 27) at Wheal Trelawny in 1864, James Skeat (aged 27) at Wheal Mary Ann in 1867 and John Bryant (aged 32) at Wheal Trehane in 1846. This early status was occasionally reached by identifying working miners of exceptional ability and success, or alternatively they might be the sons or other relations of established mine Captains. Nevertheless they would normally have served a proper underground apprenticeship to an acceptable standard.

The formality of a mine's management structure was sometimes adapted to suit the specific requirements of the concern or the expertise of the men involved and the subtlety of emphasis within different mine teams was clearly evident in Menheniot. Typical was the previously described arrangement of combining the manager and purser's posts, with Peter Clymo Jnr responsible for both duties at Wheal Mary Ann between 1846 and 1870. With equal flexibility on his death in 1870, Joseph Harris, trusted mine agent for many years, was appointed manager, whilst a Liskeard based agency in William Nettle was appointed as purser, no doubt reflecting the more limited

strengths of the new manager. It was not uncommon for managers or mine agents to hold appointments at more than one mine, travelling between them to carry out their duties. This system was of particular value to small speculative concerns, which might employ less than twenty miners at the early development stage and contract the part-time expertise of an adjacent manager or agent. Such appointments might have been sought out by enterprising agents, or where such concerns had actually been launched by an adjacent large mine's adventurers, they would positively entrust the smaller concerns in the hands of their own agents. Wheal Trelawny adventurers financed at various stages speculative development, somewhat unsuccessfully, at Butterdon, Penhauger and South Wheal Trelawny and this link is clearly evident through their mine agents. In 1853 Joseph Kemp of Trelawny was also involved in supervision on a part-time basis of all three, whilst between 1855 and 1857 Thomas Grenfell of Trelawny was similarly involved in Butterdon and Penhauger. The long-serving William Jenkin was manager or agent at South Wheal Trelawny between 1845 and 1851, whilst also appearing as agent at Penhauger in 1854, and until 1861 was mine agent at the parent mine of Wheal Trelawny. Such part-time arrangements were however not always favoured when they had been sought by the initiative of individuals in unconnected concerns and adventurers would at times complain that they required the undivided attentions of their men, particularly at a stage when a hitherto speculative concern began to consolidate its position by commencing ore sales.

A further variant was to appoint one of the several agents at larger mines, such as Wheal Mary Ann and Trelawny, as the managing or resident agent. This status, between agent and manager, was afforded when the manager's position was held by a remote Captain of such standing that the adventurers were prepared to accept his interests being split amongst a variety of mining concerns, each paying him a contracted fee, both because of the boost it gave to their company's status and because in terms of key decision-making, if not availability for day-to-day management, his worth was proven. Between 1861 and 1864 Francis Pryor of Redruth was manager of Wheal Trelawny at the same time as the important copper mine of West Caradon, St Cleer, whilst also nominally managing at least five small speculative mines in the Liskeard area and still more in west Cornwall. Despite his well-spread interests, he was known to have made key decisions which affected profitable production at both West Caradon and Wheal Trelawny. Similarly Peter Clymo Jnr had far-flung interests, although unquestionably Wheal Mary Ann was second only to his original jewel, South Caradon, and Menheniot would have received a great deal of his personal attention. Henry Hodge, agent at Wheal Mary Ann between 1847 and 1865, was given the status of managing agent in the 1860s, as was Henry Vivian in 1846 at Wheal Trelawny, both during periods of Peter

Clymo Jnr's managership.

The mine engineer was the final appointment to complement the manager, purser and mine agents. This position was not usually a direct employee of the mine, but sub-contracted to a professional mining engineering agency which looked after the interests of a number of mines. W. Mathews, W. West and Hocking & Loam figured prominently in the Liskeard district, and when Menheniot appeared on the scene established reputations and contacts with the local mining hierarchy ensured the extension of their services to embrace Menheniot. William West was engineer to the two largest Menheniot mines, Wheal Trelawny and Wheal Mary Ann, whilst also taking over the agency for Treweatha by 1862 after W. Mathews had held it for the first period of the mine's working. William West was mining engineer to at least twelve mines in the Liskeard area, was increasingly influential as the century progressed and was also a major investor in mining concerns and a prominent designer of mining engines and equipment. Both his major Menheniot contracts, Wheal Mary Ann and Wheal Trelawny, were Peter Clymo Jnr inspired developments and whilst his status was unquestionably earned, it has to be noted that William West was already closely linked with Peter Clymo Jnr through South Caradon, whilst both had been associated with Peter Clymo's father in Fowey Consols and district in their early days.

The engineering agency normally directly employed the engine house staff, but the following extract from the *Mining Journal* of 25 March 1848, although not necessarily typical, demonstrates the extent to which some sub-contract agreements went in devolving responsibility and accountability to the mining engineer. At the adventurers' meeting:

... It was resolved that Mr W. West, having proposed to bring and erect a steam whim engine on Wheal Trelawny Mine at his own expense, to draw all the attle and ores to the surface and provide all labour, enginemen, coals, hemp and every other material necessary to keep the said engine at work and in proper repair, from the 72 fathom level and all levels above, commencing from the boundary south of Wheal Trehane Mine to the northern boundary of Wheal Mary Ann Mine, for the sum of £28 per calendar month. He having also proposed and agreed that such engine should be of sufficient power to enable the company to sink 200 fathoms in depth and also to be paid an increase of £2 per calendar month for every 10 fathoms under the 72 fathom level. It is resolved that Mr West's offer be accepted.

It is intriguing to note how shrewd adventurers in a financially high risk industry had identified that by sub-contracting key areas of the developing mine at fixed price contracts the risks were spread to the sub-contractors and the adventures' commitment in this area became more predictable. Similarly with many mines using agencies for secretary and purserships, for some it

was only the manager and mine agents in the team so far described who might be direct employees.

The conditions under which the miners themselves were employed in Menheniot closely followed custom and practice that had grown up in western Cornwall over a long period and underground men were employed under arrangements known as tutwork and tribute. The former was based on the piecework principle, not just in the form of a bonus, but for the total payment and the latter almost cast the tributer in the role of a self-employed sub-contractor, negotiating a price before he started the job and heavily dependent on the value of the ore raised and the efficiency of his workmates for payment. Tutwork was less well paid, but steady work, seen as semi-skilled extension of labouring, whilst tributers were the elite of the mine workforce, both in their social standing and in their ability to vary earnings significantly, dependent on the richness of the ores in relation to the bargain they had struck with the manager or mine agents. Both systems were designed to directly link the miner's work rate and reward to the economic success of the mine, although at rates far different from the rewards an adventurer might get from a successful venture. They clearly were seen as a successful formula to overcome the almost impossible task of maintaining direct supervision over large numbers of men working in small groups at remote locations deep in the mine and in this they were to a large degree successful.[2]

The pride and independence of the Cornish miner, often romanticised in descriptions of nineteenth century Cornwall, perhaps becomes more plausible when it is appreciated that, despite all the injustices of a tough and uncompromising industry he did feel a certain independence which many thousands of his fellow industrial workers lacked when on Setting Day he, as a free and independent party, bid or of his own right chose not to bid, for work on offer for the following period at the mine. Cornish miners were also slow to organise themselves into workers associations or unions, notably so in contrast to the bitter conflicts within the coal industry during the nineteenth century. It is open to conjecture whether this could be related to the fairness of the tutwork and tribute system, despite unquestionably poor working conditions which should have fuelled industrial unrest, the natural Cornish independence or indeed the way in which the system encouraged the miners to think and work as small independent teams rather than as a united workforce. Whichever the cause and which the effect the understanding of the system of tutwork and tribute adds yet another dimension to the Cornish mining character and more specifically the mining men of nineteenth century Menheniot.

Tutwork was used for sinking shafts and driving levels and involved miners bidding for specific pitches or portions of ground to be worked, on Setting Day at an agreed rate per fathom to be sunk or driven. The criteria here was quantity and speed rather than quality, the work normally being to open up that portion of the mine in readiness for later ore extraction under tribute. In larger mines tutwork was carried out under the three shift working principle, with fixed relieving times spread over the full twenty-four hours. One miner in this circumstance bid for a pitch on behalf of an agreed group of individuals.[2]

Tribute pitches were let every two months for the front line task of extracting the ore. Miners bid on Setting Day for the right to work parcels of ground at an agreed percentage of the value of ore sales for the period concerned, the likely quantity and worth of the ore being a judgement made by the tributer before bidding. Once again, one tributer would bid on behalf of a 'pare' of men (two, four or more miners) and the contract would be to break the ores, wheel them, raise them to the surface and if prescribed, also dress the ores and make them ready for market. The company would make a charge, or pay deduction, for use of machinery to raise the ores and the services of surface staff for dressing. The payment process, as a percentage of ore sales, was geared to quality rather than quantity, although the clear incentive was there to maximise extraction without prejudicing the ultimate quality of the ore raised. A tributer had greater freedom with the hours he chose to work and at most mines this conformed to a single day shift, the length being determined by the tributers themselves.[2]

On Setting Day at the prescribed time men assembled around Menheniot's several mine offices or account houses waiting for the manager and his mine agents to appear on a raised platform or balcony window to conduct the auction. The mine agents would previously have descended the mine and carefully examined and grouped the work to be auctioned into parcels and made their judgement as to the value at which each pitch should ideally be let. Likewise each miner would have had the opportunity to examine pitches in which they were interested and to make their assessment of the bids they were prepared to make. Auctions for tribute pitches were started at a high price, with miners' competitive bids progressively reducing in Dutch Auction style until an agreement was concluded. The auction was generally conducted in an orderly manner with little indiscriminate bidding or scrambling for pitches. During normal periods of working the majority of pitches would be re-taken by the parties that had previously worked, although often at a slightly varied rate, and it was said men who had a footing in the mine were generally given the preference over strangers. Clearly however the settings could be the catalyst for dissent amongst the established mine workforce if the manager sought to force the prices for the pitches downwards or significantly reduce their numbers on offer due to depressed economic conditions.[2]

Pay day was once per month and was an important date in the calendar of the whole community. The day varied by mine and was regularly published in the information columns of local newspapers. Many goods would be obtained on credit with settlement due on pay day and many miners became locked into a system called subsist, under which the mine made a wages advance after a fortnight to assist the men through until pay day. Increasing numbers would become indebted to the mine and locked into the system, partly due to the fact that on arrival they were required to work a full month before receiving their first payment, or alternatively when at any stage a poor month was encountered due to a bad tutwork or tribute bargain. There is little doubt that miners' rewards in Menheniot, by the standards and uncertainties of the time, were significantly better than in many mining parishes, with security of labour for those that chose to settle based around the two large dividend paying mines of Wheal Mary Ann and Wheal Trelawny stretching for well in excess of twenty-five years. The picture which emerges in Menheniot during this period is very much a subtle blend of near full employment at reasonable wage rates, amongst which would be a core of experienced high earning top grade tributers, but at the same time working in relatively poor conditions within a tough and hostile environment. As with any community, not all were so favoured and families affected by disability, illness or early death of family heads, an all too regular event, would have experienced far less satisfactory living conditions.

On pay day rewards were based on the complex calculations relating to the specific tutwork or tribute bargain, from which a long list of deductions were made by the mine. Many of the charges have a rather unsavoury ring to our more enlightened ears and there seems few consumable materials or tools used by the miner in the course of his employment for which he was not directly charged. In addition to debiting tributers for raising and dressing ore, where required, regular deductions made included candles, gunpowder, fuses, ropes, nails, shovels, barrows, smithy for sharpening and repairing tools, as well as the mine barber, sick club and doctor and, of course, any subsist paid in advance. Examination of mine accounts in the 1860s also reveal it was not normal practice in the Liskeard district for mines to simply pass on the charge for candles and gunpowder at cost price, but to add a profit margin before deducting from the working miners' pay. Wheal Mary Ann was no different to any other in that respect and annual consumption of candles at that time was 21,480 lbs at a cost to the company of £537 but re-sold for £716 representing a 33% mark up. Likewise, consumption of gunpowder was 20,160 lbs costing the company £504, but re-sold for £672, also a 33% profit mark up. Exceptionally amongst the area's large mines Herodsfoot, some five miles to the west of Menheniot, demonstrated a more enlightened approach under the managership of Thomas Trevillion, strictly re-selling candles and gunpowder at cost price to the working miners.[3]

One enlightened feature for the mining community was the compulsory sick club membership, it being a reasonable interpretation that the

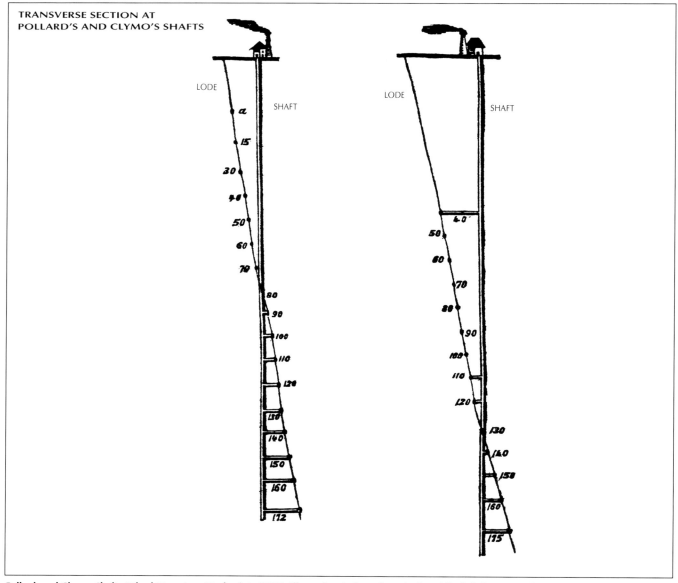

Pollards and Clymos Shafts, Wheal Mary Ann, Menheniot (1862). Illustrating shafts sunk vertically, whilst lode is at an angle or 'underlie'. Levels were then driven horizontally to follow the lode – usually at 10 fathoms (60 feet) intervals.

compulsory nature of the scheme was in fact in the miners' favour by removing the temptation to cancel membership when times were hard and cover even more essential for the miner and his family. At a typical mine, for the payment of 6d. per week miners received medical attendance when ill or suffering an accident at work. For 1s.3d. per week the cover was extended to his family and he additionally received a weekly cash payment whilst he was unable to work. Each mine contracted the services of a particular doctor to administer the scheme. Another quaint tradition perpetuated throughout Cornwall was the compulsory deduction for the mine barber, which was standard practice at larger mines throughout the district, including those in Menheniot.[4]

Lastly, in this introduction to Cornish mining organisation and practice we turn to the formation of the mineralised ground itself and the basic methods followed in sinking shafts and driving levels within the mines, both large and small. These principles will be seen put into practice time and time again in the history of individual mines which follow and this basic introduction is designed to ease interpretation of that detail. A dictionary of contemporary mining terms is shown in Appendix A.

Lead was to be found in vertical veins or lodes, usually very narrow in width but sometimes stretching for miles in length before dividing and petering out into fine stringy veins or capillaries at each end. Similarly they could reach down to considerable depths, although quality could vary and rarely remained consistent throughout its depth. This could result in a mine reducing in value after promising shallow indications or alternatively a long period of development with moderate returns could be rewarded with considerably increased value in depth; all part of the uncertainties of metal mining for the intrepid adventurers. Menheniot's deepest mine, Wheal Mary Ann, successfully followed their lode to a commercially viable depth of at least 250 fathoms or 1,500 feet and Wheal Trelawny was only fractionally shallower. Often similar lodes to those initially developed could be found running in parallel and all generally followed a consistent direction, in Menheniot's case north to south, with the centre of the parish around the two largest mines the richest mid point. These veins or lodes were literally fissures or cracks in the rock, formed during the original cooling process of surrounding rock formations. Various molten mineralised solutions passed up these cracks from below during that process, crystallising as cooling continued and finally becoming intermixed with decomposed or disintegrated rock deposits in the tightly compressed fissures. Other non-commercial minerals were to be found alongside the viable ones and in Menheniot's case the lead ore had a high silver content which paid a valuable supplementary income and was worth separation from the lead ore.[2]

The long narrow mineral lodes were additionally not precisely vertical, usually being inclined at a slight angle or underlie, the angle of which became an important calculation when determining the correct point to sink a shaft. In Menheniot the north to south aligned lodes inclined easterly in depth by a few degrees. Shafts might be started from surface at an inclined angle on the course of the lode, but this could prove problematical in the long term and the best shafts were sunk vertically from a point to the side of the lode, with the intention of meeting it at a prescribed depth from surface (see diagram p. 20).[5] This was usually where it had been calculated the initial trial was to be made. When the lode was met, levels would be started north and south along its course to prove its worth.

At depths which were deemed worthy of exploration above or below that optimum point (see diagram p. 20) a crosscut would be driven from the shaft at right angles towards the lode and then, when encountered, north and south levels would be driven from that point as before. Levels were therefore to be found along the course of the lode, crosscuts through usually barren ground at right angles to meet them. Such levels would be successively tried at depths around 10 fathoms apart and in large mines a considerable number of levels might be worked simultaneously. Progress was often slow and six feet per week was not thought poor progress under certain conditions. Crosscuts and levels varied in size but were typically five to six feet high and three feet wide, only more so if the width of the lode justified it. Shafts sunk between two levels but not extended upwards to the surface, known as winzes, were to be found in most Menheniot mines and aided communication and ventilation.[2]

Shafts were commonly referred to as either whim or engine. Whim shafts were specifically for raising ore to the surface, the dimensions being relatively less and a smaller engine generally sufficed. On smaller mines separate whim shafts were rarely provided. Engine shafts were principally for pumping water from the depths of the mine and often doubled as general purpose shafts. The largest engines on the mine were always here, pumping being the toughest task and such engines could often be tested to their limits in wet winters. Responsibility for both the engines and their attendant staff rested with the mine engineer.

Engine shafts were typically ten feet by fourteen feet in size with two compartments ten feet by eight feet and ten feet by six feet divided by timber, which was also used to line the shaft. The smaller would be described as the whim compartment for raising ore and the larger the engine compartment for pumping. The engine compartment commonly also contained the miners ladders for entering or leaving the workings. A classic example of this standard layout was Pollards Shaft at Wheal Mary Ann. Occasionally separate shafts were provided for the ladderway, usually carrying the name Footway Shaft, but these were less common and small in construction. One existed at Wheal Mary Ann to a shallow depth, where the men walked along a short level and continued downwards through an abandoned shaft sealed at the surface. Another existed at Treweatha, its precise location no longer known.[3]

Water wheels were common at surface, often used for driving machinery on the dressing floors, but their water source was more likely to be the vast quantities of available water pumped from the mine than naturally stream fed. Most surface workings included a reservoir on a high point of ground to more precisely control water availability, Wheal Trelawny's still clearly identifiable, a vast rectangular depression now deeply buried in natural vegetation.

Adits were tunnels horizontally driven across mine setts from valley floors, where mine locations were significantly higher than the surrounding ground. Such adits could be driven for considerable distances and their prime purpose was to provide natural drainage from levels which lay above the adit as an alternative to expensive pumping from surface. Their success was totally dependent on the topography of the area and in the main they only made a moderate contribution within Menheniot, generally cutting the workings at fairly shallow levels. Whilst drainage was their main purpose they were often used as a secondary means to explore the ground across the sett, with ore being extracted if productive ground was met. They also provided valuable auxiliary ventilation in many mines, to supplement air naturally circulating from the shafts. Adequate ventilation was a desperate problem in most mines, worsened by smoke and dust filled levels after blasting and a prime cause of miners disabilities. It is against this general background of mining organisation and practice that we now move on to look more closely at each of the main concerns.

CHAPTER THREE
WHEAL TRELAWNY

I and my poor brother were laughed at
for thinking to have a mine in Menheniot
PETER CLYMO JNR. 1859

IN JULY 1805 Richard Sobey, who owned land in the parish, granted permission for Richard Whitehead of Liskeard, Gentleman, William Geake of Plymouth, Innholder, James Skerry of Plymouth, Gentleman and James Tapper of Plymouth Dock, Innholder, to search for tin in, upon and out of the field known as Olver's Tenement, mis-spelt as Oliver's in the original document, in the parish of Menheniot. The field was described as being bounded on the east by Olver's Wood and can be traced today as adjacent to Trehunsey Bridge on the Menheniot parish border with Quethiock in the east of the parish.[1] Nothing more was heard of this venture and it is presumed that after a brief investigation the project was abandoned. Despite these early hopes, tin was never found in Menheniot and it was the discovery of another metal, lead, over thirty-five years later which was to change the face of this rural community.

Nineteenth century mining stories, like fishermen's tales, tended to grow in size and romanticism with each telling. That surrounding the discovery of lead in Menheniot was no different. The initial discovery directly resulted in the opening of Wheal Trelawny in 1843 and the key figures were to be the leading Liskeard mining team of Peter Clymo Jnr and his brother James. It was said that a labouring man exposed a shallow lode by chance whilst cutting a parish road near Menheniot church and pointed out the discovery to Peter Clymo Jnr. Peter Clymo then was said to have immediately applied for and obtained a lease to the land which became Wheal Trelawny.[2] A wonderfully simple and romantic story, which in fact only dates from a *Mining Journal* report in 1856, when Peter Clymo's success had become legendary within the local community. In reality Menheniot did not make his fortune, more correctly increasing it, for that had already been done by South Caradon some years before and it seems unlikely that the circumstances and relationship with the original discoverer could have been quite as informal as described.

A contrasting version has more recently been uncovered in an open letter to the *Mining Journal* in November 1846, much closer to the event and written by an anonymous writer described as 'A Shareholder'. There is clearly mischief intended by the writer and whilst this story too, for that

reason, has to be treated with some caution, the ruthlessness portrayed carries a certain credibility in a tough mining world which had seen the Clymos rise to a position of wealth and supremacy in the Liskeard area. It was said the lode had been discovered by three working miners who were obliged to seek out a responsible person to join them, to enable them to apply for a lease to the mine. The nominated person was named as J. Carpenter, who was certainly not a practical mine agent and his qualities must have been principally financial support. Whilst the arrangements were being made it was said that James and Peter Clymo also entered the fray, scenting a favourable sett was about to be granted through the passing of confidential information from another labourer, and both parties sought to meet Charles Trelawny, the landowner and mineral lord. Charles Trelawny at that meeting is said to have enquired as to who had first discovered the lode, to which James Clymo replied it was his party. It was said the landowner instantly detected a falsehood and turning to the working miners said 'My men, you shall be fairly treated'. He ultimately decided to grant one third each to Peter Clymo, James Clymo and J. Carpenter, the latter representing some lesser shareholders as well as the working miners. Carpenter still believed they had a strong claim as the original discoverers but lacked finance to put into the undertaking. When the company was formed it was alleged the Clymos said to Carpenter, 'Throw the first discoverers out or give them any part you choose from your share'. Carpenter was said to have been incensed and sought a reasonable percentage of shares from each of the parties to distribute to the original working miners. Eventually the Clymos reluctantly agreed to each of three working miners receiving three shares, the undertaking being in 130 shares, which proportionately gave two thirds of the remainder to the Clymos and one third to Carpenter and the lesser adventurers.[3] Clearly this was a major coup for the Clymos who, by the rules of the cost book, stood to make a huge return on what they were confident was a promising undertaking, either by placing a percentage of their shares on the open market or retaining them in the hope of a high financial return. In the latter case they had to be prepared to pay calls proportionate to their shareholding until the mine became profitable, but this they clearly had amassed funds to do from previous successes.

The final version is given by Peter Clymo Jnr himself, when he rose to speak at an account dinner in Menheniot in 1859, having just been congratulated on his management, first of Wheal Trelawny and then of Wheal Mary Ann. Turning to the assembled company he said

I and my poor brother [who had died in 1849] were laughed at for thinking to have a mine in Menheniot. The mine was discovered by a man named Richard Sowden and he and some of his companions applied for a sett before anything was said to my brother. Mr Trelawny however would not grant a sett without a responsible man came forward [inferring someone with proven mining management expertise and sound financial backing]. Then Trelawny was commenced.[4]

Here at last is probably the emerging truth, whilst an element of fact runs through all three stories. Clearly a small group of practical miners, possibly prompted by a labourer making a discovery whilst digging a parish road, applied to work the sett. It was quite normal for a mineral lord to take some care that those to whom he was leasing had both the management expertise and finance to fund proper exploration. This was in his direct interest, for his own future income from granting the lease was to come from a percentage of ore sales rather than a fixed rental. The proven abilities of the Clymos would have clearly been seen as preferable to a group of practical miners of unproven organisational ability, whatever sympathy he held for their circumstances. Equally in the fast moving cut and thrust world of mining the Clymos negotiating stance on the allocation of shares demonstrated a shrewd and determined style which, despite their own humble origins, was probably central to their success. Negotiations having been completed and a lease obtained in 1843 for 21 years at 1-15th dues, the ground stood ready for practical exploration to commence and Menheniot's mining industry was thus born, with Wheal Trelawny its flagship setting the way for others to follow in future years.

This birthplace of serious mining in the parish lay just over half a mile north of the village, by way of the steep, later to be called Mine Hill, leading up from the square. On the brow of Mine Hill the now barely identifiable site of the second great parish stalwart Wheal Mary Ann lay on the left before the lane wound downwards until on the right hand side as the road began to climb again, hidden by a thickly wooded slope, lay the site of Wheal Trelawny. The dressing floors, walled shafts and scant structural remains have now blended into the garden and grounds of the private residence still called Trelawny, itself adapted from the original account house. Phillips Shaft, walled and capped, lies immediately in front of the house and Trelawny Engine Shaft, the principal and deepest shaft, 125 yards north of the former in the now thickly-wooded section of the property. Sadly no dramatic engine houses remain on this original site, later known as the southern mine and completely abandoned since 1874, but in recent years remains of the dressing floors, the powder house and the extensive main reservoir, or engine pond, have re-emerged from well over a century of vigorous reclamation by thick natural ground cover and trees. It should be remembered however that this important historical site is now in the grounds of a private residence.

Returning to that first year of mining in 1843, Peter Clymo Jnr had been appointed manager and purser whilst James Clymo, who was already fully committed as manager of South Caradon, chose to take a less prominent role, confining his interests as a shareholder to membership of the committee of management. There is little doubt however that his practical expertise was never far away in the decisions supporting the early development of the mine. The Clymos with their wider interests would have worked from their Liskeard town office, although they were regularly to be seen on the Liskeard to Menheniot road riding out to check on progress at the mine. In an astute move they brought in their uncle Henry Vivian, an experienced Camborne born mine captain then aged 52, as combined surface and underground agent, placing day to day control in his capable hands. He, like the Clymos, had spent many years mining in the St Austell area after leaving his native west Cornwall, but soon settled with his wife and daughter in the village, where he continued to live after his eventual retirement.

Initial development may have appeared slow to uninitiated observers but in reality the opening out of any mine, particularly one being set up with long term prospects in view, required a considerable outlay and preparatory work both on surface structures and in initial trials to determine the best position for sinking the shaft. By May 1844 the engine house, blacksmiths and carpenters workshops and the account house had their foundations laid and walls partly up, whilst the first engine shaft (later to be known as Phillips Shaft) was being steadily sunk and a shallow level being driven. Meanwhile a 22-inch engine had been obtained and was shortly to be installed in the engine house. Serious ore production had yet to get under way, with underground work concentrating on sinking and opening out the first shallow level, but an initial parcel of eight tons of ore was ready for sale. A promising start for a brave new venture in a new and unproven ore district.[5]

By the end of 1844 £1,500 had been spent, but the mine was almost reaching the point where ore sales equalled current expenditure and it was confidently expected that Wheal Trelawny would enter the dividend lists during 1845.[6] The adventurers were already in no doubt that their faith in Menheniot was to be admirably rewarded and with it the prospects were presented of considerable expansion and the creation of major opportunities for a rapidly increasing mining workforce. Shareholding was already diverse, with local investment supplemented by an increasing holding on the London market; a link to become increasingly dominant as the period progressed.

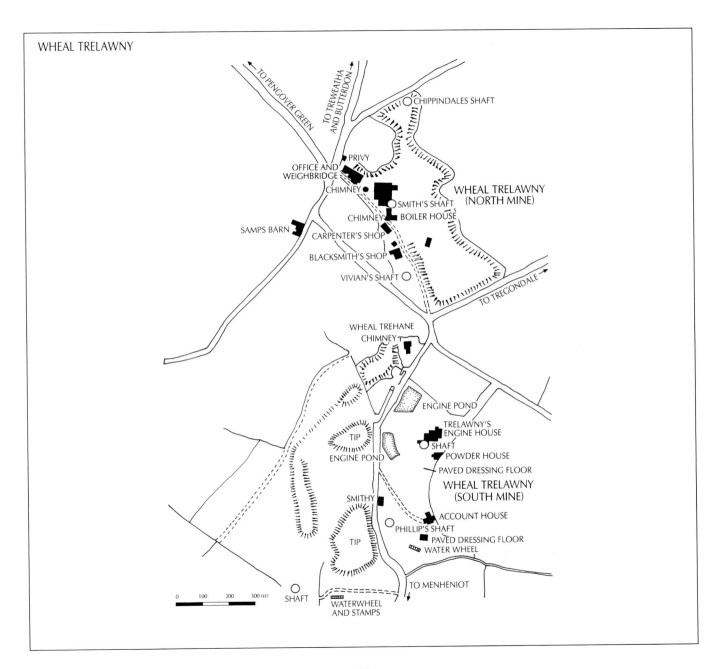

WHEAL TRELAWNY

TO PENGOVER GREEN

TO TREWEATHA
AND BUTTERDON

CHIPPINDALES SHAFT

PRIVY

OFFICE AND
WEIGHBRIDGE

CHIMNEY

SAMPS BARN

CARPENTER'S SHOP

BLACKSMITH'S SHOP

VIVIAN'S SHAFT

CHIMNEY
SMITH'S SHAFT
BOILER HOUSE

WHEAL TRELAWNY
(NORTH MINE)

TO TREGONDALE

WHEAL TREHANE
CHIMNEY

ENGINE POND

TIP

ENGINE POND

TRELAWNY'S
ENGINE HOUSE
SHAFT
POWDER HOUSE
PAVED DRESSING FLOOR

WHEAL TRELAWNY
(SOUTH MINE)

SMITHY

ACCOUNT HOUSE

TIP

PHILLIP'S SHAFT
PAVED DRESSING FLOOR
WATER WHEEL

0   100   200   300 FEET

SHAFT

TO MENHENIOT

WATERWHEEL
AND STAMPS

July 1845 found Phillips Engine Shaft sunk to the point where 12 and 22 fathom levels were being worked north and south on the course of the lode and paying ore deposits found in each of the levels.[7] By this time the young mine consisted of an adit driven 90 yards north and 60 yards south of the shaft, a 12 fathom level driven 128 yards north and an unprescribed distance south, whilst the deepest 22 fathom level had reached 12 yards north but a full 96 yards south. Each of the ends were productive and development was continuing on what was still a small undertaking.[8]

February 1846 was to prove an important milestone in Wheal Trelawny's history when the first dividend, of £1,040 or £8 per 1-130th share for the quarter ending December 1845, was declared at a meeting of adventurers in Liskeard. Phillips shaft had now reached a depth of 32 fathoms, where the next level would be started, whilst the existing 12 and 22 fathom levels were proving as productive as ever. Most of the mine's adventurers attended the meeting, including some from London, and after the official business was concluded a convivial dinner took place, culminating in formal speeches and toasts, the latter particularly offered to the manager and the non-resident shareholders from London.[9] The welcome returns were indeed to prove the first of four successive two monthly dividends of £1,040 halted only by the need to divert funds into further expansion of the mine.

July 1846 saw the first reference to a new engine shaft, to be known as Trelawny's, located 125 yards north of Phillips, which had reached a token depth of three fathoms by that time.[10] A 50-inch engine had been ordered from John Hodge's foundry at St Austell, set to dwarf the original Phillips 22-inch and a brave investment in the long term future of the mine, providing with some foresight capability to pump water from a considerable depth. By the end of October the engine house was complete and the roof on, with the engineer expected to begin heaving in the engine the following week.[11] It had been hoped to have it working by the end of the year, but in reality it was late February 1847 before this was achieved.[12] In fact Trelawny Shaft had continued to be sunk without the benefit of the new engine and a depth of 22 fathoms had been reached without apparent drainage problems.[13] This somewhat unusual achievement may have been helped by a dry autumn, but was more likely due to the short term ability of the Phillips 22-inch engine, which was draining that shaft to the greater depth of 42 fathoms, to naturally unwater shallower ground over a wide area. The mine workforce by now numbered 130 and was still increasing.[10]

If we now follow the history of these two shafts, their development continued in parallel with importance moving steadily away from Phillips and towards Trelawny Shaft until the latter became the sole working engine in that part of the property. Initially both continued to be sunk with Phillips reaching 52 fathoms by July 1847, 62 fathoms by March 1848, 72 fathoms

by September and an ultimate depth of 82 fathoms by August 1849.[14] Meanwhile Trelawny Shaft, started some two years later, sought to overtake its older neighbour, reaching 42 fathoms by November 1847, 62 fathoms by January 1849 and 72 fathoms by August 1849 when Phillips had reached its final depth.[15] Located only 125 yards apart on the same north to south lode, the levels driven from each shaft eventually met, offering through communication. This process continued downwards, level by level, and between August 1849 and November 1850 the 82 fathom level from Phillips Shaft was relentlessly driven northwards until it became the final link with Trelawny engine shaft. At this point the decision was taken to dispose of the Phillips 22-inch engine, leaving both drainage and whim haulage for that part of the mine in the capable hands of the Trelawny 50-inch engine.[16] The Phillips engine was sold for £399 and removed from the mine some time prior to September 1851.[17] Despite ceasing to perform any central role after 1850, Phillips Shaft remained open, easily identifiable to the present day and may have been used as a footway shaft for miners descending into the workings. Trelawny Shaft reached a depth of 94 fathoms by the time the 82 fathom level from Phillips had communicated with it in November 1850.[16] Sinking continued over the next twenty years to a depth exceeding 200 fathoms, where we shall return at a later stage of our story.

The powerful engines, in their impressive houses, were central to a mine's survival and kept workings unwatered, often in a precarious relationship with nature, particularly during the inevitable wet winters. Failure of the pumping equipment brought serious and immediate consequences to underground workings, well illustrated when in February 1849 the main rod in Trelawny shaft broke. The water rise, although relentless, did not endanger life, but within several days the 62 fathoms deep shaft, with associated levels, was completely flooded below a depth of 39 fathoms, equivalent to 138 feet of standing water.[18] Although repaired within days, well over a week was lost before pumping made the levels accessible again and men were able to return to the dark, dripping depths with walls, floors and ladders slippery and sodden.[19]

Barely four months later a serious fire occurred in one of Wheal Trelawny's boiler houses, which was discovered to be well alight at two o'clock early one June morning. Fortunately the fire was contained, the engine house and other buildings unaffected and no serious disruption to production resulted. The underground clothing of fifty miners was nevertheless lost, but part of the replacement cost was paid by the adventurers. The cause of the fire was never established.[20]

In 1847 Henry Vivian was continuing to manage the day to day affairs of the mine on behalf of Peter Clymo Jnr, reference being made in January to the need for the former to clear both the disposal and price of any surplus scrap or materials on the mine with the purser and to ensure any sales were passed properly through the mine's accounts.[12] Clearly the intention was to foster a tightly run concern, not always the case in Cornish mining circles. Serious personality clashes were however brewing between the Clymos and in particular the distant London shareholders. The previous year had seen a bitter legal dispute between these two parties on the rights to development and share ownership of the adjacent Wheal Mary Ann, recounted fully in the section on that concern. A bitter taste and a severe mistrust of the Clymos by the London adventurers clearly remained.

Despite the Clymos' continuing significant shareholding Peter Clymo Jnr resigned as manager and purser in May 1847 when an advertisement was placed for a successor.[21] From that point the Clymos ceased to be involved in the practical management of Wheal Trelawny, although they continued as shareholders in the company with the rights which that brought. A very different situation to the adjacent Wheal Mary Ann, where Peter Clymo Jnr remained in direct control as both manager and purser for most of its life and indeed until his own death in 1870.

Peter Clymo Jnr's replacement was to be a young 33 year old mine agent by the name of John Bryant, who had for the past year been the resident agent at the adjacent and smaller Wheal Trehane.[22] Initially he took full responsibility as manager and purser, but in November 1847 John Philp was appointed joint purser.[23] The latter was also a shareholder, had financial interests and accountancy responsibilities in a number of undertakings and had also been purser at the adjacent Wheal Trehane since its opening in 1846. Reflecting the increasing scale of responsibility surrounding the expanding Wheal Trelawny, it was specified that John Bryant should devote his entire services to the mine, holding no secondary appointments in other small concerns as was common at the time.[22] Simultaneously Joseph Kemp, a Gwinear man, was recruited as mine agent alongside Henry Vivian. The next two years saw the mine move from strength to strength, increasing in both profitability and scale, but what had been an inspired management partnership was tragically cut short when in May 1849 John Bryant, at the early age of 35, was taken ill and died of typhus leaving a young wife and family and a respectful mining fraternity to mourn his passing.[24] Due to a variety of circumstances fate conspired to ensure that Wheal Trelawny saw no less than nine managers in 28 years, a record more commonly associated with ailing concerns, whilst Wheal Mary Ann, very similar in scale and profitability, had but three over a similar period. John Bryant's death necessitated a further reshuffle and in 1849 Joseph Kemp was promoted from mine agent to manager, John Philp took over sole pursership responsibility and Thomas Ellery, a Redruth man, was recruited as mine agent. About this time Peter Clymo's uncle Henry Vivian left the mine and briefly joined Peter Clymo Jnr at Wheal Mary Ann before taking a well earned retirement in his adopted Menheniot. Thomas Ellery's health did not hold up, for in

December 1851 he accepted ill-health retirement at the age of 56 and was sent on his way with a grant of £40 from the sympathetic adventurers.[25]

Returning to the year 1847, work was about to be started on what became known as the north mine, or northern part of Wheal Trelawny. The site is marked today by the tall chimney which still dominates the area, but this in fact dates from the much later Wheal Hony and Trelawny United (1880-1884). The re-occupation by this concern has left a much more complex mixture of remains compared with the relatively simple southern site, unmolested after final and complete closure in 1874. Trelawny's two surface locations give the appearance of being quite separate concerns with green fields intervening, but in fact the workings became connected underground as increasingly deepening levels were pushed north and south respectively. The separate development of these two sites owes much to the cheeky incursion of the small but rich Wheal Trehane, which by shrewd negotiation effectively punched a hole in the side of Trelawny land by securing in March 1846 the mineral rights to a key parcel of land beneath which the lode ran between the proven northern and southern sites, the former however being still undeveloped at that time. Despite Trelawny simultaneously securing the rights to fields immediately to the east, thereby linking their two sites, the true wealth was proved to lie in the route via the Trehane property. This small independent concern made considerable profits between 1846 and 1857, but was too small to sustain long term development and was inevitably taken over by Wheal Trelawny in 1857, at last giving the latter a full and unbroken run on its main lode.

During the custodianship of Wheal Trelawny three shafts were sunk on the northern site; Vivian's to a depth of 30 fathoms located 240 yards north of Trelawny Shaft, Smith's to a depth exceeding 200 fathoms located 120 yards north of Vivian's, and Chippindale's, also to a depth exceeding 200 fathoms, located 140 yards north of Smith's. Charles Trelawny was mineral lord of the bulk of the northern site, including that beneath Smith's and Vivian's, whilst smaller parts were owned by J. Carthew, around Chippindale's, and a small section by Dr Honey.[26] Vivian's was never equipped with a steam engine whilst the large 70-inch at Smith's provided pumping power for the complete northern site. Whim haulage for both shafts was provided by a single engine conveniently located.

Despite the south mine having been worked since early 1844, it was to be 1847 before Vivian's Shaft was started in the north with a token depth of four fathoms reached by March.[27] It had always been believed that both sections held equal potential and this delay would not have been from lack of adventurers' enthusiasm, but rather one of being unable to gather the resources and finance to pursue both projects until returns were being made in the south to ease the burden. Vivian's was ultimately proven to have been sunk in the wrong place and had but a limited life, but it was to be drivings from this shaft that proved the lode and enabled the more precisely located Smith's and Chippindale's to be sunk with determination to secure the long term future of the mine.

By July 1847 Vivian's was 20 fathoms deep, crosscuts probing east and west, whilst by September the east had met the lode with a level subsequently driven northwards at right angles to the crosscut, along the course of the lode and into the heart of the northern ground.[28] By the end of 1847, barely nine months after commencement, Vivian's had reached its ultimate depth of 30 fathoms and by March 1848 a 30 fathom level was following beneath and on the same course as the 20 fathom above for a distance of 120 yards northwards. Since early April a group had been sinking the new Smith's Shaft from surface, to plans laid down by manager John Bryant. The location of Smith's was 120 yards north of Vivian's and clearly it was no coincidence that beneath them the 20 and 30 fathom levels had already reached that same position. The sinking of Smith's to a depth of 30 fathoms took barely seven weeks, an exceptional rate of progress aided by miners below working upwards or rising the shaft, from the levels driven from Vivian's. Foul air severely curtailed progress but this was resolved by boring a ventilation link through 18 feet of rock downwards from the then base of Smith's to the levels below. With at least token air circulation the shaft was widened to its full dimensions and sinking to 30 fathoms completed.[29]

Smith's Shaft continued to be sunk below this level, with 40 and 50 fathom levels working by the end of 1849.[30] The original 30 fathom level from Vivian's which had once finished at Smith's was pushed on northwards towards the distant boundary leaving Smith's perfectly situated at the centre of the northern sett.[31] In these circumstances the relevance of Vivian's Shaft faded away and no further reference was made to its use other than as a footway shaft. Attention now having moved towards Smith's with a logical programme of development under way in the 30, 40 and 50 fathom levels, it was with some surprise that in May 1849 John Bryant in his report to the *Mining Journal* made a simple but significant statement, 'We have commenced driving two levels from Trehane boundary - the 45 and 55 fathom'[24] No explanation was given as to how Trelawny men miraculously appeared at that depth, with no shaft adjacent and no levels driven from existing workings. Reference to working the 45 and 55 fathom levels however continued, to which a 68 fathom level was added in 1850 within the same area.[32]

The missing piece of the jigsaw was to be found in Wheal Trehane. When research moved on to that mine it became clear that whilst Wheal Trelawny's northern operation was still in an infant state in 1849, Wheal Trehane had reached a depth of 78 fathoms and was indeed working 45, 55 and 68 fathom levels from its own Kellys' Shaft right up to the Wheal

Trelawny boundary, where the lode crossed into that sett. Clearly Trelawny's men were driving these levels from the Trehane side, gaining access both for themselves and for sending out ore via Wheal Trehane. In reverse Trehane was paying Trelawny for the use of their engine to additionally pump Kellys Shaft, barely 160 yards away, by means of flat rods, there being no engine on Trehane at the time. In addition a separate charge was made to Trehane for supplies of additional water for dressing purposes. This proved a lucrative deal for Wheal Trelawny until Trehane invested in its own engine some years later. It was at this time that Trelawny was gaining access to the 45, 55 and 68 fathom levels enabling early returns to be made in that part of the mine in advance of expensive works on the Trelawny side. It remains odd that no identifiable charge was raised for this important concession bearing in mind that both were independent concerns accountable to separate shareholders. The arrangement lasted from May 1849 to at least July 1850, when the 50 fathom level south from Smith's communicated with the 55 north from Trehane, after which Smith's 50 was renamed the 55. The arrangement may have lasted a further year, despite this communication, for deeper 68 and 78 fathom levels were being worked in April 1851, when Smith's Shaft had still only reached 65 fathoms.

Between March 1847 and February 1851, when a magnificent 70-inch steam engine was set to work at Smith's Shaft, no steam power was used for drainage or whim haulage in the north, despite Smith's having reached a depth of 55 fathoms and Vivian's 30 fathoms. As early as May 1848 John Bryant had stated that the mine must make provision for the erection of an engine on the northern part of the sett, to complement the significant potential there.[29] It was indeed exceptional in this district for such provision not to have been essential at a very much shallower depth, the only explanation being that natural drainage was occurring toward Phillips and Trelawny Engine Shafts in the south and Wheal Trehane on the south west. Horse whims would have been used in this interim period for raising the ore, with the men descending as ever by conventional ladders.

The final shaft in the north, Chippindale's, was commenced in 1853, 140 yards north of Smith's on the same lode. Like Smith's it was sunk onto levels which already existed below, these having been driven north from the latter, which had now reached a depth of 97 fathoms with levels at approximately 10 fathoms intervals.[34] This enabled good progress to be made, the shaft reaching 30 fathoms by October 1853 and no less than 70 fathoms by June 1854.[35] The practice of rising from levels below was again employed to complement traditional sinking. A single engine for whim haulage served both Chippindale's and Smith's shafts. We now leave the northern part of the mine, initial development having been completed and the site under steady production. Both Chippindale's and Smith's were to be worked consistently for another twenty years to depths exceeding 200 fathoms, as the rich lead lode was exploited to the full.

Until 1849 shareholders meetings were regularly held in the Fountain Inn, Liskeard, after which they moved to Webbs Hotel on the other side of The Parade, both places still prominent today. The 1850s saw steady progress of a now large and well established concern, with 408 underground and surface workers employed in 1851. Dividends were regularly declared, a luxury not shared by many mining concerns, although their level and occasional absence was influenced by prices on the lead market, variations in the richness of the levels and the need for further investment in equipment or extension of the workings.

1854 was a less successful year, culminating in the departure of Joseph Kemp as manager. Between 1854-1861 reports carried the joint names of agents William Bryant, William Jenkin and Thomas Grenfell, the first named regarded as managing agent. By the latter year William Bryant, from Perranuthnoe, was living in Castle Gardens, Liskeard; William Jenkin, Illogan-born, in Barn Street, Liskeard; and Thomas Grenfell, Crowan-born, in Addington Place, Liskeard. Each rode out to the mine daily to direct operations. Young Thomas Grenfell, aged 35 on his arrival, was to remain with Wheal Trelawny until its closure seventeen years later, holding the post of manager in its final year, clearly both a practical and loyal mine servant. John Prince briefly appeared as manager between 1856-1858, probably in a remote role for the three agents continued to control the practical affairs around the mine. However after 1858 the three were once again in charge, with William Bryant resuming the role of managing agent. To a man these were west Cornishmen, the Liskeard and Menheniot areas' source of practical expertise.

As the decade ended Wheal Trelawny could look back with some satisfaction at its steady expansion to a position of strength and standing in the mining fraternity, as could its near neighbour Wheal Mary Ann. Together they represented the cornerstones of employment in the much expanded mining community of Menheniot and their stability in turn reflected upon the prosperity of the village itself. Miners came and went, as was their transient nature, but experienced men who chose to stay with their families now found stability of employment whilst the best tributers became a recognised elite within the community and an asset to the mine. Wheal Trelawny declared consistent but unspectacular dividends year after year and made no calls between 1851 and 1861, the latter a difficult year to which we will return. Ore production remained high throughout the period, the silver content increasing with depth. Detailed production figures are set out in Appendix B.

So often, in looking back, interest is centred upon the fortunes of the working miner, but battles fought behind the closed doors of company offices, as shares and influence changed, proved to be the real influence in any mining company's affairs. As the 1860s dawned Wheal Trelawny's shares, as happened with many of the larger mines, moved more and more under the control of London interests and the true Cornish influential presence waned. London money had always been a prominent feature of Wheal Trelawny, but previously local interests were well represented on the committee of management and the local purser retained more direct responsibility. The manager and his experienced underground and surface agents however remained truly Cornish, cornering the market on practical expertise to the very end. However, convincing distant management of the correctness of future direction the mine should take, along with dependence on distant decisions for the supply of much needed investment, became an increasing burden on those to whom the working miner turned and was dependent for his livelihood. The working miner could not, nor could he be expected, to appreciate the wider considerations which weighed heavily on the manager and purser as they went about their business in Liskeard or as they passed along the lanes of Menheniot riding to and from the mine.

Significant changes following this trend began to occur starting when John Philp, Liskeard born purser and book-keeper of many concerns, tendered his resignation in 1861 at the ripe age of 78. A life long bachelor, living in Barn Street, Liskeard, with his niece as housekeeper, he remained very active in the years up to retirement, chairing most of the Trelawny meetings during this period. An important Liskeard influence went with his retirement. Another major influence to disappear from 1860 was Charles Chippindale of Regents Park, London. He was a prominent committee man and Chairman from the very earliest days of the 1840s with interests in Wheal Mary Ann and Wheal Trelawny. He was also prominent in the speculative Menheniot ventures of South Wheal Trelawny, Butterdon and Penhauger. Chippindale's Shaft at Wheal Trelawny was named after this well-respected individual, who visited the area many times to attend account meetings, despite the problems associated with journeys from London before the through rail link was established in 1859.

His departure may however have been significant in releasing shares in large numbers to be taken by those who wished to become the new influence in Wheal Trelawny's affairs. That new influence was to forge a previously undiscovered shareholding and management link with the large and influential West Caradon, in St Cleer parish - only second in importance to the large and rich South Caradon. Whether this was a consciously organised coup or the coincidence of a closely knit group of London financiers independently following each others advice in taking up a shareholding will never be known. It was however to have a profound effect on the appointment of future Trelawny managers and agents. Visible evidence of this joint influence began to emerge as the same leading figures appeared on both mines committees of management. Richard Hallett was prominent as committee member and Chairman of West Caradon between 1859 and 1865 and of Wheal Trelawny between 1862 and 1866, whilst William Nicholson of London was Chairman of West Caradon in 1867-68 and of Wheal Trelawny from 1867 to 1869, where he had also been a committee man as early as 1857. He died in 1870 at the age of 83, demonstrating that age was no barrier to Victorian business influence. Likewise W. Page was recorded as committee man and Chairman of Wheal Trelawny between 1862 and 1866 whilst also on the committee of a speculative West Caradon offshoot, West South Caradon, from 1861 to 1863. Finally Henry Milford, professional company director, was Chairman of both West Caradon and Wheal Trelawny in 1870. No company records have survived from this time and the patterns of influence have had to be built up from a comprehensive analysis of newspaper and journal reports over the life of the mine. The effect of intrigue and influence within the London Mining and Stock Exchanges on Cornish mining remains an area given scant attention and worthy of more in-depth research in the future.

As 1861 dawned the south mine was experiencing a weakening and more difficult lode and fortunes were beginning to dip, dividends having ceased the previous autumn, and two substantial calls becoming necessary in the second half of 1861. Whilst agents Bryant, Jenkin and Grenfell bravely reported the worsening position to the January 1861 meeting, consideration was being given to strengthening the management team by seeking the services of prominent Cornish mining man Francis Pryor of Redruth.[36] In the event the decision was postponed for a further two weeks to allow more time for reflection. The reconvened meeting, at Webbs Hotel, Liskeard, confirmed his appointment at a salary of eight guineas a month, but more significantly as the Caradon connection strengthened, this followed his similar appointment as manager of West Caradon in 1859.[37] He not only held both these positions concurrently but similarly the management of five developing mines on Caradon, all with heavy West Caradon influence and twelve other concerns stretching from west Cornwall to the Devon border. A further five spread throughout Cornwall were in the hands of Richard his young nephew, as a direct result of the Pryor influence. Francis Pryor had by now become one of the leading names in Cornish mining expertise, whose very presence fronting a company added credibility and confidence to present and potential shareholding. From his Redruth base he diligently took great personal interest in all his concerns, making inspired and influential decisions on future direction wherever he went. Nevertheless he relied heavily on each mine's resident agents for day to day supervision and control, which he ensured was entrusted to men he knew and, indeed, more often than not, were also close relations.

Francis Pryor had been born in Crowan in 1819, the fifth son of a Captain William Pryor, and became a shrewd working miner, gaining the attention and confidence of influential mining people, who promoted him quickly to more responsible positions. He eventually attained the position where he could wield significant financial as well as practical influence and was by 1861, at the comparitively early age of 41, respected throughout Cornwall and more importantly in London. He died in 1870 at the age of 51, like Peter Clymo Jnr married but childless.[38]

His first progress report in April 1861 carried an unprecedented six signatures consisting of Francis Pryor, his nephew Richard Pryor, James Brown one of the West Caradon agents and the ever-faithful Trelawny team of William Bryant, William Jenkin and Thomas Grenfell. This disguised a somewhat prickly transitional period which by the end of 1861 had firmly resolved itself in favour of a new team of agents. Francis Pryor weeded out the older men leaving nephew Richard, aged 32, with Thomas Grenfell, still only 42 as the experienced link with intimate knowledge of what had gone before at the mine. Despite the traditional Cornish picture of trusted and senior white-coated agents, it is clear that young teams of mine agents were not uncommon in the district at this time. On his arrival Francis Pryor insisted upon a significant call to be made on the shares, in his words, to set the concern up properly and from this base the scene was set for the mine to move forward into the tough but, at least initially, marginally profitable 1860s.[40] The degree to which this uncertainty and change permeated through to the working miner must be a matter of conjecture, but undoubtedly rumour and concern would have surrounded the sudden departure of Jenkin and Bryant, two familiar figures at the mine and around Menheniot village.

W. J. Dunsford, West Caradon secretary since 1858, was appointed London secretary to Wheal Trelawny in August 1861, forming yet another common link with that mine, both positions being held until his sudden death in November 1864. He was secretary to 47 companies at that time, an indication of how such positions were truly agencies in the broadest sense of the word. W.J. Dunsford had a reputation for honesty and gentlemanly conduct and his sudden death was, according to his colleagues, linked to overwork in connection with his business affairs.[41]

The need for change to the direct management team continued to haunt Wheal Trelawny, starting in May 1864 when Francis Pryor resigned as manager, part of a systematic withdrawal from his east Cornwall interests to ease his business commitments. His three years had however been both influential and beneficial and he left the mine a stronger concern as he departed. The Chairman of the May 1864 adventurers meeting, in accepting his resignation, added that Francis Pryor had offered his continuing informal support and had subsequently accepted a seat on the committee of management, where his wide experience would no doubt prove invaluable.[42]

Francis Pryor's nephew Richard Pryor was promoted at age 35 from agent to manager, in November 1864, but before he had any real opportunity to demonstrate his worth, and only six months after his appointment, he was thrown from his horse and died shortly afterwards from injuries he had received. He left a young wife of only three months and the incident shocked a close knit mining fraternity, who were quick to acknowledge that a young man of considerable ability and energy had been lost to Cornish mining. It was all the more ironic following earlier manager John Bryant's similar untimely demise in 1849. Only three days prior to this London secretary W.J. Dunsford had also died, leaving the affairs of Wheal Trelawny in turmoil at both the London and Menheniot ends.[43]

The influential and steadying hand of the London shareholders quickly came into play and the proven experience of West Caradon manager William Johns was secured to become manager of Wheal Trelawny as well.[43] William Johns, a Redruth man, had been brought in by Francis Pryor in 1859 as an agent at West Caradon at the age of 42. When Francis Pryor resigned his managership of West Caradon and Wheal Trelawny in 1864, William Johns had been promoted from agent to manager at the former just as the now deceased Richard Pryor had been at Wheal Trelawny. Yet again it superficially appeared West Caradon was in effect managing Wheal Trelawny. This was strictly speaking not so, the appointments were separate but acceptable dual responsibilities, the link being in reality common shareholding and secretaryships which had led to solutions inevitably carrying a common influence.

William Johns lived on the mine at West Caradon, in the mine house, with his wife and eight children, aged from 16 years down to 10 months. His wife was from Tywardreath, near St Austell, whilst his children had been born in Redruth and Gwennap, tracing a pattern of movement around mining centres before his arrival in St Cleer. On most days he rode to Menheniot to check on progress at the mine, whilst the now indispensable local knowledge of Thomas Grenfell, his resident agent, was supplemented by the appointment of John Pryor, Camborne-born brother to the late Richard and at 27 maintaining the now established youthful make-up of the Wheal Trelawny team. As 1864 drew to a close a stable team of agents emerged which would remain together for the next six years, Thomas Grenfell and John Pryor additionally seeing out Trelawny's last year before closure as an independent concern in 1871. Thomas Grenfell was to have the doubtful honour of the managership in that final year. Wheal Trelawny's complete team of managers, agents and pursers are shown in Appendix I.

The inspectors for Lord Kinnaird's inquiry into the condition of mines visited Wheal Trelawny in December 1863, offering a valuable opportunity to review the facilities which now existed at surface, particularly those for the benefit of the working miners and mine girls. At the south mine two

Powderhouse, Wheal Trelawny. Hidden deep in undergrowth, the inside stone walls still show evidence of wood lining.

S. Bartlett 1989

drying and changing houses were provided, where up to 100 men and boys changed and in winter the mine girls were permitted to eat their dinner there. A large fire was provided, probably of metal stove design, with a long warming tube provided to supplement heat to the room. An aperture existed around the fire for warming dinners. Their were also raised planks around the room for the men to stand on whilst changing. Chests for the men were provided against the outer wall of a powder room across the yard.[44]

A second smaller drying and changing house was set at right angles to the first at the end of which small separate rooms were provided for pitmen and sumpmen, the former with wooden floors and a fire. Ore dressing, wet and cold work in winter for the young mine boys and girls, was mostly carried out under roofed sheds. They may not have been as comfortable as inferred, such sheds often being without side protection providing little cover from bitter winter weather. The north mine was less fully described. It was noted that dressing was under sheds, but that there was no provision for girls to warm their dinners except in the engine house, a potentially unsafe and undesirable location.[44]

Three working shafts were noted during the visit; on the south mine, Trelawny Shaft with its 50-inch engine was sunk perpendicularly to a depth of 170 fathoms and fitted for pumping and whim haulage, the latter with two kibbles used with chains. In the north Smith's and Chippindale's were sunk at an underlay of one foot per fathom and were 180 and 160 fathoms deep respectively. They were both described as for whim haulage with one kibble in each worked by the same engine. The latter description was not entirely complete as Smith's pumping role with its 70-inch engine was inexplicably omitted. Two ladder ways for miners' access to the workings were listed. Only Vivian's can be identified with certainty as one of the now dedicated footway shafts, the other is either the otherwise disused Phillips' or alternatively Kelly's Shaft, the latter at the by then integrated Wheal Trehane section of the mine.[44] Other equipment located around the mine, set amongst the ever growing and encroaching waste tips, included two 20-inch winding engines, a large 36 feet by five feet waterwheel for crushing and two further waterwheels driving 32 heads of stamps; the waterwheels were fed by surplus mine water stored in the nearby open reservoir.[45]

By 1862 Wheal Trelawny employed a workforce of 450, the ranks no doubt swelled by the integration of Wheal Trehane as well as general expansion in activity both underground and at surface.[46] The mine now entered what could be best described as the difficult 1860s and we shall follow the large concern's struggle year by year to control costs, whilst maximising output and desperately seeking to maintain some sort of a dividend for its shareholders. Between 1862 and 1867 this was achieved but

Miners drying and changing houses, Wheal Trelawny. 100 men and boys changed in No.1 dry, whilst in the winter females ate their dinner there.

Kinnaird inquiry report 1864

each year quarterly dividends of 12s.6d. or 10s. per share noticeably reduced to 5s. or 4s. as the latter year approached, with gaps when none could be declared. Gone were the glorious days of the 1850s which had seen quarterly dividends rise to £2 per share. 1867 was to see the last dividend and between then and 1871 calls became the order of the day for worried shareholders, until ultimate closure loomed over the parish giant. Mining reports however reveal a decade when the management team fought resolutely to strengthen the mine's position, never contemplating defeat, and manager William Johns with agents Thomas Grenfell and John Pryor continually sought new directions and recommended positive sinking to find stronger lead lodes as the only way to retrieve the situation. The working miner, for once, remained relatively protected at least in numbers if not remuneration during this period, with the workforce still as high as 363 in 1868 and 355 in 1870. The 1868 total was made up of 206 underground men on tutwork and tribute, 25 trammers and fillers underground and 132 men, boys and mine girls on surface work.[47] This high retention of workforce, despite a worsening financial position, was an inevitable recognition that with high fixed pumping costs and an extensive deep mine,

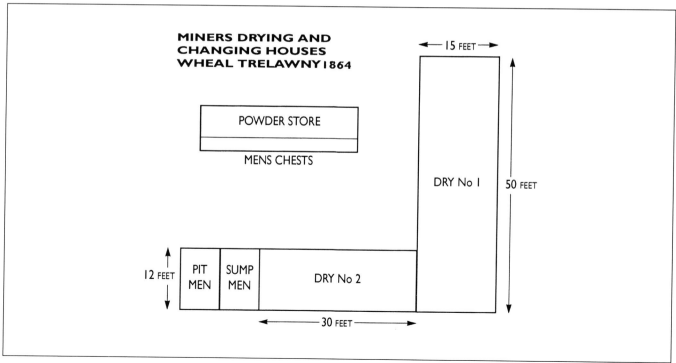

MINERS DRYING AND
CHANGING HOUSES
WHEAL TRELAWNY 1864

POWDER STORE

MENS CHESTS

←— 15 FEET —→

DRY No 1

50 FEET

12 FEET

PIT MEN | SUMP MEN | DRY No 2

←— 30 FEET —→

where any hopes of new ground lay at the deepest levels, development and ore extraction levels had to be kept high if the mine was to have any hope of achieving a return for the shareholding.

By February 1864 an extensive underground operation was being controlled, with Trelawny Shaft sunk to 166 fathoms, Smith's Shaft 186 fathoms and Chippindale's 172 fathoms. Trelawny had recently completed a phase of sinking to enable a 162 fathom level to be started that spring, whilst the 132 and 152 levels were being driven north. Smith's was being enthusiastically sunk by nine men, whilst 172 and 182 fathom levels were also being driven north and south of the shaft. The northern levels would be taken under Chippindale's shaft and on to the northern boundary. Chippindale's continued a consistent pattern of steadily being sunk on to or raised from each Smith's level after it had passed beyond the shaft. Smith's Shaft was to be the driving force taking the north mine ever deeper whilst its southern levels sought to meet those from Trelawny coming north.[48]

The mine followed a responsible policy of opening out reserves along the length of these levels well in advance of ore extraction by tributers, the practice in Trelawny being to drive levels beside rather than through the lode in readiness for subsequent controlled removal under tribute. One of the manager's key roles, aided by the detailed underground inspections of his agents, was to match the degree of controlled ore-extraction with demand and market price, an increasing problem in a difficult market situation. Despite the mine's positive approach, the informed observer would have noted a disturbing trend towards the quality of the ore and therefore the lodes falling off; a timely warning of ever increasing difficulties for the mine.

The positive response of successive managers was to recommend sinking deeper, the rate controlled more than they would have liked by the availability of finance for what remained slow and expensive work, but upon which the long term hopes of the mine depended. In this the experience of the adjacent Wheal Mary Ann encouraged the shareholding; a mine significantly deeper having passed through similar difficulties at a comparable depth. Now Wheal Trelawny hoped for that same improvement as they too sank. However enthusiastic the present management were the fact remained that, despite commencing over a year later, the well-managed Wheal Mary Ann was now at a significantly greater depth and more buoyant financially despite having to face the same cost and market difficulties. One is left with the feeling that two mines with very similar background and potential were gradually drawing apart, not for lack of present enthusiasm, but reaping a legacy of lost opportunity in the good times when good dividends were paid but which left Wheal Trelawny less well equipped to face the difficult times through which they were both now passing.

In March 1865 the committee confidently reported they were about to secure a lease on an area of new ground to the north, owned by Dr Honey. Their only concern was that existing mineral lord, Charles Trelawny, felt he was entitled to a royalty should this ore be brought to the surface via a shaft on his property.[49] This aside may partly explain the reason for two shafts, Smith's and Chippindale's being originally located only 140 yards apart on the same lode and both used as whim shafts; the former being on Trelawny land, the latter on lesser mineral lord, J. Carthew's land. However, despite all their efforts, the June meeting reported that Dr Honey had, after all, refused his consent, much to the consternation of several of the shareholders. J.Y. Watson complained that he and others had bought extra shares on the assumption that the lease would be granted.[50]

The inability to secure ground to the north restricted Trelawny's development to one of depth; an expensive option. This much sought northern extension represented a proven continuation of the lode, with each of Smith's levels down to the present 182, worked up to and against the northern boundary. This failure to secure led more than any other single factor to the ultimate closure of Wheal Trelawny, whilst the land's eventual release many years later was the cornerstone of the reworking of the northern part of Trelawny as Wheal Hony and Trelawny United from 1880 to 1884.

Between September 1865 and September 1866 Smith's was sunk by nine men from 196 to 210 fathoms despite contending with significant water problems, severe weather and heavy rainfall which almost brought work at the deepest levels to a standstill in January 1866. Sinking was suspended that September whilst the shaft was consolidated, the immediate objective having been reached, whilst the 196 and 210 fathom levels were progressively opened out. Meanwhile Trelawny Shaft which had been at 166 fathoms, with a 162 level the deepest worked, since February 1864, was resumed in September 1866, being also sunk by nine men.[51] The coincidence of Smith's sinking suspended and Trelawny restarted suggests a common labour source.

As each of Smith's levels coming south and Trelawny's north were progressively linked, illogicality and indeed inaccuracy in the titling of levels between the north and south mines became increasingly apparent. The 132, 142 and 152 levels north from Trelawny in fact met the 152, 162 and 172 levels coming south from Smith's; a 20 fathoms perceived discrepancy where they met, whatever the accuracy might have been at the point of sinking. It was next intended that the 162 Trelawny and 182 Smith's should join, but surviving mine plans show that the 182 and below it the 196 found the lode badly disordered by a slide as it approached the south mine, from which point the increasingly mistitled 182 angled downwards and the 196 upwards until they were linked by a winze, after which the combined level adopting the 196 title met the 162 coming north from Trelawny.[52] In a final act to confuse latter-day mine historians as to the true ultimate depth of

Trelawny shaft a decision was taken in 1867 to adopt common level naming, standardising on Smith's titles, throughout the mine below a level of 152 fathoms. As a result Trelawny 162 overnight became the 196 level, itself up to 10 fathoms shallower than claimed due to the steeply graded level as it progressed through the slide towards the south mine. Deliberate misrepresentation was never alleged nor necessarily intended but conveniently the overstatement of depth by at least 25 fathoms was quietly forgotten and would have misled prospective shareholders right up until closure, Trelawny's depth throughout the final period being quoted according to the revised terminology without qualification.

By March 1867 one of the drawing engines was considered life expired and potentially unsafe and March 1868 saw a new engine about to be set to work with a further burden of payments having fallen on the mine.[53] The spring of 1867 had been unusually wet and costs heavy due to an exceptionally high coal bill, as Smith's and Trelawny engines sought to keep the mine drained. A 4s. per share dividend was declared at the June 1867 meeting, somewhat unwisely in hindsight, for by December 1867 a £1 per share call was necessary and the June concession was to be remembered as the last dividend ever to be declared by the mine.[54] It was ironic that 1867 had seen lead ore production up almost a third to 1,272 tons, a tribute to William Johns' positive management and continual persuading of shareholders to authorise yet further sinking. But in an extensive deep mine like Trelawny high production equated to proportionately higher costs and whilst low market prices and moderate ore quality prevented sales overtaking costs then the good times remained as far away as ever. Whilst William Johns pondered his next move towards real profitability the established agents Thomas Grenfell and John Pryor urged the working men and creaking machinery to still greater efforts.

The committee now turned their attention to the mineral lords and initiated a campaign to seek suspension of dues, on the grounds that the shareholders were now bearing all the heavy risk and expense. The customary practice of paying dues as a percentage of ore sales, rather than fixed rent or on profits, worked well whilst a mine was at the initial development stage, with high cost but little ore production providing automatic relief, but badly when an established high production mine, such as Trelawny, was ailing. Here shareholders were now paying calls, but because production was high the mineral lords were still reaping a positive return at no risk to themselves. The shareholders threatened that if they found themselves unable to continue the mineral lord would receive nothing from an abandoned sett, but the latter pointed out that the shareholders had been quick enough to accept dividends over many years, so why should they not now bear the costs. The latter was true up to a point, but real help was now needed if the faithful parish stalwart was to continue in production.

Wheal Trelawny was becoming in danger of talking itself into its grave.

In March 1868 Chairman W. Nicholson reported that Charles Trelawny, with his accustomed liberality, and also J. Carthew agreed to give up their dues, but only if Dr Honey did so as well.[55] By June it was reluctantly confirmed that Dr Honey was immovable and that J. Carthew was also therefore unwilling to proceed, but that Charles Trelawny had offered full remission initially for twelve months.[56] Not for the first time Charles Trelawny had demonstrated a sympathetic attitude to both the company and the men on whom the parish depended, an attitude which must have been remembered around many a flickering fire in the cottages of Menheniot. In September William Johns strongly urged the shareholders to permit him to recommence sinking both Trelawny's and Smith's, the former having been at a stand for six months, the latter for almost two years.[57] In this he was appealing against a vote taken in June to suspend all further sinking until a satisfactory agreement was made with all the lords.[56]

The committee relented and Trelawny Shaft recommenced sinking in September 1868 'through beautiful ground' reported a relieved William Johns. The manager however was not satisfied and chided the committee that it was also of absolute necessity that he resumed sinking Smith's Shaft. Committee member Peter Watson however was adamant that the Trelawny decision was directly linked to Charles Trelawny's liberality, whilst equally they could not recommend the sinking of Smith's without some equal concession from all in the north. As the argument continued yet another £1 per share call was made.[58]

William Johns had set nine men to sink Trelawny shaft and by the following summer the 230 fathom level had been reached and work stopped while a crosscut was made in readiness for extending the new level. He continued to press the case for Smith's, stating in December 1868 that it was useless to contemplate sinking now, due to the relentless flow of water, but a restart had to be contemplated shortly. Chairman Peter Watson reluctantly conceded that despite no concession in dues the committee were seriously considering restarting the sinking of Smith's.[59] Throughout the dispute existing levels were under full production at Smith's, but without this commitment horizons could only be short term.

In early summer 1869 sinking was recommenced, after a two and a half year gap, coincidental not for the first time with Trelawny shaft reaching a natural pause for crosscutting at 230 fathoms and suggesting transfer of the nine man gang involved. Positive finds were needed, for by the end of 1868 production was down to 756 tons after the previous year's 1,272 tons. The sinking of Smith's proceeded more rapidly than expected, but in September William Johns had to admit some of the best tribute pitches in the mine had fallen off and returns were down.[60]

The shareholders invited Edward Rogers of Great Western Mines to make an independent inspection and report on the condition of the mine in December 1869. He reported the mine as well ventilated, the shafts well located for carrying on operations and powerful machinery was at surface capable of carrying on the working for several years. He felt that extending deeper levels, below those which had proved productive earlier for the mine, ought to offer a fair chance of meeting with something remunerative.[61] The report, published in the Christmas Day edition of the *Mining Journal*, could best be summed up as acknowledging a well equipped concern but rather guarded on prospects. 1869 production was up 100 tons to 875 tons, whilst 355 miners continued to be employed in 1870.[62] Between mid-1867 and mid-1869 calls totalled £4 on each of the 1,040 shares, many individuals being somewhat painfully in possession of large blocks which now held little value. The December 1869 meeting recommended and approved the sub-dividing of the 1,040 shares into 6,000.[61]

By March 1870 Smith's had reached its ultimate depth of 222 fathoms. William Johns reported the 210 level south of Smith's was being taken down by a pare of men, but sadly it was not turning out as he had anticipated compared with the level above. However, he did not despair that the end would ultimately lead to a successful result. It was emphasised that all the mine's bills were paid up to date.[61]

Local concern was evident in July 1870 when The Liskeard Gazette reported that, due to the illiberality of the lords in refusing to give up dues, about 1,000 shares had been relinquished in the past few days and it was feared that the mine would be wound up at the meeting of shareholders the following week. The report added that the decision would have serious consequences on the district.[64] In fact shareholders voted to continue and when they met again in October underground operations were still as extensive as ever and the sinking of Trelawny Shaft had been resumed. Finances were however still critical when respected shareholder Samuel Mocatta rose and stated he had been a shareholder for many years and would be sorry to see the workings suspended before Trelawny Shaft was sunk a further 15 fathoms. Secretary W. J. Lavington somewhat ominously clarified a further ten months would be needed to reach that depth. Another 642 shares were reported as relinquished. William Johns appealed for time and a further moderate outlay to enable his plans to be accomplished. The meeting having taken into consideration the encouraging reports decided to continue working the mine for the present, also accepting as a consequence a further 7s.6d. per share call.[65]

Shortly afterwards William Johns resigned, whilst overheads were contained by simply promoting senior mine agent Thomas Grenfell to manager, retaining just one agent in John Pryor. With Thomas Grenfell the mine was in sound and experienced hands, but he must have felt mixed emotions in presiding over a final and exceptionally difficult year.

Ore production in 1870 had dropped from 875 to barely 390 tons, despite the positive efforts of the local men. The sinking of Trelawny Shaft was nevertheless restarted in the Autumn at 234 fathoms and the now familiar nine man pare had reached 238 fathoms by January 1871. Thomas Grenfell also reported that 70 tons of ore were ready for sale, but that this had been delayed due to the severe frost. Optimistically he reassured shareholders that their two pumping and two winding engines were in first class condition and that other machinery and pitwork were in good working order. A brave body of shareholders accepted a 10s. per share call.[66] Whilst sympathy traditionally falls on the working miner in such situations, the financial commitment which was now facing many professional men whose fortunes were dependent upon the ailing mining industry is often forgotten. Some undoubtedly could afford to lose, others were showing exceptional resolve in supporting call after call, which in far off Menheniot ensured essential support for a large and totally dependent mining community.

Thomas Grenfell desperately sought to maintain an atmosphere of calm and long term commitment during that last spring of 1871, his regular reports to the *Mining Journal* being factual and unemotional but ensuring the scale of operation and effort was appreciated. As late as April 1871 he reported that Trelawny Shaft was sunk to 242 fathoms the ground being all that could be desired for the production of mineral. The latest parcel of lead ore had been bought by the Burry Port Smelting Company, near Llanelli, west Wales, and was being shipped that day.[67] However a crippling £2 per share call had to be made at the April 1871 meeting.[68] It was not altogether unexpected when only a month later a special general meeting decided to wind up the company with all possible speed.[69]

Wheal Trelawny. Excavations reveal the base of the engine house chimney and flue after many years buried in deep undergrowth.

G. Crocker 1989

Withdrawal from the deep workings was orderly and necessarily so if a responsible winding-up was to occur. The bringing to the surface of machinery and underground equipment with a resale value was pursued and whilst development stopped immediately, tribute work continued on a limited scale to ensure easily worked deposits were brought out during the final period of working, to maximise final ore sales. Samuel Mocatta and W.J. Lavington acted as liquidators and their astute management of the process, which was done outside the Stannaries Court, brought a vote of thanks from the shareholders and a resultant distribution of 17s.9d. per share to those who had remained faithful to the end.[70]

The bulk of the workforce, which had been last reported as 355 in 1870, were released soon after the May 1871 decision, a visitor in July 1871 reporting the sad site of a rear-guard workforce consisting of two agents, one clerk, three dressers and only thirty tributers, half of them being boys. He was critical of a tough directive by Thomas Grenfell that the men would get no money except that resulting from ore that was in future produced and that all cost they could must be stopped. The correspondent felt it unfair the burden should fall totally on the working classes, pointing out that both agents and a clerk were still in the employ of the company despite such a restricted operation.[71] It must be said the criticism expressed had a ring of truth.

With this all reports and reference to Wheal Trelawny ceased. Menheniot's mining community was unquestionably in turmoil with worse to come, as Treweatha collapsed in 1872 followed by Wheal Mary Ann in 1874. At abandonment the deepest levels being worked were the 222 at Smith's Shaft, 210 at Chippindale's and 230 at Trelawny's. Smith's Shaft had bottomed at 222 fathoms, but Trelawny was actively sinking at 242 fathoms when abandonment occurred. Trelawny's deep levels and shaft depth were, as previously explained, overstated by at least 25 fathoms although Smith's measurements were from surface, whereas Trelawny's original depths were below adit. The mine's true depth therefore is considered to be an absolute maximum of 230 fathoms from surface.

The silence which fell over Trelawny was however not to be permanent. Wheal Mary Ann faced an immediate crisis, for with Smith's and Trelawny pumping engines stopped the whole weight of pumping the immediate area would have fallen on them, the underground water level showing no respect for mine boundaries. Their reaction was swift, taking over the Trelawny lease and pumping capability with almost immediate effect. Somewhat surprisingly it was not only pumping that was retained at both the north and south mines. Active mining and ore extraction was restarted at both and continued until Wheal Mary Ann succumbed in 1874. This final period of working is covered under the Wheal Mary Ann chapter. For the south mine site around Trelawny Shaft, 1874 was to be the ultimate end, but the north mine was to re-emerge as Wheal Hony and Trelawny United (1880-1884), dealt with in a later chapter.

So Wheal Trelawny slipped into the pages of history, the early battles of the first adventurers long forgotten. It is easy to forget that memories of Menheniot, its lush rolling landscape and Trelawny itself would have been carried by the hundreds of miners who now sought their fortunes in the far corners of the world - Moonta, South Australia being one of the favoured destinations. Our last memory comes from there almost forty years later, as an ex-Trelawny miner recalled but slightly misquoted the stirring rendering of the Cornish ballad Trelawny by the mine's workforce so many years before. It is a fitting end to the Wheal Trelawny story sung by Trelawny's men, not the Cornishmen of the ballad but an army of miners who for almost three decades were the lifeblood of the great mine and the Menheniot community.

And they shall scorn Tre, Pol and Pen,
And Shall Trelawny die?
Then forty thousand Cornishmen
Shall Know the reason why,
And shall Trelawny die, brave boys?
And shall Trelawny die?
Then forty thousand Cornishmen
Shall know the reason why.[72]

CHAPTER FOUR
WHEAL MARY ANN

It would give you great pleasure to go over and see Wheal Mary Ann
with its masses of bright shining lead ore on the surface.
ABINADAB CROOTCH 1857

WHEAL MARY ANN (1845-1874) was the second of Menheniot's large mines and marginally the more successful. It too was a Clymo enterprise, but unlike Wheal Trelawny, which lost the brothers direct management influence after initial development, here the Clymo name remained the driving force through conception, development and on to the sustained management of a large and consistently profitable concern. Peter Clymo Jnr was purser from that early start in 1845, quickly succeeding his brother James as manager and becoming joint manager and purser from 1846 until his death in 1870, within four years of Wheal Mary Ann's own demise. A strong influence, never far from the heart of the story of one of Menheniot's two largest mines.

Wheal Mary Ann was not an easy mine to work profitably and yet profitably worked it was throughout most of its life. Time and time again astute financial and practical management was to be a feature which ensured a long term future for the mine and steady if unspectacular dividends for the shareholders. This influence extended beyond the Clymo name and was equally evident in a succession of long serving mine agents who ensured that consistent hands were in control of practical mining affairs throughout Wheal Mary Ann's life. One such man was Sithney born Henry Hodge, brought in by Peter Clymo shortly after commencement and an ever present influence for more than 18 years.

Wheal Mary Ann was just over one third of a mile north of the village, the first of the northern group of mines and located past the White Hart Inn and up steeply graded Mine Hill. A visitor today would find little changed on the early part of that walk but as the top of the hill was reached the gentle sloping field on the left, which today marks the site of the former surface workings, presents a very different picture to that found at the height of the mine's development in 1863. It is during that period that we set the scene on the second great Menheniot mine. Then the activity and noise would have provided a dramatic contrast to the rural surroundings, as would the dirt and dust which lay across the site. Then burrows spread out in long snaking lines northwards and westwards along the site boundaries. On the far side more spoil spewed over and ran down the steeply falling slope which formed a

natural containment to the central site area. The surface workings stretched some 300 yards to the north, parallel with the lane from the village, whilst averaging between 150 and 200 yards in width. Starting at the southern or village end a visitor would have first been confronted with Clymo's engine house, an impressive structure built in 1854, housing a massive 80-inch pumping engine and flanked by its adjacent boiler house. The rectangular shaft measured 15 feet by 11 feet and was divided into timber-lined pumping and winding compartments. The engine compartment was principally for pumping but was also equipped with ladders staged in 18 feet lengths each with a four feet square timbered base to enable miners to pause briefly during the long ascent from the depths far below, already exceeding 200 fathoms (1,200 feet) by 1863. The winding compartment contained skips, for raising ore, attached by flat hemp ropes to the winding gear.[1]

Pollard's engine house lay 145 yards north of Clymo's. Built in 1847 it contained a 46-inch pumping engine which had performed sterling service but had now been made partially redundant by Clymo's, although whim haulage and access remained important. The shaft, slightly smaller at 14 feet by 10 feet, was also of the dual compartment type, timber-lined and divided into pumping and winding compartments.[1] Between these two large engine houses lay a smaller one containing a 24- inch double-acting whim engine, which provided the power for haulage in both main shafts. Elsewhere on the site was a 22-inch horizontal engine for crushing and stamping ores and no less than six water-wheels provided further power for dressing and other operations.[2] An engine pond was located in the centre of the site, which would have been fed by water pumped from deep underground and used to power the waterwheels as well as for ore dressing. An old waterwheel and stamps still lay rotting and rusting in the small valley marking the northern boundary well into the 1890s, long after closure.[3]

Whilst not part of the original workings, by 1863 a Footway Shaft with a small covering house had been sunk 100 yards north of Pollard's, containing ladders in the same customary short lengths giving the men access to the northern part of the workings. This narrow shaft only reached adit level, where the miners walked some distance underground before using the former Barratt's shaft from that point to the 90 fathom level, after which further descent was through winzes between each level. Ten levels had to be descended in this way to reach the lowest level being worked at that time. This tortuous descent gives some idea of the efforts expended by Menheniot's miners reaching and returning from their work place every day. Meal breaks were taken underground, without any facilities in the accepted sense.[1]

Barratt's shaft, by then long covered over at surface by waste tips, lay adjacent to the northern boundary and had been sunk with enthusiasm in parallel with Pollard's for the first five years. The area around and right up to the northern boundary continued to be worked, but ore was now more economically brought out via Pollard's. Barratt's had never been equipped with an engine of its own and clearly a decision had been taken some years earlier to work the whole mine through Pollard's and Clymo's shafts.

Between Pollard's and Clymo's engine houses a visitor to the site would have seen a large drying and changing house, measuring 52 feet long by 18 feet wide. It had two windows, a ventilator in the roof and was equipped with a stove and rudimentary heating pipes, providing changing accommodation for 70 to 80 men. Another 30 miners changed in the roomy main boiler house whilst fillers, landers and trammers changed in the whim boiler house. Pitmen changed in another shed whilst two further small sheds existed for shaftmen. Status was clearly a feature even within the hierarchy of the working miner.[1]

The dressing operations, wet and cold work in winter, were carried out under sheds, most of which were provided with moveable hanging sides to protect the dressers against wind and rain. Here were to be found the mine girls and boys, some as young as ten years of age. We know there were 74 mine girls living in Menheniot in 1861, 78% of them teenage or younger and no less than 46% being between ten and fourteen years of age. One shed was completely boarded in and provided with a fire and seats, where the women and girls warmed and ate their lunches.[1]

Further north between Pollard's and Footway Shaft was the smithy, with its own tall chimney, whilst for safety reasons in the remote northwest corner lay a small powder house. Between this extensive group of engine houses and buildings of all shapes and sizes lay bare ground carpeted with ore and waste dust. Despite attempts to maintain a tidy site, discarded and rusty ironwork of various descriptions would have lain about; the typical flotsam and jetsam of a working mine.

To this scene now had to be added the people and the noise, the latter probably the most difficult to recreate in these now quiet rural surroundings. The two pumping engines were the work horses of the mine, their steady rhythmic thumping being kept up night and day, year after year, as the task of draining the mine was relentlessly maintained. The whim engine by way

of contrast either sat silent or clanked into furious activity as ore or deads were wound up to the surface.

Equally distinctive was the noise of the steam driven hammers and machinery which supplemented the ore crushing and dressing operations, their sound carrying across the fields long before the mine was reached. From various boiler and engine houses white excess steam leaked and whisped, whilst dirty smoke trailed from the tall engine house chimneys. The over-shot water-wheels, turning quietly and elegantly, almost seemed to belong to another age, although even they could not escape the concentrated mining setting in which they were placed.

The last ingredient to the scene would have been the surface workers. A visitor in 1863 gazing down across the site from the top of Mine Hill would have seen the greatest concentration of activity around the dressing operations whilst enginemen, surface labourers or blacksmiths might be seen leaving or standing at the doorways of the various buildings. At several points horses and carts waited patiently for loads, possibly having brought in south Wales coal from St Germans or Looe quays to fuel the engines' voracious appetites. Finally the mine clerk might be seen standing at the account house door, watching nervously for the return of mine agent Henry Hodge, perhaps with a visiting shareholder or from a visit into Liskeard to meet Peter Clymo.

We have perhaps departed from tradition by not beginning at the beginning, as classic stories should, but the image of a working mine is a powerful one not always easy to recreate in the mind's eye. Yet this is how a mine like Wheal Mary Ann should be remembered; a living and breathing force, dirty and noisy and the lifeblood of over 300 miners, in turn supporting up to 1,000 family dependents. A generation later nature and agriculture between them conspired to reclaim those spoils and the mine, which had breathed life across the parish, blended back into nature, first as weathered ivy clad ruins, then building by building, gradually disappearing as stone was reused, tips grassed over and farmers reclaimed what industry had taken away. Here nature and man conspired to cover up more and indeed more quickly than occurred high up on Caradon Hill or on the wild cliffs of western Cornwall. It is however to the early days of mining exploration, with optimism high, to which we now return.

By 1845 exploration in the adjacent Wheal Trelawny, which had been leased in 1843, had proved beyond all possible doubt both the value and direction of the Menheniot lead lode. Peter Clymo Jnr was both manager and purser there, whilst he and his brother were also major shareholders, having been prominent members of the original group who secured the lease. However, many shares had by now been sold on the London market and Wheal Trelawny's ownership was broadly based with a strong lobby in the far-off capital. Such diverse shareholding caused tensions in many mining

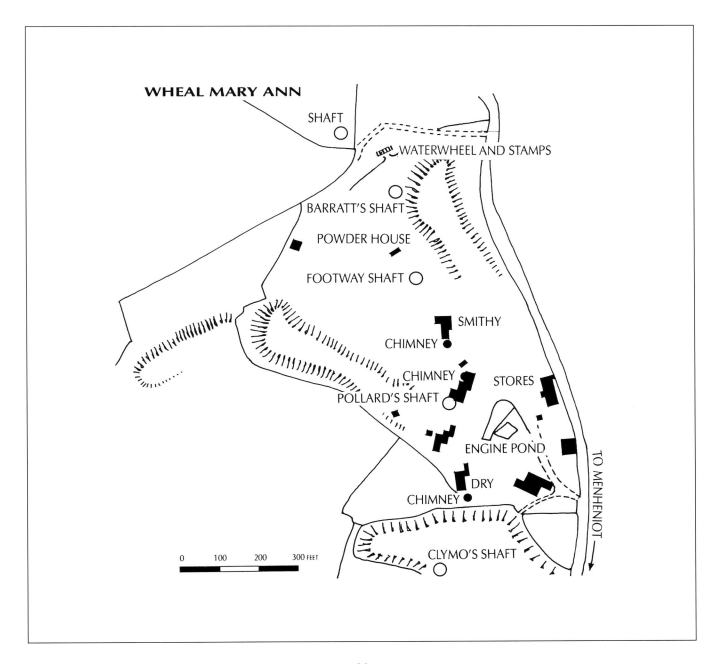

WHEAL MARY ANN

SHAFT

WATERWHEEL AND STAMPS

BARRATT'S SHAFT

POWDER HOUSE

FOOTWAY SHAFT

SMITHY

CHIMNEY

CHIMNEY

STORES

POLLARD'S SHAFT

ENGINE POND

DRY

CHIMNEY

TO MENHENIOT

0   100   200   300 FEET

CLYMO'S SHAFT

39

concerns, with London investors reluctantly acknowledging local Cornish expertise but equally jealous of their inside knowledge which in a fast moving industry could be used to unfair advantage in business affairs. It was precisely that spark which ignited controversy and bitter recriminations over the leasing of Wheal Mary Ann and once again it was to be the Clymos, pleading innocence throughout, who moved quickly and some said illegally in securing yet another lucrative property, this time Wheal Mary Ann.

The land in question belonged to 81 year old spinster Mary Pollard, who owned a modest 41 acres and lived quietly in Menheniot village with her 80 year old sister and two house servants. This small agricultural holding was about to yield sustained riches for Mary Pollard and her descendants, the mining lease finally being granted in 1845 at 1-12th dues. Miss Pollard would have had her business affairs managed by an agent and this she would undoubtedly have needed as astute mining men moved in to negotiate hopefully advantageous agreements.

Over a period of months the Clymos negotiated for a lease on behalf of the Trelawny adventurers, indeed clearly recommending the Trelawny company to purchase two parcels of land, hemming in what was to become Wheal Mary Ann, in an effort to sterilise the main sett in such a way that it had to be purchased by Trelawny.[4] Subsequent study of maps however reveals the purchases were not as critical as claimed at the time. However, negotiations for the lease became protracted and at this point confusion enters the proceedings and controversy begins.

Quite unexpectedly in the summer of 1845 the Clymos emerged triumphant with a lease secured in the names of Peter Clymo Jnr, James Clymo and Edward Lyne, Solicitor. The deal included a down payment of £1,000 with a further £1,000 payable out of the first ore sales. The mine was divided into 256 shares, 12 of which were held free of calls by Miss Pollard and her relatives, whilst dues of 1-12th would be payable. Wheal Trelawny was already divided into 256 shares and common practice dictated that existing Trelawny shareholders might have expected to be given priority in purchasing shares in the new undertaking on a pro-rata basis.[4]

In fact the three Liskeard men, proudly holding their lease, magnanimously offered the Trelawny shareholding 130 shares whilst, after allowing for the 12 complimentary ones, retained the option on the remaining 114 themselves as signatories to the lease. They were insistent that Miss Pollard had repeatedly stated that she would never grant a lease to the Trelawny company and that they, thinking it to be foolish to let it go into other hands, secured the lease by the best possible means. They now offered a reasonable proportion to the Trelawny shareholders who would not otherwise have benefited at all. They believed the offer to be fair in the circumstances.[4] The author has subsequently uncovered the text of an account house speech made by Peter Clymo Jnr in 1859, many years later,

in which he still claimed this to be the case and that he and his brother had acted honourably.[5]

The London shareholders were incensed, pointing out that as manager and purser of adjacent Trelawny Peter Clymo Jnr was an employee of that company and as such party to privileged information on the nature of the mineral ground. Any interest in an adjacent property using that knowledge could, in their view, only be used as an agent of the company. Edward Lyne was also, it was pointed out, Solicitor to Wheal Trelawny and was considered to have broken faith too. The situation was clearly complex as the men could equally demonstrate that they were independent speculators and investors in many business ventures in the Liskeard area and considered Wheal Mary Ann to be no different. Peter Clymo clearly did not take kindly to any suggestion that a technicality should limit the development of his wider business interests.[4]

It must be said that most surviving contemporary reports come from the London based *Mining Journal*, which clearly favoured the distant shareholders, but soon the power of the law supported their case and legal claims were registered by principal Trelawny shareholders, Messrs.

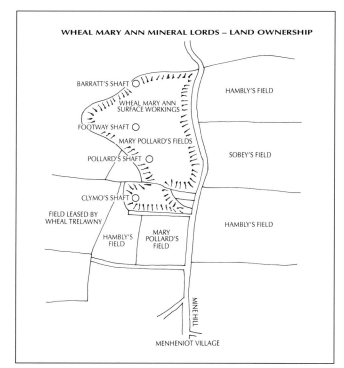

WHEAL MARY ANN MINERAL LORDS – LAND OWNERSHIP

BARRATT'S SHAFT

WHEAL MARY ANN SURFACE WORKINGS

HAMBLY'S FIELD

FOOTWAY SHAFT

MARY POLLARD'S FIELDS

POLLARD'S SHAFT

SOBEY'S FIELD

CLYMO'S SHAFT

FIELD LEASED BY WHEAL TRELAWNY

HAMBLY'S FIELD

MARY POLLARD'S FIELD

HAMBLY'S FIELD

MINE HILL

MENHENIOT VILLAGE

Chippindale, Andrew, Mount and Smith. Eventually the case went to arbitration, where it was decided in favour of the Trelawny adventurers, the precedent being used in future similar Cornish mining disputes.[5] Costs amounting to £1,500 were paid by the three Liskeard promoters, the judgement being that shares in the new company should be offered pro-rata to shareholders in Trelawny, although Wheal Mary Ann would still be constituted as a separate cost book company. In fact the two concerns always maintained totally independent management and except where sound economic practice dictated, such as for joint agreements on drainage or underground access, they pursued independent objectives with few favours given. Over the years shareholding changed and very little, apart from their adjacent situation, suggested a common bond.[4]

The final twist to this story is that despite the inference of the judgement, the Clymos remained both powerful and at the centre of respected professional life within Liskeard, Peter Clymo Jnr being a partner in the Liskeard District Bank, Mayor on several occasions and for many years a Justice of the Peace. Furthermore despite the acrimony, he remained purser at the new mine and soon succeeded James Clymo as both purser and manager. He had clearly retained a major shareholding himself and this can only be explained by the fact that, as a major existing shareholder in Wheal Trelawny, he retained a significant entitlement within Wheal Mary Ann even under the new agreement. We do know however that as a direct result of the dispute the London shareholders forced his resignation at Wheal Trelawny in 1847, but clearly they either could not or did not wish to challenge his presence in Wheal Mary Ann. It is probable that the London element soon realised that the experience and commitment of Peter Clymo would work very much in their favour and that it was best to let sleeping dogs lie.

By June 1846 the serious business of opening out what was considered to be a valuable property was well under way. The engine shaft, which became known as Pollard's, had reached a depth of 15 fathoms below surface and had almost reached adit level. The adit level itself, where initial exploration had commenced, now extended on the course of the lode for a full 100 fathoms and had done much to confirm the adventurers commitment to the property. Barratt's Shaft had also been started about 20 yards south of the Trelawny or northern boundary and had reached a depth of nine fathoms from surface, the lode having been cut at a depth of only five fathoms.[7]

One month later it was recorded that 15 men were employed at an average wage of 55s. per month, the number indicating the limited operations at that stage which were concentrated upon sinking the two shafts and extending the adit. The mine needed neither engine nor water power for drainage, its shallow workings being naturally drained by the adjacent Wheal Trelawny. This was a temporary bonus, for the full costs of pumping an ever deepening mine were soon to be a fact of life for Wheal Mary Ann too. The sett from north to south was 450 fathoms, or just over half a mile, long and was centrally positioned on the single lead lode which stretched the length of the sett, although the strength of the lode in the southern part was as yet unproven.[8]

October 1846 was a significant month, as the mine celebrated the sale of its first parcel of ore; 43 tons at the relatively high price of £21.1s. per ton. It was reported that the ends and stopes were looking well and that sinking was proceeding below the 15 fathom level on a good course of ore.[9] Progress was steady and soon the 15 fathom level had been driven 90 yards south of Barratt's Shaft on a very promising lode. It was found that the southern part, worked from Pollard's Shaft, was not so productive at a shallow depth but this did not unduly worry the management team who were confident that this part of the mine would rapidly improve with depth.[10] The road to profitability was a long one for most mines and in this Wheal Mary Ann was no different, but in the early years calls were relatively infrequent and usually coincided with major investment in machinery, as ore production if not yet profitable at least funded development in the undertaking and avoided the need for regular calls.

In January 1847 it was recommended and agreed that the original 256 shares be sub-divided into 512. At the same meeting it was announced that Wheal Mary Ann's first engine house at Pollard's Shaft, was almost completed and that the parts for the 46-inch Sim's combined cylinder pumping engine were daily expected by sea at St Germans Quay.[10] April saw all the parts on the mine and erection proceeding with all possible speed. It was said that it was hoped to have the engine working within a month.[11] It is clear that at this stage most returns were coming from Barratt's Shaft, although Pollard's would soon assume that role. By May the steam engine had been put to work and Peter Clymo was indicating that Pollard's shaft would now be sunk below adit level with all possible speed and that, with the pumping capability now provided, the way lay open to establishing a good and lasting mine. Adventurers meetings were held at this time and for some years to come at The White Hart Inn, Liskeard.[12]

September 1847 saw a 30s. call being necessary, principally to meet a £650 payment to Harvey & Co. towards Pollard's engine.[13] Two months later Peter Clymo announced the raising of mine agent Henry Hodge's salary to £6.6s. per month and at the same time reported that twelve men on extended hours were sinking Pollard's Shaft with all possible speed and intended to cut the lode, at 30 fathoms under adit, by the following February.[14] Interestingly when Peter Clymo Jnr's. own salary was reviewed in March 1848, from £3.3s. to £5.5s. for his managerial and purser's role, it proved less than that paid to Henry Hodge his mine agent. This reflected the full-time commitment of the resident agent as opposed to the part-time responsibility exercised by Peter Clymo from his Liskeard office, where he successfully managed a wide range of business concerns.[15]

The mine purchased further equipment in May 1848, when a second-hand 18 feet water wheel with six heads of stamps attached was obtained at the Silver Valley sale. Concurrently a crushing machine was purchased from Wheal Gill which was intended to be worked from the same wheel. It was considered that the acquisitions would soon pay for themselves by offering a great saving in the cost of ore dressing.[16]

With a single strong lead lode passing through first Wheal Trelawny and then Wheal Mary Ann, on a north to south alignment, it was inevitable that both mines would work levels right up to their common boundary. With these at 10 fathoms intervals throughout the depth of each mine communication occurred at most levels although, as separately structured companies, the boundary was strictly respected. Ore was taken out via separate shafts and under normal working conditions there was no real dependence of one on the other, although differing activity over the years could effect the pumping workload as water, which respected no boundaries, found its own level between the two.

By July 1848 Barratt's shaft had reached a depth of 40 fathoms and the 30 and 40 fathom levels were being driven on the course of the lode. However in adjacent Trelawny, started two years earlier, Phillip's shaft was sinking towards a 72 fathom, level, whilst its 52 fathom level had been driven 200 feet south from the shaft towards the Wheal Mary Ann boundary. This was over 10 fathoms deeper than any point so far reached in Wheal Mary Ann. In an effort to speed up development Mary Ann's adventurers passed a resolution in July 1848 empowering Peter Clymo Jnr to negotiate with John Bryant at Trelawny to offer to contribute to the cost of driving the 52 fathom level more rapidly to their boundary and through into the Wheal Mary Ann sett. There it was intended that the latter's men, gaining access via Trelawny, would push on southwards to a point below Barratt's shaft where they would commence rising towards its bottom, some 10 to 12 fathoms above.[17] A deal was struck and worked progressed as planned, with the level reaching within six feet of the point where the rise towards Barratt's was started four months later.[18]

Similarly, in May 1849 a winze was reported being sunk from a 50 to a 60 fathom level in Wheal Mary Ann, when both the mine's shafts were hardly 52 fathoms deep.[19] Again, in September 1850 reference was made to the value of the lode in the 70 fathom south of the boundary at a time when both Wheal Mary Ann's shafts were barely 60 fathoms deep.[20] Both descriptions could only be attributed to levels being driven from Wheal Trelawny. This however seemed to be a feature of early development only and no references have been found to the practice after 1850.

By 1849 Peter Clymo was able to report enthusiastically that he was currently driving no less than five levels on the course of the lode throughout the mine. Ground was being opened up much faster than they were taking ore away and it was clear that this was part of a prudent and deliberate policy to improve the value of the mine by keeping proven reserves.[18] Informed observers nodded approvingly at a management that knew where it was going and was clearly placing long term prospects before short term gain. Peter Clymo may have been a fast mover in acquiring properties, but when it came to direct mine management his practical skills always placed the well being of the mine first, whilst shareholders learnt that if they were patient they would reap the benefits of a solidly profitable property built on firm foundations.

He maintained firm control of both practical direction and the management of the mine's finances, and his style and authority shone through in the way in which he steadily, and without seductive early dividends, led the mine towards profitability. The first dividend was not declared until November 1849, nearly four years after commencement, a not unusual period however in the world of mining. After that point dividends were rarely suspended and became a steady and reliable feature of the mine's working. Prior to that first dividend few calls had been made whilst carefully managed ore extraction funded development work, but was never allowed to deflect underground staff from the prime objective of opening up the property. From the beginning of 1849 the signs of long awaited success for the shareholders began to build. A rising credit balance of £129 declared to the January meeting became £557 by May, £1,018 by August and £1,987 by November. Then and only then was a modest dividend of £640, or £1.5s. per share, declared and £1,000 paid to Mary Pollard in final settlement for granting the lease.[21]

From that point steady dividends became a feature of the mine's operation, with a significant balance always held back, and often used to cushion unexpected fluctuations in fortunes underground or on the metal market, thereby presenting a more consistent performance to shareholders and with it greater confidence in the undertaking. This practice was never used recklessly and any long term change was addressed in the proper manner.

Meanwhile surface infrastructure was expanding, reflecting the more established status of the mine. Engineer William West was authorised to erect a steam engine for the crusher in August 1849.[22] Later in November preparations were made to erect an engine house for a steam whim, and mining labourers, previously employed underground driving the 15 and 30 fathom levels, were temporarily withdrawn to raise stones for the proposed building, which was soon under construction. The steam whim, also supplied and erected by William West, was brought into operation during 1850. The number of miners employed in Wheal Mary Ann rose from 15 in

1846 to 125 in 1849, but had reached 422 by 1851 as an increasing number of levels were brought into production and surface activity expanded. Lead ore returns illustrated the development period well, with initial annual production of 166, 192 and 334 tons respectively between 1846 and 1848 being followed by significant rises to 873 tons in 1849, 1,186 in 1850 and 1,265 by 1851. The silver content of Wheal Mary Ann's ores was always high and provided valuable supplementary income throughout its years of operation.

Little is known about the surface and underground agents who supported Peter Clymo Jnr as manager and purser and Henry Hodge as resident agent during the first ten years. After this, published mining reports acknowledged the names of the wider team. We do know however that Henry Vivian, Peter Clymo's uncle who had been resident at Wheal Trelawny in the early days, briefly joined Wheal Mary Ann in August 1849 at a salary of £7.7s. per month, but soon took retirement in the village where he lived out his final years. In the same month Mr Roskilly was appointed mine clerk at £5.5s. per month, a high rate suggesting a semi-purser's role.[22] P. P. Roskilly was recorded as a mine agent in both 1853 and 1854. Robert Knapp was an agent between 1855 and 1858, whilst at the same time holding the appointment of manager of the adjacent Wheal Ludcott, St Ive. This interesting character set himself up as a consultant to a number of small concerns, managing up to five different speculative ventures which came to little in the wider Liskeard area during this period. He followed the mining calling to Nevada, U.S.A. in 1865, returning to the Liskeard area in 1872 when he again offered his services as a consultant to mining concerns.[23]

By November 1850 both Pollard's and Barratt's shafts had reached a depth of 70 fathoms below adit, with a 70 fathom level being enthusiastically extended across the sett. However in that month it was reported that flooding problems were being experienced in the 70 as a result of Trelawny agents damming up the water which had flowed naturally towards their sett. This clearly had been a useful supplementary form of drainage to that being performed by the Pollard's pumping engine.[24] Two months later it was again reported that the 70 fathom level had been under water for six weeks, but that it would be drained in a few days.[25] Clearly a difficult winter at depth for Wheal Mary Ann, although fortunately productive levels lay above the troublesome 70 to ensure continuity of production. Sinking proceeded well the following summer and beyond with Pollard's shaft reaching 80 fathoms by August 1851, 91 fathoms by April 1852 and 101 fathoms by that September. Considerable potential lay ahead, with a depth of around 250 fathoms being worked twenty years later. In September 1852 £200 was paid to Mr Hambly for a small extension of ground to the mine.[26]

A further addition to surface equipment was made in Autumn 1852 when a steam whim was purchased for £200 from the small Penhauger Mine in the north of the parish. It was said the additional power would be used for crushing ores as well as whim haulage. The autumn of 1852 proved to be exceedingly wet, the whole district suffering from heavy rain which had inundated the countryside for the previous two months. Consequently pumping expenses were increased whilst surface operations were retarded.[26]

The adventurers meeting of June 1853 reported news of the most important project since the sinking of Pollard's shaft; the start of a new shaft to be called Clymo's and located 145 yards south of the former.[28] By September it had already reached 17 fathoms below surface and by October 20 fathoms.[29] Sinking continued, but it was not until March 1854 that a decision was taken to purchase a large 80-inch steam engine and in June tenders were received from John Hodge of St Austell for £3,090, Perran Foundry for £3,150 and Harvey & Co. for £3,587. The order was placed with John Hodge and all dividends were suspended until this large item of expenditure was cleared from the accounts.[30] The new engine house was completed by September 1854, when it was reported that installation of the engine itself would shortly commence.[31] William West, the mine's consulting engineer, supervised its erection. Throughout 1854 and the first half of 1855 a water pumping charge of £112 per quarter was raised by Wheal Trelawny against Wheal Mary Ann and its cessation probably coincided with Clymo's engine being started up to support Pollard's in the ever present task of keeping the mine drained.

Clymo's shaft continued to be sunk with a depth of 75 fathoms being reached by February and 90 fathoms by August 1857.[32] By the end of the year 95 fathoms had been reached, but sinking was temporarily suspended whilst Clymo's sumpmen cut ground for bearers and cistern.[33] Throughout this period Pollard's shaft continued to be sunk with 143 fathoms reached by February 1857 and 160 fathoms by July 1858, maintaining sinking well ahead of Clymo's as a result of its seven years earlier start.[34]

By 1862 however the difference had disappeared and indeed at 186 fathoms Clymo's was marginally the deeper. Some 15 levels, each at 10 fathom intervals, had now been extensively worked throughout the mine and efforts were concentrated on the deeper levels with the 160 and the new 172 Pollard's, 175 Clymo's receiving extensive attention. Returns were still reported as excellent but an informed observer noted that when a mine, particularly a lead mine, has to sink smartly to maintain its returns at depths comparable to those being reached by Wheal Mary Ann, then profits generally become 'small by degrees and beautifully less'.[35] In fact dividends per quarter had fallen slowly over a period of six years from £2 to £1 and then 10s. per share. It has to be said, however, that never once during this period did a dividend fail to be declared and this reflected much on the continuing quality of the mine's management which was continually tested

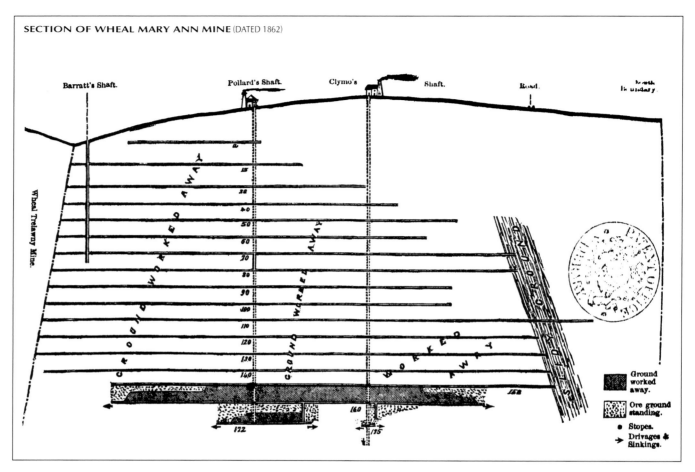

and never experienced the luxury of easy profits offering reflected glory.

An alternative to pursuing ever greater depth as the single source for exposing new lead ground did however exist. The single, strong north to south lead lode had been worked up to the Trelawny boundary in the north at all levels and no potential existed here for extending the sett. Likewise to east and west enough was understood of the lead bearing lodes of the district to hold out little hope of parallel lodes existing to either side. The great unknown lay to the south towards the village. Most levels had been worked in this direction to a point near the boundary where the lode became lost in slidy ground which was repeated at every level so far tried. It was believed that such a strong lode would not just peter out and that after being

disordered it ought to continue southwards. The problem was rediscovering its position, when driving was frustratingly slow and expensive and particularly when nature conspired to offer clues which often frustratingly bore no reward.[35]

It was known that the ground to the south was readily available for lease beyond the present sett boundary and a local observer in 1861 noted that shares in Wheal Mary Ann were fairly flat but currently an excellent buy, with a considerable rise in value anticipated should a discovery to the south be made.[36] A trial was agreed southwards penetrating the slide at the 110 level and this was already under way by September 1860.[37] Work was reported as continuing in December and again in March 1861.[38] December

1861, well over a year later, saw the trial still under way and now extending a significant distance southwards, with crosscuts east and west hoping to intersect the elusive lode. Branches of the lode had been met with more than once, but no sooner were hopes raised than they were dashed again as the traces petered out. By 1862 the trial had been suspended after several years of committed exploration and Peter Clymo was faced with the reality that future prospects were now totally confined to exploiting ever deepening levels in the main part of the mine.[35]

Shaft drainage was not always as straight forward as might be expected and that from Clymo's deepest level particularly so. In 1862 two eight inch bucket pumps lifted the water from the 186 to the 160 fathom level, where the water flowed back along that level to Pollard's. Here one eight inch bucket pump and two nine inch pole pumps, which raised the water by a shammel lift, took the water to the 110 where it ran back along that level to Clymo's shaft again. From there it was brought to the surface powered by four 13-inch pole pumps worked by Clymo's engine. It was said that when the 172 level was communicated between Clymo's and Pollard's that it was proposed to do away with all the lifts in Pollard's, leaving the complete drainage task for the mine in the able hands of the Clymo's 80-inch engine. The Clymo engine was described as amongst the finest in the county and kept in splendid order, but had been asked to perform comparatively little work despite having been erected for eight years. Clearly the mine was well equipped for future deeper sinking, which would soon be needed, but had not been presented with as heavy a drainage problem as had been originally anticipated. The suspicion remains that adjacent Wheal Trelawny was doing more than its fair share of keeping the district's water level under control.[35]

The September 1859 adventurers meeting was a grand occasion marked by a presentation to Peter Clymo in recognition of his able management of the undertaking from its commencement to the present time. The assembled company, including many Liskeard mining principals, took the opportunity to stand in turn and add their congratulations to this leading member of the Liskeard mining and business community. During the first thirteen years of operation Wheal Mary Ann's shareholders had seen dividends amounting to £48,512 or £47 per 1,024th share; individual reward being significantly greater since most were multiple shareholders. Over the same period calls had amounted to little more than £3 per 1,024th share and these had only occurred during isolated periods, most expansion being funded out of profits and before dividends were declared. A slight cloud did however hang over the present proceedings, reports on the lower levels of the mine being disappointing, but overall it was said the shareholders could congratulate themselves on a sound undertaking.[5]

Originally it had been intended to commission a portrait of Peter Clymo to hang in the account house, but ultimately it was decided to present him with a 24 inch by 20 inch silver tea tray, with a rich tudor masked border and an elaborately engraved centre, bearing his name and the sentiments of the adventurers. It is a pity that the portrait option was not pursued as no likeness of Peter Clymo has been handed down to the present day. Perhaps one day the engraved silver tea tray will reappear in some private collection and be set in its proper historical context. During his speech Peter Clymo took the opportunity to recount his version of both the discovery of Wheal Trelawny and the Wheal Mary Ann controversy, which are detailed elsewhere and add a personal flavour to the story. A toast to neighbouring mines was responded to by John Philp, 76 years old purser of adjacent Wheal Trelawny and a respected senior member of the local business community. Such events were always managed with some style and were accompanied by a sumptuous meal and leisurely after dinner speeches, as only Victorian business communities knew how.[5]

As the 1860s dawned it is worth looking closer at the team of mine agents which were to take Wheal Mary Ann through the final phase culminating in closure in 1874. Senior resident agent Henry Hodge, controlling day-to-day affairs since 1847, remained in charge until his death in March 1865 at the age of 54. He is buried in Menheniot churchyard. The way had been paved for his successor by the arrival of 42 year old Camborne born Joseph Harris in 1859 who became senior agent in 1865 and ultimately manager in 1870, on the death of figurehead Peter Clymo. In

The gravestone of Henry Hodge, Menheniot. Henry Hodge was Peter Clymo's faithful resident agent at Wheal Mary Ann for 18 years from 1847–1865. He lived in Menheniot village.   *S. Bartlett 1990*

1861 Joseph Harris lived in Addington Place Liskeard, within a few doors of Thomas Grenfell, mine agent at Wheal Trelawny. Joseph Harris's wife and child had been born in St Blazey, suggesting he had arrived in the Liskeard area via the St Austell mining district. His period of tenure was a challenging one as economic difficulties multiplied.

James Stevens joined the team of Henry Hodge and Joseph Harris one year later in 1860 and remained faithful to the company right through to closure in 1874. Aged 39 on his appointment and St Agnes born he superficially appeared to have been another imported western agent. However, closer inspection reveals a rather different story, based on the birthplace of his eight children, which indicates he had been living in Menheniot since at least 1844, which by coincidence was the period of the first influx of Wheal Trelawny working miners and over a year prior to Wheal Mary Ann's commencement. Then aged 23, he is likely to have been one of the mining vanguard, now at last being promoted probably via tutworker and tributer to a position of authority. Still relatively young his recent practical experience would have strengthened the team. In 1861 he was living in Merrymeet, north of the village, with 15 and 19 year old sons already working miners and a third entering the ranks by 1871. His four daughters however were spared the trials of becoming mine girls, one in later years working as a milliner in either the village or Liskeard.

The last man to join the team of agents was James Skeat in 1867 and he too saw out the last days of Wheal Mary Ann with James Stevens. James Skeat was only 27 years of age on appointment, was St Blazey born and with a Tywardreath born wife and four St Blazey born children had genuine roots in the St Austell mining district. He lived in Menheniot village and added youth to the Wheal Mary Ann team.

The twenty one year lease on the mine was due to expire in 1866, but as early as December 1862 negotiations were initiated by the adventurers both to secure a guaranteed long term future for their investment and most importantly to seek a reduction in the 1-12th dues on ore production currently paid to the mineral lord. The economics of the concern were far from secure at this time and the threat of uncertain terms for lease renewal would have added further pressures on Peter Clymo and his fellow adventurers. A committee was formed to undertake the negotiations consisting of Peter Clymo, Tom Kittow and J. C. Isaac, all major shareholders and important members of the Liskeard business community.[2]

Negotiations became very protracted and whilst an agreement based on 1-15th dues looked likely, the proposed compensation for damage to surface land of £100 per acre was proving totally unacceptable to the adventurers.[2] By way of a veiled threat the June 1863 adventurers meeting resolved that all speculative operations on the mine be suspended until the dispute was resolved.[39] In practice the sinking of Clymo's shaft continued, but the point

had never-the-less been made that unless the terms were favourable enough to enable profitable operation, then the continued working of the mine was far from guaranteed.

In December 1863 it was reported that a new lease had indeed been granted at 1-15th dues, but clearly the report was premature for in June 1864 a guarded statement was issued that a settlement was within days of being made.[40] Still later in September that year it was reported that it was believed that the new terms were now agreed upon and that a draft was anticipated shortly.[41] Negotiations had now dragged on for almost two years, although in practice the present lease still had over one year to run. A relieved mine management reported final confirmation of renewal in the early part of 1866. Times were by now truly hard, as costs increased and production levels, due to underground difficulties, became increasingly difficult to sustain. The lease represented but one problem resolved of many facing the concern at this time.[42]

During the difficult 1860s it was to the credit of the mine that not one single call became necessary. However dividends grew progressively less and were indeed suspended from time to time, whilst the price of shares remained depressed. This would have been acceptable in the short-term, but it became increasingly clear as the years went by that no instant road to recovery was in sight, for the mine was deep, costs were high and expansion into new ground had been ruled out. Production could only be increased by sinking deeper, the quality of the ore in depth was proving only moderate and nationally the lead market did not present exciting prospects. Nevertheless 350 miners were still employed in 1862 and to observers in Menheniot a large established concern continued to face the detailed challenges of day-to-day operation resolutely. Undoubtedly there would have been an atmosphere of tight cost control locally and yet the need to maximise production to cover high fixed pumping and maintenance costs was equally always present.

To set this in context it is worth looking closer at dividends and production between 1862 and 1870, after which storm clouds began gathering in even more determined fashion. Dividends were indeed at an all time low between 1862 and the summer of 1866, fluctuating between 10s. per 1,024th share per quarter and actual suspension. After that they gradually increased to 12s.6d, 15s. and ultimately 17s.6d. by 1868 before dipping again stage by stage to 10s. per quarter by 1870. Gone were the heady days of the £2.5s. per share dividends of 1857 and 1858, although once again it says a great deal for the efforts of the mine management that no calls became necessary during the period, despite the obvious difficulties encountered. It has again to be remembered that in interpreting dividends many adventurers were large shareholders with the effect on their personal income multiplied significantly upwards and downwards as dividends rose and fell. It was the pressure of the adventurers that the management team remorselessly felt whilst re-examining every option in an uncertain business in order to maximise day to day productivity.

Lead ore production never the less fell during the period, mainly due to increasing difficulties in obtaining the right quality ore and the need to divert significant quantities of labour to sinking of the main shaft and driving of cross-cuts to new levels which became slower and longer as depth increased. Peak production of 1,597 tons in 1857 had fallen to 910 tons by 1862, reducing still further to 729 tons by 1865, before steadily climbing again to 1,048 tons by 1867, 1,139 tons in 1868 and dropping a little to 941 tons by 1870. The recoverable silver content of the ore by now represented a far higher percentage than in the boom years, possibly due to more refined smelting methods, and this at least was a valuable boost to much needed earnings.

Pollard's shaft had not been sunk beyond the 170 fathoms below adit reached by 1862, with all efforts now concentrated on Clymo's shaft as the principal communication with the mine at depth, although levels stretched the full length of the sett including extending from Clymo's below and beyond Pollard's shaft to the northern boundary. Significant expense and effort went into sinking Clymo's, reaching 186 fathoms below adit in 1862, 203 fathoms by June 1864, 215 fathoms by June 1865, 226 fathoms by December 1866, 239 fathoms by June 1868 and a maximum 253 fathoms below adit by March 1870.[43] During this time 180, 190, 200, 210, 220, 230 and 240 fathom levels came into production. The 250 fathom level itself did not begin to yield ore until March 1872. At some stages sinking of two fathoms (12 feet) per month was achieved, at other times progress was much slower, whilst after an intended new level was reached sinking was often suspended so that labour could be diverted to driving a crosscut to meet the lode. The problem of the inclined lode, illustrated on page 20, was now becoming an increasing imposition at depth. Clymo's shaft had passed through the lode at 130 fathoms and now, as the latter drifted further to the east in depth, each level required a longer easterly crosscut of no productive value until the lode was met. After the crosscut had reached the lode, productive north and south levels were pursued at right angles along its course. In 1867 the 220 crosscut involved 26 fathoms or 156 feet of unproductive driving taking over a year, whilst in 1870 the 240 crosscut took between 18 months and two years to drive between 35 and 40 fathoms.[44] This more than amply illustrates the agonizingly slow process in opening out a hard rock mine, consuming valuable labour and time when shareholders impatiently expected early results.

One brave decision taken in 1868 was that to install a man-engine in Pollard's shaft at considerable expense. Interestingly South Caradon, Peter Clymo's other great venture, took a similar step in the 1860s. This ingenious system enabled men to be conveyed to considerable depths in short stages of about 10 feet, a platform being located at each stage to enable men to step off and rejoin the next stage. The simple principle was based on vertical rods connected to a beam engine at the head of the shaft. The rods rose and fell with and were limited to the length of the stroke of the beam, men descending travelled downwards on a small platform attached to and with the downward stroke of the rod. At its downward limit, which coincided with a platform on the side of the shaft, the men stepped off, rejoining the rod from below when it reached the top of its stroke which on its return would enable them to travel down to the next stage. In this way multiple stages enabled men to reach considerable depths. A dramatic improvement for the men, their introduction was never the less slow and piecemeal throughout Cornwall.

By June 1868 preparation work for the man-engine had been started and it was said that repairs to Pollard's shaft had been completed, inferring that the shaft had fallen into partial disuse since Clymo's had taken over the full pumping task after 1862. It is however likely that Pollard's had remained in use as a ladderway for the men and for whim haulage. Installation of the engine was contracted to William West & Sons, who handled so much of Wheal Mary Ann's engineering needs.[45] It had been hoped to have the engine working by September 1868, but this date was eventually put back with completion finally taking place in December.[46]

Regrettably within three months it was being reported that the engine was not equal to the task and William West undertook to install a more suitable one free of further expense, except for the building of a new engine house to accommodate the replacement.[47] This was achieved with remarkable speed and the man-engine was reported as completed and working by June 1869.[48] It had been confidently stated that the outlay on the investment would rapidly repay itself, by significantly reducing the time spent by the men in descending and ascending from the mine, as well as increasing their productivity through eliminating the fatigue brought on by the taxing activity previously experienced in reaching their workplace underground. This remained the only man-engine installed in the Menheniot area and one of the few in the wider Liskeard district. Inadequate attention to the welfare and conditions experienced by the working miner, if only seen in the hard economic sense as a road to greater productivity, remained the Achilles heel of Cornish mine management over the years. If the financial returns were as quick and as great as suggested by Wheal Mary Ann's manager, then it remains surprising that action was not taken earlier or on a wider scale.

It is now worth looking at the final and significant changes which took place to the Wheal Mary Ann management team in the years leading up to the mine's demise. As 1867 dawned the ever present Peter Clymo Jnr was manager and purser, Joseph Harris principal resident agent and James Stevens and James Skeat mine agents. However in November 1867 Peter Clymo Jnr collapsed whilst attending the account day at South Caradon and was carried home paralysed. He was bed ridden for the next three years and died at the age of 69 in July 1870. With him went a piece of Liskeard's mining history and this was fully recognised in the town, as indeed it was in Menheniot. Liskeard was in mourning on the day of his funeral and 600 miners from South Caradon and Wheal Mary Ann led a funeral cortege of 1,100, including town dignitaries, watched by a further 1,000 spectators. This sad event is covered in more detail in a later chapter.[49]

Peter Clymo Jnr had chaired almost every quarterly adventurers meeting since commencement and his dominance of affairs meant that less is known about other shareholders than was the case with Wheal Trelawny. His enforced immobility brought fresh names to prominence, although one suspects most had been investors for many years. Of the nine meetings between June 1868 and June 1870 five were chaired by John Isaac, two by James Cock and one each by James Dymond and Tom Kittow. Dear old Tom Kittow deserves a special mention. He was 82 years old when he chaired the June 1868 meeting, 90 years old when he eventually retired as South Caradon purser, after 50 years, in 1876 and 100 years old when he died in December 1886. Tom Kittow was one of the original 1836 adventurers in South Caradon, with James and Peter Clymo, although not a practical miner but a farmer of Browda, Linkinhorne, north of Liskeard. His name is mentioned in connection with a Wheal Mary Ann committee in the mine's first year 1845 and clearly, as a close friend of Peter Clymo, his money had probably been involved in the very first shady deals surrounding Wheal Mary Ann. He left £40,000 when he died in 1886, which considering this was after the mining collapse leaves one wondering as to his worth in the 1860s. He was not alone in amassing a fortune from mining speculation in the Liskeard area.

Even more significantly all these latter-day meeting chairmen were Liskeard men, which might appear of no great significance until one recalls that Wheal Trelawny, which was often thought of as mirroring Wheal Mary Ann in production, profitability and style, was by this date dominated by London investors amongst its chairmen, with quarterly meetings having moved to the capital. Likewise a London secretary by now dominated the financial management of Trelawny. We will see Treweatha Mine go the same way in a later chapter, typical of a general trend that was emerging in Cornwall. It is now becoming equally clear that Wheal Mary Ann, despite being one of the larger mines, remained firmly under the Liskeard influence, despite being quoted on the London market, with shares changing hands there as well as in Cornwall. One is left to speculate how the common influence between the two mines separated over the years, bearing in mind

that the judgement at Wheal Mary Ann's commencement was that Wheal Trelawny shareholders were entitled to the new Wheal Mary Ann shares in proportion to their holding in the former.

Returning to the direct mine management team, Peter Clymo's death in July 1870 prompted the need for formal changes and Joseph Harris was promoted to manager at £10.10s. per month whilst William Nettle succeeded as purser at £8.8s. per month. William Nettle held a number of such appointments in the Liskeard area, whilst also happening to be the late Peter Clymo's nephew, son of his sister Jane. Peter Clymo's special attributes in matching a practical mining background with financial management ability had allowed him to comfortably embrace the joint post of manager and purser. The new separate appointments reflected the more practical strengths of the new manager, which needed the support of an independent purser.[50]

The team of mine agents was not strengthened following Joseph Harris's promotion and one suspects the latter retained his direct resident role; not being a man of multiple business interests as his predecessor had been. He managed through the difficult final years, including the enforced takeover of Wheal Trelawny in far from ideal circumstances, as we shall shortly see. However his tenure was short lived and he died at aged 57 in September 1873. Circumstances at the mine were clearly grim by this time and mine agents James Stevens and James Skeat, whilst never formally referred to as managers, saw out the last year of what was by then a reduced operation as joint managing agents.

As 1871 dawned Wheal Mary Ann, despite its difficulties, was still declaring a small dividend of 10s. per share quarterly. This however disguised poor long term prospects which deteriorated still further when the mine's long term and adjacent partner Wheal Trelawny announced its intention to cease operation. Quite simply, without the latter's major contribution to pumping the surrounding area, Wheal Mary Ann faced a rise in the water table with which it had no hope of coping. Action was swift and a special adventurers meeting in August agreed to negotiate to buy out Wheal Trelawny. The deal specifically included purchase of machinery and materials with the express purpose of maintaining the latter's pumping capability.[51]

A month later the quarterly adventurers meeting confirmed the decision and made preparations for paying an estimated £3,000 to Trelawny's liquidators, which was later raised to a finalised payment of £3,600. A £1 call per share was made, which was very low considering the scale of payment that was involved. The call produced £968, showing a default by holders of just 56 out of the 1,024 shares, a surprisingly loyal response from adventurers who must have realised the major step being taken in extending the mine's commitments. Additionally small profits of £603 and £780 from the last two quarters were applied to the settlement, the rest being found from the cash balance usually carried over. In fact, Wheal Mary Ann had done extremely well in only using £968 of new adventurers money to complete the £3,600 purchase. The legacy was a high risk balance carried over of only £855, which offered no bolster against future debt whilst future uncertainty as to the likely effect on costs of the enforced enlarged operation loomed large in the minds of investors and management alike.[52]

Wheal Mary Ann's intentions proved to be positive to say the least and those who had believed that the only future activity which would be seen on the Wheal Trelawny site would be around the Trelawny 50-inch and Smith's 70-inch pumping engines were very much mistaken. By the end of December 1871 Joseph Harris reported that repairs to Trelawny shaft were indeed complete as was preparatory work at the former 240 fathom level, which Wheal Mary Ann intended to retitle the 210. Smith's Shaft was also being cleared with completion expected within the following few days. Joseph Harris having completed his review of Trelawny believed that many of the levels in the old mine could be extended and paying lead ore found.[53] None of the former Trelawny agents were retained and it is not known the degree to which Trelawny miners were re-engaged or Mary Ann's redeployed. Over 300 jobs had been lost at Trelawny in little over a year, whilst in 1872 the third parish stalwart Treweatha Mine also collapsed declaring more than 170 miners redundant. Catastrophic social problems were clearly manifesting themselves and Wheal Mary Ann now carried the hopes and fears of the whole mining community within Menheniot.

Joseph Harris was faced with miles of worked out levels in the two mines whilst other areas, particularly at the deepest levels, held some potential for further exploration. The choices were many but his economic resources inevitably limited which could be pursued. During 1872 the extent of these re-workings became clear. Clymo's shaft on the original Wheal Mary Ann site remained the centre of activity with 190, 200, 210, 230, 240 and the bottom 250 levels being worked. On the Trelawny southern site the retitled bottom 200 level was in production, whilst on the northern site Smith's 190 was being driven north with optimistic views being expressed.[54] The winter of 1871/72 had, however, proved the wettest for many years with Smith's 190 flooded for several months whilst the whole mine had faced unprecedented pumping demands. Inevitably this pushed costs up and depressed dividends, which from an unacceptable pre-merger level of 10s. were now down to 5s. or even 4s. per quarter. One suspects the experienced Clymo reaction, had he been alive, would have been to build up the financial security of the mine by suspending such small dividends. Nevertheless in terms of production, if not profit, 1872 proved a good year with 1,254 tons of ore being raised; up one third on 1870 and the highest production figure since the late 1850s. The difference however was that by

now costs in the deep mine were on a quite different scale and the market place far from buoyant. Regrettably such production levels no longer reflected enhanced profit.

In November 1872, an advertisement was placed for the sale of the Pollard's 46-inch pumping engine, presumably now redundant with pumping on the original site in the safe hands of Clymo's 80-inch engine.[55] By December 1872 and again in March 1873 the high price of iron and steel work for mine equipment was reported as causing concern, whilst serious fluctuations in both the quality and price of south Wales coal, due to strikes in the latter area, was equally placing a heavy unplanned burden on the mine.[56]

An erroneous but as it proved perceptive report in April 1873 suggested the mine was not expected to last the winter through, whilst by August another unofficial report suggested that lodes were being speedily worked upon, inferring preparation for abandonment.[57] Meanwhile manager Joseph Harris had been taken ill and died, leaving James Stevens and James Skeat in sole charge of practical affairs on the mine. Their reports of October and December 1873 confirmed a significantly reduced level of activity in the ailing mine. They described working confined to the 240 and 250 levels in the original Wheal Mary Ann section, reflecting withdrawal from shallower levels in the intervening months. Trelawny's shaft was no longer being worked at maximum depth, confined to a shallower 170 level south, whilst Smith's on the northern part of the former Trelawny mine, was still being worked at the 190, but at a reduced level. None of the lodes were particularly productive.[58] At the end of the year annual production figures were revealed as indeed being dramatically down from 1,254 to 759 tons.

It was perhaps not surprising when a special meeting of adventurers, held at Webbs Hotel, Liskeard, in April 1874, resolved that the mine should be abandoned, although it was noted withdrawal should be in an orderly fashion to ensure losses were minimised. Purser William Nettle added that the owner of land adjoining Charles Trelawny's had been approached for an extension of the sett, which had however been refused. This was regarded as the final nail in the mine's coffin and strengthened the recommendation for abandonment.[59] It is presumed the land referred to was Dr Honey's, north of Wheal Trelawny, which the latter mine had cast equally envious eyes upon in the run up to its closure. The eventual granting of this land some years later led to the ambitious but short lived Wheal Hony and Trelawny United (1880-1884), described elsewhere.

Despite the decision being taken in April 1874 it was to be the last Saturday in September before operations were finally suspended.[60] During the intervening period development work ceased, expense was curtailed and easily obtainable ore worked and raised with all speed. It is likely that the pumping engines were progressively slowed, economising on fuel, whilst materials of value were drawn to the surface in readiness for auctioning. The old mine was dying and as the beat of the pumping engines slowed and with a final gasp stopped, so the life of the mine expired too. An eerie silence fell over Menheniot, not heard since 1843, as the last pumping engine in the parish ceased operation. Latter-day concerns were to flicker briefly, but to all intents and purposes the mining era was over. How the miners and their families responded to this final calamity we shall explore later.

A succession of site auctions started in November 1874 when the Trelawny 50-inch pumping and adjacent Trelawny 20 in. winding engines were sold to F. W. Michell of Redruth for £625.[61] The next three day sale in February 1875 saw an impressive array of engines up for auction including Clymo's 80-inch and Smith's 70-inch pumping engines, the 45-inch man engine, 26 and 24-inch winding engines and a 22-inch engine with 12 heads of stamps.[62] Three engines, including the largest Clymo's 80-inch, were sold to the shortly to be reworked Wheal Wrey, Ludcott and North Trelawny Mine, located just across the parish boundary in St Ive. These are thought to have never been moved due to the collapse of the prospective company. The Smith's 70-inch remained unsold, being taken by South Caradon in June 1875 for £1,015.[63] A final engine disposal was a 22-inch winding engine in May 1875.[64] One of the longest surviving Wheal Mary Ann engines was a small 11-inch, built for the mine in 1850 and sold in one of the 1875 sales to Liskeard Brewery, where it survived until 1938[66]. All the sales included auctioning of a variety of stamps, pitwork, water-wheels, crushers, dressing machinery, boilers and eventually the account-house furniture. The number and size of these auctions, notably the February three day sale, serves as a final reminder as to the complexity and extent of surface operations across the hill from Menheniot village. Shortly only the giant engine houses, chimneys and buildings would be left, stripped of anything of value, like the bleached bones of some giant beached whale.

That February 1875 sale was followed by a luncheon in the account house attended by the principals. Food and drink was liberally partaken and through a smoky haze after dinner speeches progressed in true account house style. It was clearly a time for nostalgia for the long standing shareholders present. Prominent Liskeard businessman Thomas Allen rose and reminded the assembled company that they were met '... to bury an old tried and valued friend, the wife of their bosom, the dear old Mary Ann'. He then took the opportunity of a captive audience to invite their attentions to be re-directed from Wheal Mary Ann

... to three wealthy and blooming young widows, Wheal Wrey, Ludcott and North Trelawny to whom he had been making love for some time and now intended to marry. Unfortunately he could not cope with them all and needed their support.

The final comments were delivered amid ribald laughter from the assembled company.[65]

It would be nice to draw the Wheal Mary Ann saga to a romantic Victorian conclusion, but somehow the light hearted and sumptuous account house proceedings pall somewhat when the large numbers of destitute miners and their families resident close by are remembered. Perhaps even sadder it later emerged that both Thomas Allen's enthusiasm and the many purchases he made for Wheal Wrey, Ludcott and North Trelawny were for a concern which was never to see the light of day. He was subsequently accused of dubious practice in soliciting and obtaining funding for a concern which was never financially supported to the degree he claimed. It seemed a rather unseemly end for Wheal Mary Ann; a concern which once had held its head high within the Liskeard area.

It will remain a matter of conjecture whether Wheal Mary Ann or Trelawny was the greater mine. Wheal Mary Ann's period of operation between 1845 and 1874 closely matched Trelawny's from 1843 to 1871. Production figures, miners employed, profitability and ultimate depth were all similar. However more detailed analysis has to award the accolade to Wheal Mary Ann with slightly higher production, marginally greater depth and greater and more consistent dividends over longer periods. Indeed Trelawny at an earlier stage than Wheal Mary Ann experienced wild fluctuations between profit and calls with which it seemed less able to cope. That steadiness over many years has to bring us back to the name which was associated with Wheal Mary Ann for so long - Peter Clymo Jnr. His influence began in 1845 at the mine's opening and he remained manager and purser until his death in 1870, within four years of the mine's demise. His practical mining and business ability will be remembered principally in Liskeard for the fabulously rich South Caradon. Those who knew Menheniot and its mines understood that what he achieved here, with the deep and notoriously difficult Wheal Mary Ann, with a far less valuable mineral in lead than South Caradon's copper, was perhaps a technically more accomplished achievement. At the very least perhaps the names Peter Clymo and Wheal Mary Ann will now be acknowledged by a wider audience over a century later for their key role in the Menheniot mining story.

CHAPTER FIVE
WHEAL TREHANE

*This is one of the most extrraordinarily
valuable little mines in the County*
SAMUEL RICHARDS, MANAGER 1854

WHEAL TREHANE (1846-1857) is best described as the almost forgotten dividend mine of Menheniot. Collins[1] gives Wheal Trehane but four lines of print and Dines[2] mentions in passing that the exact location is uncertain, but that it probably lay immediately to the west of Wheal Trelawny. In fact this plucky little concern, its boundaries too confined for a long term future, employed over 100 miners at its peak and maintained regular dividends for most of its life. The year 1846 proved to be both lively and traumatic for Menheniot's young mining industry as shrewd members of the Liskeard mining community negotiated with somewhat bewildered landlords for the right to mine minerals beneath their land, adding individual or groups of fields to their setts as mine managers pondered and used both experience and judgement to predict what course the elusive lead lode would take beyond their immediate boundaries.

The lease for Wheal Trehane was signed on 25 March 1846 with Thomas Kelly, the owner of the mineral rights, for a period of 21 years at one-fifteenth dues and for which a premium of £500 was paid.[3] By coincidence on that same day in 1846 Wheal Trelawny was fighting its bitter battle in the Rolls Court with the Clymos over ownership of Wheal Mary Ann, whilst Wheal Trelawny itself, then the deepest mine in Menheniot, had yet to reach 45 fathoms, a trifling depth compared with that which the larger mines ultimately reached.[4] To this young scene came Wheal Trehane which, much to the surprise of its larger neighbours and informed mining opinion, earned its place in the dividend lists for almost ten years alongside the larger and better known Wheal Mary Ann and Wheal Trelawny. Wheal Trehane would unquestionably never have existed as an independent mine had not a party of Liskeard adventurers spotted what they were convinced was an error of judgement by Wheal Trelawny in attempting to purchase land to follow their highly productive lead lode northwards from their original sett and towards an independent northern part of the mine where the lead lode had again been proven. Between these separate parcels of land lay several fields, but under two separate owners, the easterly side by Dr Honey and the westerly by Thomas Kelly. The Trelawny agents were convinced that the lode ran through Dr Honey's land and paid a premium of £1,200, refusing

Thomas Kelly's. At that point, John Philp, a shrewd Liskeard adventurer, businessman and purser of mines, stepped in and after paying a premium of £500 for Thomas Kelly's ground formed a separate company under the name Wheal Trehane to work the ground. The difference in premium paid suggests a carefully played hand by John Philp, who would have brought the prospective adventurers together, packaged the deal and completed negotiations, based on expert but confidential advice from qualified mine managers. John Philp himself was not a qualified miner, illustrating well the complex business and practical relationships which made up the Cornish mining scene at this time. John Watson, the London share-dealer, visited Menheniot two months later in May 1846 and vividly describes the Trelawny agents surveying their land and feverishly placing pegs across the surface of Dr Honey's field, marking out the anticipated run of the lode to link their two setts, whilst concurrently expressing the opinion that the Trehane men working on the adjacent land were little better than madmen. Meanwhile the new Trehane team probed their ground and prepared to sink an exploratory shaft. Quite what the local Menheniot farming community thought of all this strange competitive activity is not recorded.[3]

By June 1846 Kelly's Shaft had been sunk 20 fathoms and men were driving a level to meet the lode.[5] By August 1846 the lode had been cut and Wheal Trelawny sadly reflected on what might have been as the Trehane adventurers sat back and awaited the first sale of ore. However one fear remained. The sett boundary lay barely 25 yards to the east of Kelly's Shaft and the lead lode ran parallel to this eastern boundary, beyond which lay the Trelawny sett. Lodes rarely ran precisely vertical, tending to swing away from the vertical in depth, or underlie as it was known, and it was cautioned that this lode tended to underlie to the east, potentially taking it right out of the Trehane sett and leaving them with barren ground.[6] The Trehane adventurers remained solidly behind their investment and three years later were to note that in reality, the underlie east had been trifling down to the 55 fathoms level and that the agents considered a further 100 fathoms as a practical objective.[3]

However that lay far ahead and far more important in the short term was the October adventurers' meeting, held to review the six month old mine's progress. Key figures were John Philp, adventurer and purser throughout the mine's life, and Captain N. Faull, the mine manager. Captain Faull reported on the extent of the workings and stated that in about three weeks he would have around 30 tons of rich silver-lead ore ready for the market. John Philp spoke next and one can imagine the 63 year-old bachelor's chest swelling proudly as he announced that in view of what had been said, no further call was at present necessary and neither did he anticipate such an event. The sale of the forthcoming ores would be sufficient to meet all demands on the mine, including the cost of labour and materials for October. It would also cover the balance of the premium owed to Mr Kelly and at the same time allow a handsome sum to remain in his hands for contingencies of any kind or to be paid to the adventurers as a dividend. A final decision on the latter would be made nearer the time.[7]

At the same meeting it was resolved that the interests of the mine would be further enhanced by having a resident captain on the mine, inferring that Captain Faull was attending in a part-time capacity only, as was common practice with smaller mines in the district. The purser was requested to advertise for an agent.[7] At the next adventurers' meeting in December 1846 the appointment of Captain John Bryant of Altarnun as resident agent was confirmed at a salary of £6.6s. per month.[8] However, barely six months later he was to successfully apply for the combined position of manager and purser at Wheal Trelawny and he was succeeded by Captain Samuel Richards, who was to begin a long association with the practical management of the mine, lasting from 1847 to 1855.[9]

In May 1847 a lease was signed for a further two fields from St Germans School for 21 years, at 1-15th dues and for a premium of £100. The land adjoined their existing sett to the north west, giving an additional 30 fathoms run on the lode.[10] In March 1847 a first dividend was declared of £1 per 1-256th share, followed by a second £1 dividend in June.[11] By the end of 1848 £10.15s. per share or a total of £2,752 had been divided on a paid up capital of only £320 or £1.5s. per share.[3]

A combination of good fortune and shrewd management kept costs down in the early years without impairing the mine's progress. Very early on the adventurers passed a resolution that all materials required for the mine should be tendered for, undoubtedly mindful of deals which benefitted agents and merchants, but not the adventurers at certain disreputable concerns.[8] In August 1846 it was stated that the mine was drained naturally by the adjacent Wheal Trelawny and that only a horse whim was needed for raising ore.[12] As the depth increased, the expense of a steam engine was still avoided, despite drainage becoming necessary, when an arrangement was entered into with Wheal Trelawny in the autumn of 1847, to lay horizontal rods the 160 yards between Kelly's Shaft at Wheal Trehane and Trelawny engine house, to enable the latter to pump Wheal Trehane as well. In December 1847 Captain Samuel Richards reported that since October he had completed the bob beds, bobs, pulley frames and other works for laying 80 fathoms of horizontal rods to connect the pumpwork in Kelly's Shaft with the Trelawny engine and that on the whole it answered remarkably well. With this machinery it was stated the shaft could be sunk at the same rate as having their own steam engine on the mine.[13] Wheal Trelawny accounts confirm this arrangement, showing a £16.10s. monthly pumping charge up to December 1848, then £27.10s. monthly up to February 1850 when payments ceased.

Two shafts existed on the mine, the principal shaft being Kelly's. By December 1847, soon after the horizontal rod scheme linking with Trelawny engine house had been started, the shaft had reached a depth of 44 fathoms with work having been completed on dividing and casing the shaft with timbers down to the 35 fathom level. Levels had been horizontally driven from this shaft at 20 fathoms and 35 fathoms and the prospects of the mine were considered to be very good.[13] By June 1848 the shaft had reached 55 fathoms and by January 1849 61 fathoms with additional levels being driven and worked at 45 fathoms and 55 fathoms.[14] By December 1849 the mine had been sunk still deeper and a depth of 78 fathoms had been reached, with 62, 68 and 78 fathom levels being horizontally driven and worked.[15] Throughout this period of considerable activity dividends had continued to increase, amounting to £1,280 in 1847, £1,472 in 1848 and £2,688 in 1849, whilst Captain Samuel Richards continued to direct the practical working of the mine.[16] About 100 miners, labourers and mine boys and mine girls were employed at this time.[3]

The hidden riches of this little mine appear to have been as underrated in the mining world of 1849 as it is forgotten today. The *Mining Journal* of 17 November 1849 remarked that the mine was in 256 shares, with a market price of £28 to £30 each, whilst dividends averaged £9 to £12 per share per annum or about 30 per cent. This exceptional rate of return could have led many to suppose it might not be lasting, but the *Journal* was at pains to point out that although small, costs were low due to its lack of dependence on expensive machinery, the ores raised were rich, particularly in silver and realised well above the average price for the county. With hindsight we know Wheal Trehane's limited boundaries and underlying lode always posed the threat of losing the ore in depth into Wheal Trelawny ground, but in reality this hidden jewel had proved a banker to its original adventurers and it would be 1857 before its luck was finally to turn and considerable profit was left to be made at this time.

It had now become clear that on this scale of operation Kelly's Shaft required its own steam engine and in December 1849 Samuel Richards reported that the engine house was ready to receive the 22-inch engine and

Mining Machinery & Materials for Sale.

Mr. GEORGE SEALY

IS INSTRUCTED TO OFFER FOR SALE,

BY AUCTION

On Tuesday and Wednesday, the 20th and 21st days of October instant,

AT ELEVEN O'CLOCK IN THE FORENOON OF EACH DAY,

AT TREHANE MINE,

IN THE PARISH OF MENHENIOT,

About 3 Miles from the Borough of Liskeard,

THE FOLLOWING VERY EXCELLENT

MACHINERY AND MATERIALS

A 45 in. Cylinder Pumping Engine,

Eight feet stroke, with equal Beam, Boiler 1¼ tons, Balance Bob and connections complete;

A 22in. Cylinder *Whim Engine,* Boiler 9-tons, Fly-wheel 11 tons, Winding Cage, &c., complete;
Spare Boiler, 9 tons, nearly new; 1 large Crusher in excellent order; 1 Portable Crusher,
used on Dressing Floors;

400 fms. Tram road Iron and wooden sleepers	5 12ft. 7in. Plunger poles	1 Large centre cog wheel, 7ft. diameter
4 Tram waggons	3 8¼ft. 7in. ditto	18 Wheel and hand barrows
12 9ft. 9in. Pumps	5 Bucket prongs, clacks, seatings, &c., complete	1 Grinding stone
2 11ft. 9½in. Workings	25 fms. 1½in. Bucket rods	2 Smiths' bellows & anvils
2 9ft. 9in. Windbores	130 fms. 7 & 9in. Main rods, with strapping plates, bolts, staples, and glands	1 Vice and screwing stock
2 9in. Doors and Door pieces, with seatings complete		Screwing tools, 5 cwt. steel borers
7 9ft. 8in. Pumps	140 fms. Knocker line	A lot of Iron and Smiths' tools
75 9ft. 7in. ditto	200 fms. Iron stave ladders	4 Scales, stands, and weights
4 9ft. 8in. Windbores	1 Iron & 2 wood matching pieces	Iron tube in changing house
4 8in. H pieces & doors	60 fms. Air pipes & launders	1 Crab winch
4 8in. Top door pieces and doors	60 fms. 5-8 Whim chain	3 Tons scrap wrought iron
4 9in. Working Barrels	260 fms. 5½ & 6in. flat whim rope	2 Tons cast iron
4 9in. Stuffing boxes and glands	185 fms. 9in. Capstan rope	Turning lathe and apparatus
	2 Whim Kibbles	A lot of shovels & other mining tools
	Shears, poppet heads, & pulleys	Wooden House
		4 Houses or sheds on dressing floor
		Jigging machines

Tyes, Strakes, Hutches, Kieves, Round Buddle, Brunton Frames, Hand Frame, and Dressing Tools of all kinds.

Also, a large quantity of New and Old Timber; an excellent Dial; and the Account House Furniture, &c., &c.

MARAZION, OCTOBER 1st, 1857.

ROWE, LETTER-PRESS & COPPER-PLATE PRINTER, BOOKBINDER, BOOKSELLER, &c. PENZANCE.

Wheal Trehane's closure was followed by a sale of materials in October 1857. A rare surviving poster lists a vast array of surplus equipment available for disposal.

J. Brooke collection

that some parts were on the mine.[15] By January 1850 it was noted that the principal parts of the engine were on the mine and were now being put together.[17] Somewhat despairingly in February 1850 Samuel Richards stated that a few small parts of the engine were yet to be sent from the foundry, but were promised that week. He was confident the engine would be set to work the following week.[18] By the end of 1850 Kelly's Shaft was down to 90 fathoms, but the dividend was down from £2,688 in 1849 to £896 in 1850, no doubt partially held down by the expense of the steam engine installation.[19] From this point onwards the adventurers were faced with the full scale costs of an ever-deepening mine, needing maximum ore yield to maintain profits against the cost of pumping and drawing ore from the increasing depths. It must have seemed an age since the days of a single horse whim with no drainage being necessary, but in reality Wheal Trehane had come a long way in five short years.

The mine then settled into a period of steady working, with the inevitable periodic fluctuations caused either by market movements in the price of lead ore, the curse of all metal mines, or temporary changes in costs or production. Dividends climbed back to £1,024 in 1851, then plummeted to £128 in 1852, before three glorious years dividing £2,048 in 1853, £3,072 in 1854 and £2,048 in 1855, the last annual profits the company was in fact to see.[16] The original 256 shares were subdivided into 512 in 1851, 1,024 in 1853 and finally 2,048 in 1854. In July 1854 Robert Daly was appointed London secretary at the time of the division of the company into 2,048 shares, the need for an agent close to the London share market an essential feature of Cornish mining by this time.[20]

The September 1854 adventurers' meeting expressed the highest praise for Captain Samuel Richards' management, whose recommendations in every instance, it was said, had been confirmed.[21] However, Captain Richards left the mine soon afterwards and Captain Thomas Woolcock took over the management during 1855 and 1856. Finally Captain M. Edwards took over during 1856 until the mine's closure as an independent concern in 1857. *Tredinnick's Share Circular* in July 1856 reported that Trehane was all

but commercially valueless and this, combined with the evidence that no dividend was declared at all in 1856, the first complete year without a dividend since opening, indicated that real difficulties were being encountered.[22] These were unquestionably linked to the old boundary problem with Wheal Trelawny, for that concern took over the company in 1857 and continued to work Kelly's Shaft and integrate the underground workings with the extensive Trelawny sett. Interestingly John Philp, whose drive and initiative had led to the forming of the company and had been purser throughout Wheal Trehane's life, had in fact also held the purser's position at Wheal Trelawny for some years, although not at the time of the great controversy which led to Wheal Trehane's appearance as an independent concern.

An auction was held on the mine in October 1857 when a 45 in pumping engine, a 22 in whim engine, boilers, crushers, 400 fathoms of tramroad iron and wooden sleepers, pipes, 140 fathoms of knocker line, 200 fathoms of iron stave ladders, tools, Brunton frames and account house furniture were offered for sale.[23] Clearly demand was not great for as late as April 1859 the boiler and crusher were again offered privately and with the unsold materials were put up for auction in May 1859, when they were bought by Thomas Bartlett, a London share-dealer, through Robert Daly, the former London secretary of Wheal Trehane. John Parsons Jnr, a Wheal Trehane adventurer, challenged Daly's right to sell the materials, as he had been paid off as secretary in June 1858.[24] A sad end to a mining company that had shown drive, initiative and provided results from a confined mining sett in distant Menheniot. These company arguments seem a long way from those heady days of 1846 when Menheniot scratched its head and wondered at the activities of a small group of people who believed that a field in Menheniot held the key to a mining fortune, which they were determined to find. Their judgement was to be proved unquestionably sound and earned Wheal Trehane a rather special place in Menheniot's long lost mining heritage.

CHAPTER SIX
TREWEATHA MINE

How much longer are shareholders to be satisfied with weekly reports of water being out,
of valuable lodes being cut again, of water getting in and stopping further working.
It is sad to see the mine in such a depressed state.
A FRUSTRATED SHAREHOLDER 1865

THE FOURTH OF Menheniot's larger mines was Treweatha (1852-1872), which despite lacking the consistency and profitability of its neighbours contributed to the village mining scene for no less than twenty years, only closing when the parish stalwarts too were failing, following Wheal Trelawny in 1871 and a little ahead of Wheal Mary Ann in 1874. Treweatha was the furthest from the village and the most northerly of this group, located on the edge of the rich central mining area, which should have brought it the riches associated with its larger neighbours. 'The mine that should have been' is an apt description of Treweatha, for the scale of its operations always rightly placed it on a higher plain than that of its poor northerly neighbours Butterdon, Penhauger and Wheal Venton, which were truly speculative in nature and rarely employed more than 20 to 25 miners. Yet at the same time, despite its significant scale of activity, there were to be none of the rewards of regular dividends which were enjoyed for so many years by those who invested in Wheal Trelawny, Wheal Mary Ann and even Wheal Trehane for the latter's short lifetime. Treweatha was indeed a somewhat strange undertaking in many respects, said to be largely financed by London and Liverpool shareholders and prone during its life to periods of relative secrecy when the mining press had great difficulty in establishing the true state and prospects of the company, which in truth fluctuated considerably. Despite raising 4,371 tons of lead ore in its lifetime, calls were continuously made, the only dividends ever declared in twenty years being between 1854 and 1857 and even these were interspersed with a substantial call in 1855. The mine failed to declare a single dividend during the last three quarters of its life, whilst patient shareholders continued to finance development in new and different directions, always seeking that elusive success. As with all the larger Menheniot mines silver was found in association with the lead ore, but this valuable secondary source of income was never able to contribute more than containment of what would otherwise have been larger financial losses.

A high cost mine like Treweatha was however far more important to the economy of the local community than its poor financial performance might suggest. It was after all the distant shareholders who faced the worries of funding the concern and, providing they continued to do so, the scale of activity on the mine itself was to the benefit of the local merchants and the miners themselves. The bulk of stores and materials were purchased locally through merchants who imported much of the essentials via the local ports of Looe and St Germans and transported them by canal, rail or road. By 1856 Treweatha employed 125 miners and labourers contributing around £1,200 in wages each three monthly period, representing some 13% of the total miners earned income for disposal within the community. Similarly the mine's merchants bill for coal, gunpowder, candles and other stores amounted to £727 over three months, whilst in addition £562 in outstanding bills were owed to the local merchants - a necessary risk taken by this canny group who no doubt allowed comfortable profit margins to compensate for at least some of the risks taken. Treweatha's expenditure with these merchants is estimated at around 17% of the total similarly spent by all Menheniot's mines at that time, making it an important if lesser partner in the mining economy of Menheniot.[1]

The story of Treweatha falls into three distinct phases, starting with early success between 1852 and 1859 when the mine struck rich at a shallow depth causing much excitement and some encouraging early returns. This resulted in the moderate dividends declared between 1854 and 1857 which were, never the less, achieved whilst costs in establishing the mine both underground and at surface were high. A not inconsiderable achievement, even if closer examination of the accounts suggest a more responsible management might have not been quite so quick in declaring dividends which on occasions seem largely the product of stage managing the balance sheet rather than genuine sustainable profit. Victorian and in particular mining accountancy practices often left much to be desired, but the fine line between genuine fraud and optimistic accounting remains difficult to differentiate. It was however an optimistic time; a new mine with a sound early start, justifiably heavy expenditure had been authorised to set the concern up for the future and a significant workforce of 125 was actively employed. With hindsight much of this optimism lay in the fact that the adventurers, encouraged by rising share prices, saw this period as the start of even greater riches to come. Indeed following some seven to nine years behind Wheal Mary Ann and Wheal Trelawny's success comparisons were quickly made, it being well known that the earlier developments became richer the deeper they became, and enthusiasm in Treweatha and its future ran high. Fate however dealt many an unexpected blow in the uncertain world of mining and in practice the strength of the lode beneath Treweatha weakened in depth.

The second stage of the mine's life cycle, from 1860 to 1865, initially saw a major reduction in scale of activity and large numbers of miners laid off. However a very positive if small scale exploratory period followed, with a workforce limited to 20 in 1862 and 37 in 1863 and trials on new lodes and in different parts of the sett genuinely sought to create what was in effect a new mine. This careful exploration paid off and the latter years, up to ultimate closure in 1872, saw a return to large scale deep mining, the workforce climbing to 174 by 1870, coupled with a new commitment to heavy expenditure in wages and consumable materials in order to maintain the extensive workings at depth. Unfortunately whilst ore production dramatically rose, particularly between 1869 and 1871, this did no more than compensate for the balancing higher working costs and no dividend was ever declared during this final period of extensive activity. Eventually a combination of the imminent expiry of the 21 years lease and the poor commercial prospects of the undertaking led to abandonment This was however preceded by a period of record production plundering easily reached reserves and stripping recoverable materials from underground in a race against time, as expensive pumping was reduced and water levels rose. This however lay a long way ahead and was far from the minds of the early adventurers who in 1852 saw a new and exciting prospect to rival those already profitable undertakings in Menheniot, a parish becoming an increasingly important centre for lead mining both in the county and in terms of national production.

Treweatha Mine was located two and a half miles north of Menheniot village and three quarters of a mile south of the Liskeard to Callington turnpike (the present A390) along narrow high banked lanes. Approached from Menheniot village the surface works occupied a long narrow site on the right hand side of the road about a third of a mile in length and one field in width, with the present day Treweatha farmhouse, outbuildings and farm cottages marking the centre of the site and effectively dividing the surface works into north and south mines.

The central area of this strip around the farm remained free from surface operations and considerably predates the mine, being the traditional farming home of the Rowe family, one of Menheniot's larger land owners and responsible for granting the rights to mine Treweatha to the proposed company. At that point in 1852 widowed Phillippa Rowe, aged 61, was in residence with her three children and four farm labourers 'living in', whilst

in the cottages close by lived her fifth labourer William Bartlett, aged 52, father to the young William Bartlett who opened our story and who had already become a young recruit to the mining industry elsewhere in the parish. Since 1841 William Bartlett Snr had moved up from Venton which was close by and also on Rowe land. By 1861 Phillippa's son, George Rowe aged 26, headed the family and was clearly regarded as somewhat more than a simple farmer, being listed under 'gentry' in successive *Post Office Directories* for the parish. At some point between 1861 and 1871 the close proximity of the mine to the family residence appears to have become unacceptable, for by 1871 George Rowe had moved to Venton House, one third of a mile north facing on to the Liskeard to Callington turnpike. Treweatha Farm had in turn by 1871 become the residence of Thomas Foote, aged 49, the Treweatha Mine manager, along with his wife and their eight children still living at home. After closure its role as a working farm was re-established and the attractive farm house still sits beside the winding lanes leading down towards Menheniot village, marking the site of one of Menheniot's long forgotten mining ventures.

Two shafts were located on the southern mine, Harris's being 350 yards south of Treweatha Farm whilst the original engine shaft, later called Ward's was situated close by, 50 yards south east of Harris's.[2] The two adjacent shafts were specifically located to work the parallel western and eastern lodes running through the property on a north to south course. A ventilation shaft is additionally mentioned on the south mine in 1856 and in 1863 and 1866 reference is made to a separate Footway Shaft for miners access, on the course of the lode, but its precise location is unclear.[3] Extensive tips, dressing floors and supporting infrastructure littered a site which has now been largely landscaped and returned to agricultural use. Undulating grassy mounds, some scattered engine house foundations, particularly around Harris's, and the remains of both shafts now hidden in undergrowth near field boundaries betray a once busy past. A waste tip stands immediately across the road, outside the boundary of the surface works, lonely and forlorn, appearing out of place in an otherwise agricultural panorama.This was clearly a later dump resorted to when available land within the site became scarce and would probably have been fed by an overhead ropeway with waste buckets strung high across the road.

The north mine, beyond the farm house, was a later development started in 1859 designed to replace the failing southern site, although the latter continued to be maintained for drainage, and indeed parallel operations returned there during the final extensive period of working prior to closure. An engine shaft was sunk on the north site, mine buildings appearing to have been concentrated in the southern corner near to the farm. The remainder of the northern site was covered by extensive waste tips. The feeling that Treweatha was shrouded in mystery is enhanced by the fact that, unlike Wheal Trelawny and Wheal Mary Ann, no plans of underground or contemporary surface workings have survived. The earliest surface map that can be found dates only from 1882, ten years after closure. Whilst this accurately depicts tips and site boundaries it nevertheless shows the area largely devoid of buildings, many no doubt having been of less than permanent construction.

Treweatha Farmhouse. Originally the home of the Rowe family, before Mineral Lord George Rowe moved to nearby Venton House. It became the Mine Manager's house and by 1871 was home to Thomas Foote, agent and manager (1861–1871).

S. Bartlett 1990

The story of Treweatha, with both contemporary silences and the loss of most records and all plans has proved one of the most difficult in the parish to reconstruct, heavily dependent on scattered newspaper reports with often incomplete descriptions. By careful cross referencing these sparse reports have begun to bring together a comprehensive picture of the mine's chequered history. A very different type of record to that surrounding Wheal Trelawny and Wheal Mary Ann, but equally important to the Menheniot story.

That detailed story commenced with a 21 years lease being obtained by the company in 1852 at 1-15th dues from George Rowe for the rights to mine beneath his land. By September the engine shaft, in what was to become the south mine, was down 11 fathoms whilst a start had also been

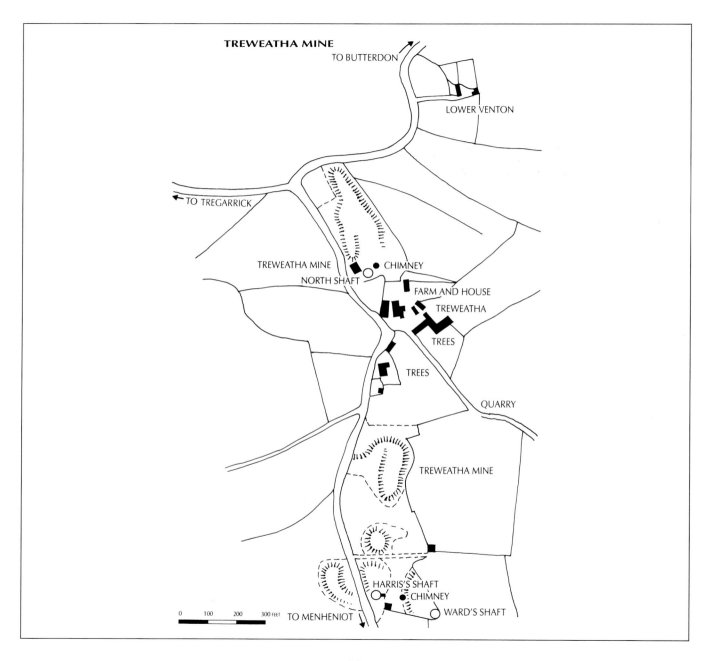

TREWEATHA MINE

TO BUTTERDON

LOWER VENTON

TO TREGARRICK

TREWEATHA MINE
NORTH SHAFT

CHIMNEY

FARM AND HOUSE

TREWEATHA

TREES

TREES

QUARRY

TREWEATHA MINE

HARRIS'S SHAFT

CHIMNEY

WARD'S SHAFT

0   100   200   300 FEET

TO MENHENIOT

made on the western shaft, where a rich branch of lead had been found at a shallow depth.[4] By the following April the shallow find had been confirmed, although somewhat surprisingly the engine shaft had not been progressed beyond a depth of 15 fathoms.

Clearly attention had turned to early exploitation of the rich shallow discoveries, for a crosscut had been driven 14 fathoms west from the engine shaft to intersect the lode, which had been located as planned and levels then driven north and south on its course for a length of about five fathoms (30 feet). The south end was in soft ground and needed careful timbering, but the ground was generally easy for driving. A modest development at this stage, but the ore being found already paid for raising to the surface for dressing and prospects were excellent.[5] A casual visitor when taken underground in August 1853, found the mine being opened out as well as any could have wished, with ore showing in every direction where the lode was to be seen. He felt however the backs were being worked rather early.[6] By October 1853 sinking had resumed and the engine shaft had reached a depth of 23 fathoms where the lode had been cut and levels were also here being driven north and south on the course of the lode. Ore was being dressed and 25 tons were presented for sale on St Germans Quay on 14 October.[7] The quality of the lode in the various ends fluctuated during the remainder of the year, but prospects remained excellent and a first dividend of 5s. per share was declared in December 1853, following three calls of 5s., 10s. and 5s. which had been incurred since the mines initial opening.[8]

Composition of the initial management team is uncertain, but by early 1853 James Osborn, who had managed the adjacent Wheal Venton since 1850, was in charge whilst William Rowe, unrelated to mineral lord George Rowe, was mine agent. William Rowe was to be the consistent early influence, directing day to day operations and the practical contact with the working miners for seven years until 1860. His presence was important during the first year, when there was management instability following the unexpected death of James Osborn in October 1853 from typhus fever, followed by a brief caretaking role performed by William George Jnr. Thomas Richards, a professional mine manager with numerous interests, was then appointed to front the mine's affairs and he and William Rowe formed a well balanced team which was to last until 1860. William Rowe always submitted the detailed weekly reports, whilst Thomas Richards presented reports to adventurers' meetings and occasionally more comprehensive monthly reports in the mining press.

During 1854 a new reservoir, dressing floors, engine house and stack were built and a 50-inch pumping engine and boiler was purchased from Bicton Consols for £1,000. This was to be located on the main engine shaft working the eastern lode, giving much needed additional pumping power for the ever deepening workings. A new 24-inch whim engine, for drawing purposes, was also purchased at this time.[9] By September 1854 masons were busily engaged in building the engine house and engineers were similarly occupied heaving in the whim engine.[10] November was to see masons engaged on building the stack and boiler house and both engines were expected to be ready to start work by the end of the month.[11] It was also noted in November that the share price had dropped of late, in consequence of the heavy outlay on machinery, but shareholders were reassured that the real value of the property had not diminished and its prospects were seen as excellent.[12] By May 1855 other projects were in hand with the dressing floors being extended and a crusher house being built.[13] In September 1855 a new carpenters shop was being worked upon and it was confirmed the crusher was now working and answering expectations.[14] This marked the end of eighteen months of sustained expansion of the surface workings, the site being a continual hive of activity with the large quantity of materials somehow being brought on to the mine down Menheniot's narrow country lanes. This scale of activity, coupled with the hundreds of miners now walking Menheniot's roads to and from work, begins to give some idea of the total transformation that had overcome this once sleepy agricultural parish, where mining was unheard of just twelve years before.

Whilst the building work was in hand underground development had continued under the direction of William Rowe. September 1854 saw the engine shaft down 39 fathoms with additional levels at a depth of 30 fathoms being driven north and south.[10] By May 1855 a depth of 44 fathoms had been reached with a 40 fathom level north and south being added to the ends being worked.[13] Thomas Richards and William Rowe reported to the September 1855 adventurers' meeting that the 40 fathom level was proving very productive and they estimated that the mine for the foreseeable future would be producing 25 tons of crop ore and five tons of seconds per month.[14] A 4s. per share dividend was declared at the December 1855 meeting. This return to the dividend lists had as predicted occurred once the heavy expenditure on machinery had been overcome. For some inexplicable reason the *Mining Journal* reporter sent to cover the December meeting was forbidden access, much to the consternation of the newspaper, who's editor openly expressed regret that the mine felt it necessary to conduct its business in secret.[15]

The next few years saw steady if unspectacular progress sinking the main engine shaft, with more levels being brought into production whilst shallower ones ceased to be worked. A depth of 50 fathoms had been reached by February 1856, 69 fathoms by December of that year and 74 fathoms by August 1857. 40, 50, 60 and 70 fathom levels were being worked and clearly the policy was to only sink when the management felt it could justify resources to work another level.[16] Containment of labour costs within existing limits was being enforced, transferring men deeper as and when it was deemed appropriate to withdraw them from the very shallow levels which had now ceased to be worked. Ore sales continued with no particular allegiance emerging to any specific purchaser; five successive parcels each going to separate agencies at this time. The first went to J. T. Treffry's of Par, the second to Joseph Walker, Parker & Co. of Chester and the third to Sims, Willyams and Co. of Llanelly, whilst two parcels of seconds went to J. Bibby & Sons of Liverpool and Locke, Blackett and Co. of Newcastle - all ore being shipped through St Germans Quay or Looe.

Fortunes, however, gradually took a turn for the worse, although at the time it was seen as only a temporary setback in the mines prospects, and the 70 fathom was to prove the last really rich level that was to be found. Meanwhile further expenditure took place in November 1857 when an additional boiler was purchased from Wheal Langford.[18] All the pitwork from the 50 to the bottom of the mine was changed at this time and when the additional boiler was attached to the engine William Rowe was able to report the new pumping capabilities answered all their expectations.[19] George Rowe had in the meantime agreed to accept half dues until such time as the mine was able to pay its way again.[20] Sinking however continued in the hope of the lode strengthening in depth, 79 fathoms having been reached by January 1858, 93 fathoms by February 1859 and the ultimate depth of 100 fathoms by December 1859.[21] Reports to the mining press became very thin in 1858, despite unchanged management personalities at the mine, a move which might have been interpreted by outside observers that all was not well. The future of this part of the mine was carefully reviewed in January 1860 and a decision taken to abandon the shaft, although it remained necessary to retain some pumping capability to prevent flooding of the complete workings as other options were developed.[22]

In fact during the previous year attention was being deflected elsewhere in the hope of finding a more profitable lode. As early as February 1859 it was said that permission had been obtained from the mineral lord to open up the ground northwards and a decision was taken to dig shallow pits and sink trial shafts on the backs of the lode in the northern ground.[23] This was to be the start of the new north mine, beyond the farm house, to be quietly developed in parallel for the first year and then the only hope for the future during Treweatha's period of regression into an extremely limited operation in the early 1860s. Early progress was encouraging, with a promising lode discovered only three fathoms (18 feet) from the surface. However problems were already being experienced with water filling the shaft and a steam engine was seen as essential to maintain drainage.[24] Initially Thomas Richards and William Rowe recommended that drainage to a depth of 30 fathoms might be economically achieved by installing a line of rods with bob and pulleys from the pumping engine on the south mine.[25] However, by September 1859 it was confirmed that a small portable pumping engine was in place and the shaft timbered and secured to a depth of nine fathoms. It was said there had been a great deal of delay in installing the engine but that it was now working very well.[26] However it was very much a case of returning to basics as an established mine being worked to a depth of 100 fathoms subsequently found itself reverting to a trial development with a single shaft barely 10 fathoms deep.

Treweatha was indeed a changing mine as 1860 dawned. First in the spring manager Thomas Richards left, followed at the end of 1860 by William Rowe marking the end of a long serving partnership. James Wolferstan, a professional mine manager from Plymouth with responsibility for Bedford United and Tamar Consols on the Devon border, took over the direction of the mine, initially supported by William Rowe but replaced in early 1861 by Thomas Foote and John Scoble as mine agents. Thomas Foote had been James Wolferstan's mine agent at Tamar Consols. After several years of remote management James Wolferstan left and Thomas Foote was confirmed as manager. In reality he had probably been performing that role, certainly as senior resident agent for some time. James Wolferstan had been aged 65 when he took on Treweatha and it is unlikely that he ever went underground. He died in Plymouth in 1864 not long after leaving the mine. The Thomas Foote and John Scoble team was to settle into a regular partnership which lasted until closure. Thomas Foote arrived in Menheniot in 1861 and, as previously described, occupied Treweatha Farm from some time prior to 1871. John Scoble, a Kea man, was aged 43 on his arrival and by 1871 was also living adjacent to the mine with his family. He was never to leave Menheniot and is buried in the churchyard, following his death in 1887 at the age of 69. His gravestone describes him as 'late of Treweatha Mine'.

The decision to abandon the south mine caused yet another change in direction on the method of draining the new mine. Despite recent installation of the portable engine it was now recommended that if commitment to the new working was absolute then the large pumping engine should be transferred from the original south to the north mine.[22] Despite the decision being taken in March 1860, by June it was stated that the masons were still working on the new engine house to contain the transferred engine, despite unfavourable weather which had caused the delay, and that the engine was nearly out of the old house. The parts had been thoroughly examined and it had been agreed that the piston rod, air pump, bucket, fire-front and steampipe were all in need of repair, whilst the boiler also required some attention. The work was anticipated to be completed by the time the engine house was ready and it was estimated the engine would be working by late July.[27] James Wolferstan, the new manager, visited the mine in July 1860 and comprehensively reported on what he found. This style of report confirms that despite his position of authority he had no regular resident role at Treweatha. He estimated that the engine would be working by late August, much of it now being in place with only minor repairs to be effected. William West was responsible for the engine's repairs. The stack was several feet above the surface and foundations were dug for the boiler house. The work had been seriously impeded by the wet weather experienced for the past two months, suggesting not all Victorian Cornish summers were sunny.

Further complications occurred for the struggling venture in January 1861 when the 50-inch engine house caught fire. An engineman discovered what proved to be a serious fire and sought the assistance of a miner who lived close by. They managed to shut down the engine, but had to retreat before the rapidly expanding fire. It did not burn itself out until the following day although it was claimed that the engine itself was not irreparably damaged.[57]

James Wolferstan had earlier assessed the extent of surplus materials on the mine which might be sold to assist funds, but proposed any sale be postponed until the engine was working and the mine drained, the extent of the water problem being uncertain.[28] The sale eventually took place on the mine three months later at the end of October 1860. Materials for disposal included the small portable engine, pumps, tram wagons, tram iron and saddles, chain sheers and a 12 feet water wheel complete with four Brunton frames.[29] A depth of 18 fathoms was not in fact reached until December 1860, despite nine fathoms having been achieved by September 1859.[30] It is clear that very little underground work had been done during the reconstruction period and most of the true mining workforce, previously in excess of 100, laid off. Fortunately Wheal Mary Ann and Wheal Trelawny were booming at this time, but it is uncertain the degree to which they were able to absorb the surplus workforce. Certainly Treweatha's reduced role was to last for some time, with only 20 employed in 1862 and no more than 30 underground and seven dressing as late as December 1863.[31] The limited workforce would have concentrated on sinking the shaft, with 22 fathoms being reached by April 1861, 25 fathoms by mid May and 36 fathoms almost eighteen months later in October 1862. For a long time only the 15 fathom level south was being cautiously exploited although the 30 fathom south was being worked by May 1862. In October 1862 it was said that little had been done in the mine for the past four months, whilst ground was cut for changing the pitwork, this being subsequently accomplished.[32]

Prospects were however gradually improving with promising ore bodies being identified in the 30 and later the 40 fathom level. Despite the need for close control over costs in September 1863 it was recommended that a waterwheel for drawing and crushing be erected at a cost including labour of £300.[33] By January 1864 it was reported the waterwheel was working well as were the shaking tables and it was hoped to get the round buddle working in a day or so.[34] Treweatha was one of the mines visited by Lord Kinnaird's Commission into the condition of mines in December 1863. The site, in its reduced northern form, was described as containing a small drying and changing house, although most men were said to change in the boiler house; a warmer but potentially dangerous location not favoured by responsible concerns. The small ore dressing facility was noted as being covered in, the activity being notoriously wet and cold in winter with a predominance of female and child labour involved.[35]

The years 1864 and 1865 were notable for increasing reference to water problems as the north mine steadily deepened, although thankfully some ore sales were taking place to relieve the financial burden on the adventurers. With the large pumping engine transferred to the north mine and a depth of little over 40 fathoms this is perhaps a little surprising, but references were repeatedly made to the depth of water in the abandoned south shaft and clearly a relationship existed between the need to contain water levels there if the north's problems were not to be worsened. In January 1864 it was reported that they were not keeping pace with drainage, so much rain having fallen during the past week.[34] Likewise in February it was said that several breakages had occurred as a result of the need to drive the engine so fast.[36] A respite during the summer was soon replaced by further worries; progress in January 1865, at a depth of 47 fathoms, being reported as painfully slow in consequence of contending with so much water.[37] At the February meeting the grave decision to temporarily stop all works for the present was reluctantly taken, again due to the state of the workings, now disappearing beneath rising water levels. A shareholder bitterly complained as to how much longer were they to suffer reports of water being out, valuable lodes being cut, water getting in again and workings being stopped. It was sad to see the mine in such a depressed state.[38] The following summer minimal reports only recorded that there was no alteration to the ground in the engine shaft and that it was still troublesome for sinking.

Adventurers in mines were an unpredictable breed and from this least likely of launching pads a period of significant investment and expansion in the mine now began, which was to restore production to levels not seen since the 1850s and with it a mine workforce which was to rise into three figures and reach a peak of 174 by 1870. The expansion was very much investment led, with necessary high calls to support it, with no evidence of anything more than promising long term signs to sustain the commitment. Certainly no rich find coincided with the decision to take the mine forward into its last period of sustained activity. The most likely explanation is a major injection of capital, or preparedness to support heavy calls as the cost book system demanded, following a major change in shareholding bringing fresh commitment and untarnished enthusiasm to revitalise the project. In fact the company's London secretary, the influential link with outside shareholders, changed in 1864 when W. J. Dunsford was succeeded by William Ward. Clearly a development beneficial to the company. Despite these changes those in control of the practical operations retained the confidence of the shareholders and the team of Thomas Foote and John Scoble took the mine forward into this new phase.

Work was commenced at surface to prepare for a new waterwheel purchased from the Tamar Mine, the wheel having been dismantled and brought to a quay on the Tamar estuary from where it was to be shipped to St Germans and brought forward by road to the mine. The ability to transport large parts of mine engines, boilers and items of supporting equipment given the condition of the roads and the limitations of available transport at the time, remains an achievement which should not be underestimated. Whilst the waterwheel was *en route* preparations for a wheel pit, drawing machine and crusher house were in hand.[40] By April 1866 it was said that the arms and wings were on the waterwheel and they would shortly start on the buckets and packing.[41] One month later a wooden watercourse had been completed from the south to the north mine, water diverted onto the wheel and work was starting on the pulley stand, poppet heads etc. from the shaft to the drawing machine.[42] January 1866 had seen the momentous decision taken to restart and clear out the old engine shaft on the south mine, to be renamed Wards Shaft, with the intention of reworking or extending the old levels. However with an ambitious original depth of 100 fathoms further sinking was not a priority and indeed never took place.[43] By April 1866 the reworked Ward's Shaft had been drained to a depth of 43 fathoms although the years of disuse had taken a heavy toll with rotten timber to be cleared and choked areas to be freed.[41] Meanwhile commitment to continuing to work the north mine in parallel remained. Annual production now began to rise from a paltry 35 tons of lead ore in 1865 to 141 tons in 1866 and 313 tons in 1867.

In July 1867 Thomas Foote and John Scoble, assessing the potential limitations of their northern pumping power, suggested reluctantly that no advantage could be gained in sinking the engine shaft below its existing depth of 50 fathoms believing it would not be possible to see the lode before the winter set in and water built up. This they greatly regretted as the 50 fathom level was seen as most promising. They did however propose to take away as much ore as possible from this level during the summer, to boost sales at the next samplings. Meanwhile it was not only Ward's shaft which was attracting attention on the south mine. Harris's Shaft was referred to by name for the first time in July 1867, clearly very much part of the Treweatha expansion plans, not apparently a new shaft although its origins are uncertain. Its location is however precisely known, 50 yards north west of Wards and 350 yards south of Treweatha farm house. Levels were already, or had previously been, worked beneath it and the newly named Harris's

either took advantage of the course of an earlier shallow shaft or was the result of rising to the surface from an existing winze or combination of levels. Either way Harris's was immediately referred to as being pushed on to communicate with a rise from the 50 fathoms level, which when accomplished would enable plans to be progressed to sink below that point, drainage intending to be by a lift attached to Ward's engine. Thomas Foote was certain this would lay open valuable new ground for working and would in effect be a new mine for a great length of the lode.[44] Calls of 10s. and £1 per share were made in March and October 1867 to sustain the mine's expansion.

The October 1867 adventurers' meeting expressed a vote of thanks to Thomas Foote for his energy and skill in working the mine under the many difficulties experienced in recent years. Production was rising, a positive sign for the adventurers and since the last meeting 105 tons of lead ore had been sold and a further 20 tons were currently being dressed. This was suggested to more than demonstrate the productiveness of the lode and Thomas Foote recommended the adventurers should seriously consider erecting more powerful pumping power to enable the engine shaft to be sunk still further and more productive ground opened out.[45] A month later Harris's shaft was reported as progressing well, the ground being more settled and timbering well in hand. Ore was being dressed towards a further sampling and the general scale of activity on the mine was increasing month by month.[46]

The adventurers heeded the manager's recommendations and Saturday 23 May 1868 saw a new 80-inch engine started on Harris's shaft christened the *Margaret Harris* to much applause before an assembled company. It was a great day for Menheniot and the culmination of an ambitious project, being as large as any engine previously erected in the parish. The *Mining Journal* congratulated the company on their commitment and foresight in what were difficult times for mining. A large party descended on Menheniot to celebrate the event including, from London, company secretary William Ward, chairman George Harris and principal shareholder G. Rawlins. The large party of guests assembled at the mine around the engine and Captain Foote, having gathered the mine workforce together, spoke to them at length as did William West, the mining engineer responsible for designing and erecting the engine. A substantial meal was laid on for the Treweatha miners who gave three hearty cheers for their manager and guests.

The formal party adjourned to the account house where a sumptuous dinner of roast beef and plum pudding was provided. The guest list included many influential faces from the Liskeard area with George Harris presiding and William West supporting as vice-chairman. Those around the table included James Seccombe Jnr, manager of East Phoenix and son of the late Samuel Seccombe, gifted manager of Phoenix, whilst Thomas Nicholls of Tavistock, Thomas Pryor of Redruth, the purser of Wheal Trelawny, T. H.

Geak of St Germans, Treweatha mineral lord George Rowe and William Johns manager of Trelawny and West Caradon, were all in attendance. The proceedings lasted long into the afternoon, the loyal and patriotic toasts being followed by hearty cheers 'for which the people of Cornwall were so well known'. William West gave 'success to the mine' and spoke at length, through a haze of cigar smoke, to the assembled company on the future prospects in which he had absolute faith. He congratulated Captain Foote on his management of the mine and the mode of working which he now proposed. Finally he had no doubt that the shareholders would be repaid for their outlay. George Harris, the chairman tried to rise but was almost deafened by the loud and continuous cheers. Mutual compliments continued and it was then the turn of company secretary William Ward to be congratulated on his energetic and competent conduct of the London affairs of the company, followed by further loud cheers. Captain Foote rose and gave what was described as a very interesting account of the mine, although concentration levels must have been a little questionable by this time. Finally Mr R. Clogg rose and gave a selection of statistics in connection with lead mining, by which time it is doubtful if many were listening with any conviction. Still further toasts were proposed before the assembled company broke up and made their way out of Menheniot and into the night. Never had confidence been so high, fuelled by the extensive celebrations of that long day. The reality of the task, when Thomas Foote and John Scoble returned to the mine the following morning, was to prove somewhat tougher but the advantages which the new large engine gave in assisting the deep working of the mine could not be questioned.[47]

A 10s. call per share was made at the November 1868 meeting, but good quantities of ore were being offered for sampling and shareholders and miners alike were satisfied with the progress the mine was making.[48] A year later activity in the mine remained high with North, Ward's and Harris's shafts all in production and efforts continuing to extend the workings. This pattern of expansion was to continue for the next few years. North Shaft had been deepened from 50 to 62 fathoms by 1869, with particular attention now being given to driving the 62 fathom level north and south, whilst continuing to work the 30, 40 and 50 fathom levels.[49] By the end of the year sinking had recommenced below the 62 and this continued during 1870, with the ultimate depth of 74 fathoms having been reached by February 1871 with the final crosscut commenced east to meet the lode at that level. The 50 fathom and 62 fathom levels north and south were also still being worked at this time.[50]

The older Ward's Shaft, previously abandoned at a depth of 100 fathoms depth in the first working, had been cleared to a depth of 90 fathoms by June 1870 with attention being given to securing and timbering. Promising levels had been tried and new ones opened as the depth increased, believing that valuable ground still remained if properly worked. The 43, 63 and 73 fathom levels south were being tried at this time.[51] By February 1871 the 43, 53, 63, 73 and 90 levels south were being worked as well as the 90 north. The engine and pitwork were said to be in good order and the water being drained well.[52] In March 1871 men were set for the final push to clear and secure Ward's Shaft from the 90 to 100 fathoms, after which it was proposed to resume driving the latter level, submerged and abandoned since 1860, north and south. The shaft was however never to be sunk below that original 1860 depth of 100 fathoms. March 1871 also saw money being spent on putting the whim engine in good order as well as erecting an 18 feet water wheel with connecting wooden water-course, intended to run some new jigging machines in connection with the dressing operations.[53]

Harris's shaft also continued to be worked and by September 1869 a plat had been cut away, to store ore in readiness for raising, at the 62 fathom level from where men were already driving north and were about to commence driving south. The lode in the 50 south, also being driven at this time, was described as poor.[49] Tribute pitches continued to be worked during 1870 and additionally by December the shaft was completed and secured from the 62 to the 74 fathom level. The 62 fathom level was being driven both north and south during this period. Machinery and engines were all working well and work had just been set throughout the mine for 93 men.[54] Despite this continuing scale of activity, involving all three shafts, in hindsight quantity rather than quality was the order of the day. This was not so much the fault of the practical management of the mine but more a reflection of the moderate quality of the lode which now remained within Treweatha's boundaries. The high cost of working at this scale continued to exceed the rising ore sales and frustrated any hopes of profits being realised, even though ore production rose to 340 tons in 1869, 356 tons in 1870 and 687 tons in 1871.

In spite of this very brave and determined final period of working, largely inspired by William Ward the London secretary and chairman George Harris, limits of the shareholders support were being reached and the renewal of the 21 years lease, which was to expire in 1873, drew ominously close. It was perhaps inevitable that an advertisement should appear in August 1872, offering a new 21 year lease for Treweatha to any interested party with engines, machinery and plant available to be purchased at valuation.[55] No offer was made and in September 1872 an auction took place on the mine, machinery and equipment being described as one 80-inch and two 50-inch pumping engines (from Harris's, North and Ward's), a 22-inch winding engine, three waterwheels (40 feet by 30 inches, 18 feet by two feet and 15 feet by 18 inches), a crusher, a double acting drawing machine, 260 fathoms of pitwork and tram iron and wagons.[56]

Treweatha's main engines were to be disposed of far and wide. The 80-inch *Margaret Harris*, still only four years old, was bought by a local agent and was to leave Cornwall, resold on to Shire Moor Colliery, Blaydon-on-Tyne. One of the 50-inch engines was destined to travel even further, shipped from Looe to the lead mines of Linares, Spain.[57]

The fact the mine was almost at its peak level of employment the year before closure must have made the final demise dearly felt within the village. It is doubtful if much respite was on offer elsewhere for the redundant miners, with Trelawny now only existing as an extension of Wheal Mary Ann's operation, which in itself was by this time contending with significant financial problems. Treweatha was never to be worked again and gradually the site became overgrown, whilst the remains of engine houses and supporting buildings deteriorated and the stonework re-used for adjacent parish projects. Treweatha Farm House remains the principal land mark to the mine's original site emphasising the relative permanency of the land, in direct comparison to Menheniot's all too brief flirtation with the fickle world of mining.

CHAPTER SEVEN

TRANSPORT COMMUNICATIONS

Transport communications for all the mines in the Menheniot area received scant comment in contemporary records and yet presented significant logistical problems. Large quantities of lead ore required transportation to the coast, for movement by sea for smelting. In return coal needed to be moved from the adjacent ports, where it would have arrived from south Wales, to feed the voracious appetites of Menheniot's engine houses. Both of these movements placed pressure on transport communications to a degree far exceeding earlier agricultural needs. Menheniot lay around six miles from the nearest shipping quays, which were at St Germans and Looe, over extremely poorly made roads made significantly worse as soon as traffic in any quantity began passing. The exceptionally difficult terrain could most kindly be described as a succession of hills and deep valleys which did not lend themselves to easy transport solutions. Very little evidence has survived directly related to transport in use at the time, but it is known that packhorses or pack mules, each slung with

The ancient port of Looe. The riverside fishing and general quays saw considerable congestion in the 19th century as coal imports and copper mineral exports from Caradon and Menheniot mines boomed. North and South Wales registered vessels were regular visitors during the mining period, alongside Cornish coastal shipping.

S. Bartlett collection

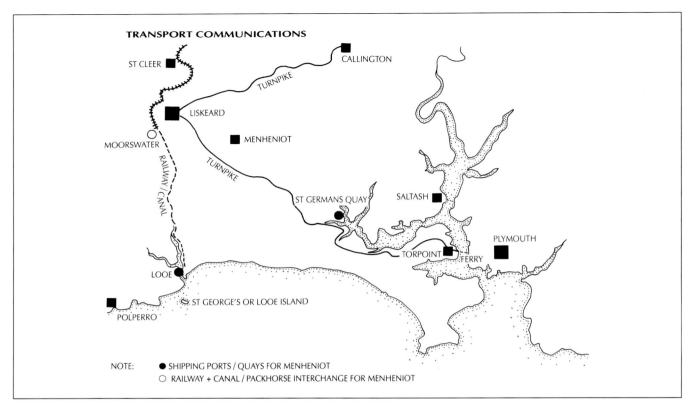

TRANSPORT COMMUNICATIONS

NOTE: ● SHIPPING PORTS / QUAYS FOR MENHENIOT
○ RAILWAY + CANAL / PACKHORSE INTERCHANGE FOR MENHENIOT

Transport communications were never easy for Menheniot's mines. Coal and mine materials inwards and ore outwards were shipped through the port of Looe and St Germans Quay, having arrived by packhorse, cart or the canal/railway interchange at Moorswater for Looe.

panniers to either side and in charge of a single man, were extensively used in the area, although horses and carts were becoming more plentiful by the 1840s.

There is clear evidence that both St Germans Quay and Looe were used, with the former having the greater historical ties with Menheniot. Whilst no dedicated rail link could ever be justified from the site of the mines to either port, during the period of principal mining activity from 1843 adjacent developments took place which enabled partial advantage to be taken of the improving transport scene in the area. In October 1853 Treweatha Mine reported a sale of lead ore was to take place at St Germans,

confirming that mine's link with the quay, whilst in 1856 it was said that most of the ores from the Menheniot district were shipped at St Germans, where a new good quay had been built at Cuddenbeak.[1] Quantities were also conveyed to Looe, where new quays had been built and others altered and repaired. The quays at Looe were described as insufficient for the trade, Menheniot traffic being exceeded by the booming output from the Caradon area. This originated north of Liskeard and was brought down on the Liskeard & Caradon Railway to Moorswater, below Liskeard town, thence via the overworked canal link to Looe.

The Liskeard & Looe Union Canal had been opened in 1828 prior to the mining boom and the Moorswater traffic interchange was showing distinct signs of inability to cope.[1] Some lead ore from Wheal Mary Ann is known to have been brought to Moorswater by road for onward transit via the canal to Looe. This confirmed the belief that Menheniot traffic which was shipped from Looe would have largely been conveyed by packhorse or cart through

Liskeard to the Moorswater canal interchange, rather than by direct road transit to Looe itself. Wheal Trelawny is known to have been renting its own wharf at Looe in 1862.[2] The canal, with the interchange point at Moorswater increasingly unable to cope with the quantity of traffic passing to and from the Caradon area, was superseded by a throughout rail link to Looe, following the canal bank, at the end of 1860. Liskeard and Menheniot traffic would have continued to have been accepted at Moorswater, whilst the heavier Caradon traffic now enjoyed a through rail journey.

At Looe itself the harbour had been deepened by the removal of rocks and loose stones from the confined tidal river bed, against which the small

quays of East and West Looe had been built some centuries before for fishing and general trade.[2] The port had strong Welsh connections, with coastwise shipping bracing the hazardous winter voyage around Lands End bringing south Wales coal in for Menheniot and Caradon with back loads of lead and copper ores for smelting. Lead from Menheniot was shipped to north Wales, Llanelly and Burry Port in west Wales and more conveniently to the local smelters at Par and up the river Tamar. Typically, in April 1861, a visitor to Looe would have found the *Brilliant* of Looe, a coaster of 81 tons, just arrived from Swansea whilst nearby was the *Phoenix* of Looe, a coaster of 126 tons, captained by John Walters of East Looe, but betraying its Welsh connections with William Lewis of Pembrey as ships mate. In April 1881 the *Ifor* of Aberystwyth, a coaster of 98 tons, had recently arrived via Briton Ferry, south Wales, plying a similar trade.

Meanwhile the strong links between Menheniot and St Germans quay survived via the tenuous road links from the mines north of the village, eased somewhat by the availability of the Liskeard to Torpoint turnpike road for

Looe. The quays were rail connected and this later aerial view shows the passenger terminus beyond the river bridge, on the right hand river bank. Sidings then crossed the road at the end of the bridge – sidings and wagons being clearly visible along the quayside.

S. Bartlett collection

part of the journey. The Cornwall Railway reached Liskeard in 1859, striding across the southern edge of Menheniot parish then on towards Saltash and the magnificent Royal Albert Bridge which took it across the river Tamar and into Plymouth, where it joined the already completed rail route to London. With far greater prizes to be won, the railway's only concession to Menheniot was an inconveniently sited station one mile south of the village and even further from the mines which lay north of that point. There has been suggestion that some lead ore was sent by rail from Menheniot Station to St Germans, where it was transhipped onto a tramway which took it down to the quay. However it is now thought the short tramway was specifically built to move seaborne construction materials for the Cornwall Railway and then fell into disuse.[3]

Summarising the effect that Menheniot's mining trade had on surrounding roads and transport links, it is clear that serious logistical problems emerged in maintaining efficient links with both St Germans and Looe over difficult and poorly maintained roads. At the same time the district was not large enough to support a dedicated transport link in the way that the Caradon area supported a dedicated mineral railway from the high moorland to Looe on the coast. Menheniot survived on the variously described combinations of packhorses and carts combined with canal or rail from Moorswater in the case of Looe; all pursued in an effort to most effectively reach the nearby coast. St Germans Quay emerges as the historic seaborne link with Menheniot, initially for agriculture, then seeing its quays expanded co-incidental with the parish mining boom. There is little doubt however that as the mining period progressed Looe took greater prominence and featured increasingly as the shipping port for the district, although Menheniot's trade was always in a supporting role to the dominant Caradon copper ore traffic.

St Germans Quay. Predates Looe as the traditional agricultural and mining port for the Menheniot area. Ore sales took place on the quay and both ports continued to participate in the Menheniot mining trade.

S. Bartlett 1993

CHAPTER EIGHT
MENHENIOT FAMILY LIFE

Between St Ive and Liskeard and below this towards the sea
is a tract of charming land as well cultivated as most in the Kingdom
MARSHALL 1806

AS THE MINING fraternity descended on Menheniot in the 1840s, the village and its rural community was to encounter change out of all proportion to that experienced before. This was not, as happened in certain moorland parishes, a mining community establishing itself in a sparsely populated landscape, but a workforce marching into a large, well populated agricultural parish with all available good quality land enclosed and under cultivation. The small areas that were not would have been thickly wooded and lush, mostly coinciding with the steeper slopes of this undulating parish. Very little has been written of the area's mining families, their fortunes and their personal tragedies and yet their story in every respect deserves setting alongside the history of the mines themselves. The vanguard found an established rural community and it is the untarnished village of 1841, just two years away from change, which sets the scene for our story of Menheniot.

Menheniot was traversed by two turnpike roads by this time, the first from Liskeard skirted the northern edge of the parish before passing through St Ive and on to Callington. The second from Liskeard skirted the southern edge of Menheniot *en route* to Torpoint and the chain ferry across the river Tamar to Plymouth. Both passed the village by with sights set on greater prizes. Menheniot village lay in the centre of the parish, remote from either main arterial route, but itself the focus of a spider's web of narrow lanes radiating from the church which dominated the centre of the village. The distancing from the two main roads gave the village a more remote and inward looking feel than its proximity to Liskeard might suggest. Some years earlier a traveller along the Callington road recorded

Between St Ive and Liskeard and below this towards the sea is a tract of charming land, as well cultivated as most in the Kingdom. I saw several women at work busy hand reaping. The produce of the enclosures is mostly wheat and barley, with some oats and turnips, with a little clover and upland ley. Some horses and oxen in carriages, but packhorses seem still to be much in use.[1]

In 1841 72% of the parish workforce was involved in agriculture, with 153 agricultural labourers, 145 farm servants, 34 farmers and eight yeomen.

The diversity of other trades in the parish however demonstrated the versatility and breadth of skills present in a rural community at this time including carpenters, blacksmiths, shoemakers and wall masons. 18 house servants and three gardeners were in service, the house servants mostly well spread in twos or threes at the larger farm houses. A school building had been erected in Menheniot village in 1835 and George Pooley was schoolmaster there in 1841. Merrymeet hamlet, in the north of the parish, was afforded status with a second parish school built in 1842 for 130 children. A registered charity to instruct poor children of the parish in learning had existed since 1753 and by 1856 as well as contributing to the salaries of master and mistress, it provided for twelve children to be taught free and the remainder to pay a halfpenny per week. It is ironic that in education at least, with two schools offering between a hundred and a hundred and fifty places each, capacity here at least existed for the unexpected influx to come. An iron foundry had been established at Roseland around 1830, initially supplying existing trades but poised to

Menheniot village. Looking towards the square, the church boundary is on the left and the former police station along the road to the right.

S. Bartlett 1991

benefit from the mining industry's needs, as would other associated trades. By 1856 Nicholls, Williams & Co. proprietors of Roseland Iron Foundry also had offices at Church Street, Liskeard.[2]

Whilst no one landowner dominated the parish, the most influential at this time both in the community and with the mining fraternity was undoubtedly Charles Trelawny of Coldrenick after whom Wheal Trelawny mine took its name. Charles Trelawny was born on 26 June 1799, became High Sheriff of Cornwall in 1822 and died on 25 August 1883, aged 84, his life having spanned the greatest years of Menheniot's mining history. He took great care in his leasing of Wheal Trelawny ensuring, despite pressure from James and Peter Clymo, that the proper entitlement went to a small group of working miners and later was more sympathetic than any other mineral lord in considering reductions of dues, to help the hard pressed mine adventurers through the bad times.

The sizes of farms in 1841 varied significantly, whilst labourers' cottages were scattered in random fashion around the parish. On the larger farms it was common for up to five or six teenage farm servants to be living in the main farm house whilst nine and ten year-olds were not uncommon. This tradition also pointed to overcrowded conditions amongst the farm labouring

workforce, with large families and meagre wages forcing the young to make their contribution to the family income at the earliest possible age.

If 1841 marked the end of an era, then 1851 was an equally important reference point, coming at a time when the population had risen from 1,221 in 1841 to 1,944 (+ 59%) and the numbers of homes from 237 to 315 (+ 33%). A full profile of Menheniot's changing population numbers, in ten year bands from 1801 to 1901, is given in Appendix D. The influx of miners was in full swing at this time and was to continue rising well into the decade. In order to reach a complete understanding of the mix within the village the details of every person recorded in the 1851 census return for Menheniot have been extracted. Appendices E to H set out the occupations of every resident and the age profile of those working within each trade, the contrast in age profile between mining and agricultural labourers being particularly telling. The occupation or status of every child under 15, in individual one-year bands, is presented in greater detail outlining the nature

Between 1841–1861 Menheniot's population doubled as experienced miners and their families migrated from all over Cornwall. By 1851 the boom was well under way and Menheniot's census return reveals the strong central and western Cornwall influence.

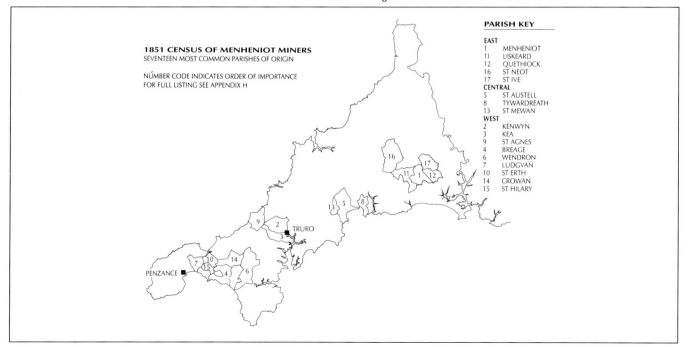

1851 CENSUS OF MENHENIOT MINERS
SEVENTEEN MOST COMMON PARISHES OF ORIGIN

NUMBER CODE INDICATES ORDER OF IMPORTANCE
FOR FULL LISTING SEE APPENDIX H

PARISH KEY

EAST
1   MENHENIOT
11 LISKEARD
12 QUETHIOCK
16 ST NEOT
17 ST IVE
CENTRAL
5   ST AUSTELL
8   TYWARDREATH
13 ST MEWAN
WEST
2   KENWYN
3   KEA
9   ST AGNES
4   BREAGE
6   WENDRON
7   LUDGVAN
10 ST ERTH
14 CROWAN
15 ST HILARY

TRURO

PENZANCE

of child labour in the parish. All miners and selected other trades have been divided by place of birth (or adjusted to birthplace of youngest child prior to arrival in Menheniot) as an indicator of the mix of immigrants moving into the parish.

Before moving on to our central subject, the mining families, Menheniot's traditional trades in 1851 exhibit a quite amazing diversity, partly due to the significantly better quality of the detail recorded in the 1851 census. Blacksmiths, carpenters, shoemakers, millers, tailors, woodmen, dressmakers, masons, drapers' assistants, waggoners, postmen, washerwomen were all present in numbers. No less than 81 female house servants, 70 of which were under 30 years of age, were attached in generally small numbers to the larger farms and houses, although very few professional men were resident in the parish. In very much smaller numbers cooks, governesses, nurses and a groom were present at only the largest houses. Numbers working in the principal trades were blacksmith 25, carpenter 25, shoemaker 16, miller 16 and mason 9. The numbers of blacksmiths and carpenters reflected traditional rural trades which would have prospered from the needs of the mining industry.

290 persons were working in the traditional parish mainstay, agriculture, including 204 labourers and 50 farmers. Of the latter only 21 were born in Menheniot, suggesting the handing down of farms from father to son was not as great as commonly believed. A similar number were born in other east Cornwall parishes, whilst the remainder were born in west Cornwall, Devon and Somerset. However, the 290 in agriculture overall compared with no less than 361 in mining, already outstripping the traditional employer and yet to reach its peak. When multiplied by miners' family dependents not working, the true impact of the mining industry on a traditional way of life can be seen. The final small group of miscellaneous professions and trades included the vicar, curate, two national schoolmasters, highway labourer, parish sexton, tollgate keeper, solicitor's clerk and errand boy. No less than 227 children were described as scholars and whilst almost equal numbers were male and female the equal distribution of the sexes did not apply to the older eleven and twelve year-olds where twice as many were girls, greater numbers of boys already finding work in mine and field respectively. 216 of the 227 scholars were aged twelve or under.

The mine agents who were to open up Wheal Trelawny in 1843, Wheal Mary Ann in 1845 and Wheal Trehane in 1846 and then gear them to full production, were faced with an immediate and chronic skilled labour shortage. There was a good local supply of masons, carpenters and associated trades for the construction of engine houses and mine buildings whilst, by offering enhanced rates of pay, the traditional agricultural labouring workforce, after some initial suspicion, provided a source for at least part of the unskilled labour requirement. In the years to come, younger Menheniot men were to graduate from mine labouring to become skilled miners, but this was to evolve over a period of time and was more a feature of the established mining period, playing no part in the initial recruitment of the essential skilled mine workforce. Wheal Trelawny from small beginnings rapidly built up to a workforce of 130 by 1846 and 300 by 1849. Wheal Mary Ann, with its later start, was employing 15 in 1846, but rose to 125 in 1849 and 422 by 1851, whilst the smaller scale Wheal Trehane had a steady workforce of 100 in both 1849 and 1851. By then, over 800 mining jobs were on offer in Menheniot where none had existed at the beginning of 1843. Numbers employed at each mine, gleaned from diverse sources, for no company records have survived, are set out in detail in Appendix C.

Not only was there no mining tradition in Menheniot, but the small start made in adjacent St Ive hardly helped and the booming Caradon area north of Liskeard, with South Caradon opened in 1837 and West Caradon in 1839 both now in full production, was absorbing the migrant west Cornwall workforce which had been channelling in via Liskeard for several years. Some western Cornish mining parishes were now experiencing mine closures and unemployment. Many were conditioning themselves to emigration to Australia and other foreign lands, whilst a welcome and less well chronicled alternative was the move up-country to emerging mining districts. Large communities had earlier built up around the St Austell area whilst others now travelled through Liskeard to establish themselves on both the Devon and Cornish sides of the upper part of the Tamar around Tavistock, Gunnislake and Calstock. The Menheniot mine agents worked on recruitment through word of mouth in Liskeard, using Caradon men returning to their families in the west and by intercepting men travelling east in the hope of finding work. Where necessary the newly appointed Menheniot agents travelled back themselves to recruit and the fact that they too had been recently taken on from western mines inevitably meant links between those parishes and Menheniot became naturally forged.

By 1851 it was clear that as well as direct migration, more complex patterns were emerging with some western men drifting back from the Devon border towards Menheniot and others moving eastwards after several years' employment in the St Austell area. A fascinating feature of this migration pattern was that at varying stages in the Menheniot mining era different parishes of origin dominated in turn and this was undoubtedly a complex combination reflecting patterns of mine closures in the west, the impact of word of mouth encouraging groups of families to follow each other and the influence of mine agents returning to specific areas to seek out labour.

Within the restrictive environment of an enclosed, already well populated district, rows of cottages began to appear both in the village and dotted at random along the lanes throughout the parish. In many cases, such as at Factory and Quarry, they were some distance from the mines, which principally lay north of the village, and no pattern of purpose-built cottages directly associated with a particular mine emerged. Larger outposts grew up around Merrymeet and Pengover Green in the north of the parish, largely dominated by mining families. Here the lanes would be thronged with hundreds of miners, coupled with noisy groups of mine boys and girls making their way to and from work, whilst the continuous noise of working engines and mine machinery contrasted markedly with the peace and tranquillity experienced today.

On the road from Menheniot to Pengover Green lay Crift Cottages and these in 1851 consisted of 18 dwellings, 16 of which were occupied by mining families. By 1861 further cottages had been built and the total number increased to 38, each one having a narrow yard for growing vegetables or keeping a pig, at the end of which was an earth toilet. Immediately below Crift was a beer retailer, in what is now known as Crift House, a rough and ready establishment opened for the miners. This was originally fronted by a court yard entered from the Menheniot to Merrymeet road. Just one line of cottages, at right-angles to the road, remains today, giving away few secrets of the trials and tribulations of the families that have gone before. Crift Cottages provided a fascinating picture of life in a mining

The lane from Crift cottages to Pengover Green. Once busy with hundreds of miners, mine boys and girls *en-route* to Wheal Mary Ann, Wheal Trelawny and Treweatha. *S. Bartlett 1991*

community in 1851 with no less that 110 people living in the 16 cottages occupied by miners. 39 lead miners, without including mine boys and mine girls, emerged daily for work from this restricted location, 13 of them being lodgers adding to the size of main family groups. Whilst undoubtedly many cottages in the parish have since disappeared, this sort of density begins to explain how a large mining workforce dispersed into the restricted number of residences available. 33 of the 39 miners were western men and only one had been born in Menheniot whilst half had been born in just two parishes, nine in Kenwyn and 10 in Kea and it was clear that many families had a common heritage and story to tell.

Crift Cottages had been built around 1849 and the evidence of recent arrivals was apparent. James Stevens' youngest child had been born only eight months earlier in St Austell as had Joseph Truern's child nine months previously. Breage man Benjamin Lukay and Redruth born William Tonkin both had children born in Liskeard three and five months earlier respectively. This is the first evidence of Liskeard acting as a transit camp for Menheniot, a subject we will return to later. All together 11 children aged one year or less were present in the 16 cottages, only two of whom had been born in Menheniot. A truly young community in every sense of the word, with but one common bond, a mining tradition. The noise of children playing around Crift and in the lane outside would have been constantly present with no less than 10 children in the age group four to seven. William Bawden, who opened our story, was one of these Crift men. He had arrived from Breage with his wife and five children and at the age of 32 was at his prime as a miner. He was to find relative prosperity and security of employment in Menheniot, but was also to find tragedy when his eldest son William James died in June 1858, aged 18. Crift Cottages were to experience more than their share of early deaths during a three-month period in 1858 when in addition to 18 year-old William Bawden, the previously mentioned William Tonkin lost a six day-old son whilst five year old Sarah Hill also died. Tragedy and early death, whether from accident or illness, was never far away in nineteenth century Menheniot.

Leaving Crift another Menheniot miner in 1851, a St Hilary man, recounted his travels prior to reaching Menheniot around 1849. He had met and married a Devon born girl and their first child had been born in New South Wales, Australia seven years previously. Within a year they were back in St Hilary in the west before travelling the length of Cornwall to Callington, near the Devon border, where they remained for several years before arriving in Menheniot two years previously. Crowan born John Prout, child of a mining family, recorded his own travels through Cornwall to Menheniot.

I could never remember anything about my birthplace, for my mother took me to Camborne when a baby. When I was eight years old I went to work at a place down from Dolcoath Tin Mine called Red

River. I had to work from seven till five with an interval of half an hour for dinner, as a tin dresser for a penny per day. Then in 1852 we went to Liskeard to live, but instead of stopping in that town we went three and a half miles out to be near the mine in Menheniot Parish. There I went to work in Wheal Trelawny Mine and had sixpence per day to start with. That was drawing lead ore.

Demonstrating how the Menheniot saga was to cross the world, John Prout's story was found not here but in a South Australian newspaper half a century later.[3]

During the first decade of the Menheniot mining era an artificially young mining community established itself, quite out of character with older settlements in the west or indeed the native Menheniot population. The missing feature were the old, sick and infirm which were so common in the traditional mining villages, although this was sadly to change over succeeding years as Menheniot accumulated its share of the casualties and flotsam of a dangerous and debilitating industry. As the area became established the age profile of miners gradually rose and this feature could be seen repeating itself, but in different cycles according to each parish's dates of expansion, in other parts of the Liskeard area reflecting that despite the mobility of miners, a hard core set down more permanent roots as long as prosperity continued. As well as the previously illustrated young married men, who within a reasonable period were joined by their families, by far the largest secondary group were unattached lodgers, a potential powder keg set to explode in bouts of lawlessness and disruptive behaviour, particularly following monthly pay days. The majority of these men were unmarried in their late teens or early twenties and, like their married colleagues, of western origin. Somewhat surprisingly no large boarding houses existed in the parish specifically providing accommodation for this group, but they were to be found singularly or in twos or threes supplementing the family income in miners' cottages or equally often with farm labourers in the parish. Frequently there would be a common bond between mining families and their lodger in parish of origin, suggesting prearranged contacts prior to leaving home to seek work in far off Menheniot or, even more commonly, younger lodgers had clearly arrived in pairs, having left home to seek their fortune in a distant mining field with the strength of companionship to sustain them.

The Liskeard area, from which Menheniot cannot be excluded, gained a reputation for unruly behaviour and drunkenness during this period and the presence of large numbers of younger miners, far from home and family ties, unquestionably contributed to this problem. As early as May 1842 Liskeard experienced trouble with Caradon men, when heavy drinking boiled over into a riot following a Saturday pay day when several hundred miners descended on the town. Following a disturbance at the Buller Arms at

Menheniot police station. An imposing structure for the size of the village. Built in 1859 at the height of the mining era, equipped with two cells and accommodation for two policemen and their families.

S. Bartlett 1993

closing time the police arrested several of the ringleaders, but responding to a cry of 'one and all' nearly two hundred miners broke down the doors and windows and succeeded in rescuing their companions. It was said the whole neighbourhood was kept in a state of fear until nearly six o'clock the following morning.[4]

An imposing police station was built in Menheniot in 1859. Today the solidly built building seems overlarge for such a small village. However both the scale and the fact the building date coincides with the height of the mining boom suggests yet another link to Menheniot's mining past. Peel Lodge, now a private residence, was built to house two policemen and their families with separate living accommodation, as well as a police office and two cells. No bathrooms and only outside toilets were provided. No doubt many a miner cooled his heels behind these grey stone walls.

Two police constables, Thomas Mutton and Joseph Voss, aged 28 and 27, were recorded in Menheniot in 1861. Thomas Mutton had only joined the force in 1860 and clearly the life did not appeal to him for he resigned in June 1861. By contrast Joseph Voss, who had been recruited in 1857 was dedicated to the force and was promoted to Sergeant in Launceston in 1865 and reached the exalted rank of Inspector in the Truro district in 1886, where he remained until retirement in 1894. He had been born in Cardinham, a labourer prior to recruitment and was over five feet 10 inches tall with dark grey eyes and dark brown hair. By 1871 Menheniot's resident police presence was still two in the form of William Beckerlegge and James Truran, aged 34 and 35. William Beckerlegge was an ex-sailor recruited in Newlyn in 1860, moving to Menheniot some time prior to 1871. He was a round faced man of dark complexion, five feet eight inches tall with hazel eyes and brown hair. James Truran was a tough ex-miner from St Agnes, recruited in 1864, a man of dark complexion also five feet eight inches tall with dark grey eyes and dark brown hair. Together they were responsible for maintaining law and order in Menheniot.[5]

It is difficult to judge the real scale of law and order problems in the parish, but the tough and transient mining workforce unquestionably brought with it the potential for periodic bouts of lawlessness, particularly linked to drinking excesses amongst the less responsible elements of the young community both here and in nearby Liskeard. Lesser crime raised its head periodically, typified one night in April 1857 when a wooden water course was cut in two and water which had been pumped from the mine flooded Mrs. Hawker's fish pond, killing both fish and vegetation; the mine water it was said being very injurious to both.[6] The Hawkers lived at Scawns and the offending mine was probably Wheal Mary Ann. Likewise, just two weeks later a sheep was stolen from the Pool Hall estate of George Roby.[7] In nearby Liskeard a reminder of the standards of the day occurred in May 1857 when

Scawns, Menheniot c.1900. The scene, in April 1857, of Mrs Hawker's fish ponds being flooded and poisoned by Wheal Mary Ann mine water.

S. Bartlett collection

James Rudner, a young man, was apprehended on a Sunday afternoon and brought before the magistrates charged with playing marbles on the Sabbath. His employer gave him a good reference and he was discharged on payment of 2s. costs.[2] A more serious incident occurred in Menheniot in July 1857 when Nicholas Grylls, a shoemaker of Menheniot, was charged by Liskeard magistrates with furiously riding along the highway and seriously injuring John Kernick, blacksmith of Menheniot, who subsequently died of his injuries. The former was committed to Bodmin to stand trial for manslaughter.[9]

Strongly balancing the wilder elements of the community was a growing family base with strengthening roots in the village, which gradually corrected the balance towards stronger sobering influences. A powerful presence throughout this period was the commitment to Methodism, as strong in Menheniot as in other Cornish communities at this time. Methodism was not brought to Menheniot by the immigrant miners, as might have been imagined, although the west Cornishmen undoubtedly brought a strong Methodist tradition with them and their sheer numbers, as with other aspects of village life, strongly influenced the growth of Methodism in the village. John Wesley made several visits to Liskeard, the first as early as 1751 and the last in 1787 and from his early inspiration Methodist Societies steadily grew and chapels were built, both in the town of Liskeard and in the surrounding parishes. Menheniot village itself boasted two chapels, one Wesleyan Methodist build in 1838, but replaced by the present building in 1905, the other United Methodist Free Church built about 1860. Taking the parish as a whole, at Pengover Green a Bible Christian Chapel was built in 1850, whilst a Wesleyan Reform existed at Pengover. The tenth anniversary of the Pengover Green Bible Christian Chapel was celebrated in June 1860 by a public tea attended by over 200 children.[10] A Free Methodist Chapel was opened at Pengover Green in November 1861, enlivened it was said by the very able choir.[11] The Wesleyan Chapel to be seen at Merrymeet today was not built until 1908, when it replaced an earlier one at Trengrove.

A feature of the Methodist tradition was the itinerant preachers, who could be seen moving around their large circuits, sometimes on foot, but more often on horseback, dominant and eloquent characters often rough and ready in manner but much loved by working men and women alike. The Methodist tradition was equally as strong amongst the mine Captains and agents as the working miners themselves, many of the former having reached their respected position from the ranks of the working miner. These strong-willed characters were to be found in many local congregations leading their men in inspired singing and worship at chapel as well as in the harsh environment of the working mine during the week. The Methodist tradition in the village undoubtedly has earlier roots and a wider base than the dates of the chapels described, with local societies traditionally meeting in houses

Merrymeet Mission Church. In the north of the parish, Merrymeet's community had a resident curate from the 1850s – the old school chapel being licensed for services from 1870. The mission church itself was not built until 1905.
S. Bartlett 1991

or barns for prayers and worship and only progressing to more formalised buildings as funds and the necessary organisation emerged. This is well illustrated by the fact that the breakaway Bible Christian Movement had by 1848 no less than three separate societies in the parish based at Butterdon Mill and Merrymeet, Menheniot Village and Pengover Green.[12] The Pengover Green Chapel of 1850 was, until recently, the only tangible reminder of the movement. In 1861 Samuel Cutts, a twenty-six year-old unmarried methodist minister born in Westfield, Sussex, was resident at Pengover Green. A man hardly built in the tough Cornish mining tradition, but one who no doubt brought his own special contribution to the patchwork quilt of nineteenth century Menheniot society.

The established church had a strong traditional base in Menheniot, with a large church seating 550 dominantly located in the centre of the village.[2] At this time it was within the diocese of Exeter, with the benefice from 1478 appropriated to Exeter College, Oxford. Prior to the nineteenth century at least four incumbents had become bishops after leaving Menheniot and during the nineteenth century the parish was noteworthy for its long serving ministries.[13] These were dominated by Rev. William Carr (1792-1830) and Rev. Richard Martin (1831-1883), the former recorded in the parish register as having died on Christmas Eve 1830. Richard Martin had been born in the Cathedral Cloisters, Exeter and was twenty eight years of age when he arrived in Menheniot to commence a ministry of no less than fifty two years, which took him to the age of eighty. He more than any other person could claim to have known Menheniot for twelve peaceful years prior to the arrival of mining, to have seen its rise, dominance and subsequent fall. His memories, if only they had been recorded, would have been invaluable. Just two incumbents collectively spanned ninety one years of service, a record of consistency rarely equalled.

Whatever competitive influence the growing popularity of Methodism might have had amongst the mining community, the established church was prominently served during this period with no less than two curates supporting the vicar, one always resident in Merrymeet. We do know something of the curates, who by their nature changed more frequently.

Menheniot Church, dominantly located in the centre of the village. The Rev. Richard Martin (1803–1883) held the living for 52 years from 1831 witnessing the rise and fall of mining in Menheniot. *S. Bartlett collection*

Henry Olver, aged 33, from Warminster, Wiltshire, was at Merrymeet in 1861 and John Bampfield, from Stoke Dameral, Devon, likewise in 1871. The present mission church at Merrymeet was only built in 1905, services previously being held in the old school chapel at Merrymeet, licensed in 1870 by the Bishop of Exeter.[13] In fact the school had been built in 1842 and early references to a resident curate in Merrymeet have been found in 1856, 1861 and 1862.[14] A major refurbishment of Menheniot church took place in this period, the completion marked by a special service on 20 August 1866, following a major extension to the east end of the church. The latter part of the nineteenth century saw the ministries of Rev. Louis Woollcombe (1883-

1887) and Charles Hammond (1887-1912) as mining fortunes receded.

Menheniot born men were beginning to drift into mining by 1851 and William Bartlett, by now a nineteen year-old miner, was lodging with George Bassett and Theophilus Hill at agricultural labourer William Richards' house at Pengover Green. This was the same William Bartlett who had been a nine year old farm servant in 1841. He had seen the first miners arrive and was himself to span the whole era of Menheniot mining, before being forced to leave with the mining exodus in the 1870s, a victim of over-dependence on one industry.

The range of mining work on offer provided employment for men, women and children, with several family members often employed at the same mine. The 422 at Wheal Mary Ann in 1851 comprised 280 men, 68 women and 74 children, significantly the latter two supporting categories comprising one third of the total workforce. At this time it was still common for young boys to be employed underground, usually working with a father or other close relative. Women were never employed underground, but bal maidens or mine girls were an essential part of the mine workforce at surface, where with mine boys and a few older male labourers they dominated the ore dressing workforce. Considerable variation occurred however from mine to mine, according to the prejudices of the manager, as to what constituted the most cost-effective workforce.

A group of influential managers meeting in Liskeard in April 1862 expressed quite diverse views, exploding a few long-held myths on the classic make-up of a Cornish mine workforce. Thomas Trevillion of Herodsfoot employed no-one under the age of 18 underground and preferred adult males on surface work; they work better he declared. Asked whether he gave older miners surface work he replied firmly that he did not, his male surface workforce being recruited from local unskilled men who had left agriculture because the pay was better. James Seccombe, who lived at Trenodden, Menheniot, and was an influential manager in the Caradon area, stated that at East Caradon he employed no-one underground under 17. His residence Trenodden still stands and he and his family have a prominent memorial in Menheniot churchyard. William Rich of Caradon Consols, a small mine with only 27 underground miners, similarly declared it was his policy to employ no-one underground under 17 or over 38, emphasising that he always picked the young and fittest men. He stated he would not employ older men in case they prejudiced the economics of his small concern.[15]

Peter Clymo Jnr, a highly respected but more traditional figure, referred to his main concern, South Caradon, but it is clear his traditional views were equally practised in Menheniot at Wheal Mary Ann and Wheal Trelawny, where the Clymo influence had also been present. He declared a willingness to employ children from seven to eight onwards, with 12 to 14 year old boys employed underground, generally with their fathers. He employed women extensively separating ores.[15] No less than half the mine girls resident in Menheniot in 1851 were aged 15 to 19, with a quarter under 15 and a quarter 20 to 29, only two were over thirty. Virtually all were single girls or younger married without children and occasionally young miners' widows. 52 mine boys and girls aged 14 or under were resident in the parish, with eight aged 10 or less, including at least one boy and girl aged seven. Child mortality in Menheniot as a whole remained an ever-present threat to young families and during a particularly bad six-week period between mid-July and the end of August 1858 of eight people buried in the churchyard all were children aged six or under.

The sheer scale of the population expansion within Menheniot might have superficially led one to presume that the parish soon became self-sufficient for mining labour. In fact a significant gap existed between the 800 mining jobs recorded as available in 1851 and just under 400 Menheniot men, women and children discovered in the census return for the same year and recorded as working in the mining industry. Parish boundaries had ceased to be a barrier to seeking work many years previously and small numbers would have been prepared to walk several miles from adjacent parishes. However the real answer to Menheniot's missing mine workforce lay in Liskeard itself. Despite no mines being open at this time within the parish of Liskeard, almost 400 working lead miners were resident in the town along with a further 93 copper miners. Evidence suggests the vast majority of these would have worked in Menheniot, indeed the bulk were resident in the relatively densely populated part of the town on the eastern or Menheniot side.

Writing about Liskeard in 1856, John Allen records that a great demand having been created for mining labour, initially by Caradon, that housing accommodation was insufficient and that small cottages and single rooms became frightfully overcrowded with 'fever and immorality' the consequence.[2] A response was made to increase available accommodation and this included high density courts, as they were known, running back behind Higher Lux Street, Barn Street as well as several other locations in the town. In 1851 there were also large concentrations of lodgers at designated boarding houses within the town and all the signs suggest that when men found work but not accommodation in Menheniot they fell back on Liskeard, which was where they had initially arrived in their quest for work. Unfortunately in doing so they met head on following groups of speculative miners homing in on Liskeard before the final search for employment in either Caradon or Menheniot. The bulk at this time would ultimately have found work, at higher rates of pay than in the west, but initially insufficient and unsatisfactory accommodation added to the problems of the new arrivals.

Lead miners resident in Liskeard in 1851 proved equally as well travelled as those setting up home in Menheniot itself. Over one third of the western arrivals hailed from St Hilary, Breage and St Agnes whilst a significant group had their roots in St Austell and Tywardreath. Two real strangers were James and Thomas Searle, 18 and 20 year old Welsh miners from Glamorgan, whilst another young married couple, miner and mine girl respectively, were from Cork, Ireland. Mobile western men were well in evidence, one born in St Agnes had a wife born in Cumberland, whilst their four children had been born in the Isle of Man, Kenwyn, Bovey Tracey, Devon, and Liskeard, the latter and youngest aged six months. Yet another Redruth miner had a two year old child born in Jersey, Channel Islands. The cycle which the lead miners went through, using Liskeard as a residential transit camp, repeated and indeed was well timed following a similar initial peak a few years earlier with the opening out of the Caradon area. By 1861, when Menheniot's mining industry had become more settled, the evidence that Liskeard was a residence of necessity rather than choice was indeed confirmed. Whilst a small increase in the Menheniot resident mining population took place, with a similar increase in available housing, Liskeard's lead mining population dropped dramatically from 384 to 181 between 1851 and 1861, its initial role during the period of rapid expansion completed. A walk through the lanes of Menheniot in 1861 would have revealed a parish that had reached its population peak a few years earlier and had settled into a sustained period of relative prosperity. Most of the small speculative mines had by now left the scene, but Wheal Mary Ann and Wheal Trelawny held respected positions with a steady production pattern and employing a large and well established workforce.

The western men were still present in numbers and whilst a few were still arriving, their age profile was rising and more were now supporting teenage families rather than the extremely young family profile evident in 1851. The dependence on this skilled group was however noticeably reducing. In 1851 western miners had formed the bulk of the skilled underground workforce with local Menheniot men recruited in a supporting labouring role both underground and at surface. However by 1861 amongst male miners aged 15 and over only some 20% were of western origin, 20% from central Cornwall (particularly from the St Austell area), the remainder being from east Cornwall, mostly farming parishes, with Menheniot men themselves dominating. These figures clearly demonstrate the emergence of a new first generation of locally developed skills. Further evidence of the integration of the mining industry into the local community can be found from the families which were now providing the continuing large numbers of mine boys and girls for the dressing floors. Where in 1851 these had largely been supplied from the immigrant mining families, who clearly regarded the industry as a family source of income to be maximised, by 1861 this group

whilst still dominating was being infiltrated by young family members of agricultural labourers with no mining tradition. No written evidence has been found of Menheniot's farms suffering labour shortages at this time, but it is difficult to imagine anything other than this having occurred, coupled with pressures on wages in the face of higher rates being offered at the parish mines. It is clear that large numbers were tempted in this period of consolidation to transfer their allegiance and this must have been more significant in an intensely farmed parish such as Menheniot than in wilder moorland parishes.

New groups of cottages appear in the 1861 census clearly indicating that building expansion continued well after 1851. We already know that Crift cottages was enlarged from 18 to 38 dwellings and between Pengover Farm and Merrymeet the strangely named Sebastopol emerged, clearly owing its allegiance to the 1854-56 Crimean War. One Sebastopol family was headed by a Redruth born miner, aged 42, with a wife and four teenage children born in the Tavistock area. Clearly a man who had made the classic trek from the far west to the Devon border and had latterly fallen back on what he considered were better prospects offered in Menheniot. The rising age profile, which brought with it larger families entering employable age, was clearly evident and illustrated well the numbers within a single family which could be dependant on a particular mine. At Merrymeet miner Thomas Eva from Mevagissey, aged 49, had seven children which included three mine girls aged 14, 16 and 17 and a 12 year old mine boy. At Trecondale William Williams, aged 38, was joined at the mine by five of his seven children, 15 and 22 year old miners and 14, 13 and 11 year old mine girls. This Cornish mining family clearly had an interesting story to tell for their elder children had been born in Bedwellty, Monmouthshire, whilst their youngest only three years earlier in Brecon.

Phillack born Paul Mitchell, aged 43, had recently arrived at Quarry with clearly itchy feet. His wife was from Marazion and had dutifully followed him with 14, 12 and 10 year old children born in Calstock on the Devon border. They then had moved west for a nine year old born in Ludgvan, west Cornwall, and a seven year old in Marazion, then back to Calstock for a four year old and finally a one year old child in Bodmin. A small but noticeable group of families in 1861 contained this Bodmin influence prior to arrival in Menheniot. Lastly and not for the first time the Channel Islands tantalisingly raised its head with a four year old Alderney born child in another mining family.

The decade from 1861 to 1871, before the final rundown of Menheniot's principal mines with the closure of Wheal Trelawny in 1871, Treweatha in 1872 and Wheal Mary Ann in 1874, is an extremely difficult one to judge from the perception of the working miner. Clearly at some point the community began to lose faith in the future of its mining industry and began initially in small numbers to be tempted by the prospects of other mining fields or indeed emigration to distant lands, particularly Australia. What is clear is that this was not, as might have been supposed, a response to wholesale mine closure but an emerging feature running well in advance of any substantial job reductions. Whilst the number of resident adult lead miners did drop by one third between 1861 and 1871 this would largely have occurred in the latter years of the decade and still left a large workforce up to the bitter death throes in the three years following 1871.

The 1860s saw the name Menheniot change from one which strangers came towards to find work, to a village with links and which was remembered with nostalgia by men who increasingly found themselves in different mining fields and different continents. By this time local Cornish newspapers were full of advertisements by shipping lines offering attractive passages to Australia and other prospective countries currently attracting Cornish emigrants. Agents were active from time to time recruiting for specific projects with financial incentives or assisted passages and most influential of all, letters and stories were published of fortunes being made and rich men returning, although no mention was ever made of the many more who only found hardship, deprivation, sickness and were either stranded or returned home penniless. The news would initially be made by men from other already depressed mining areas, but once a few were prompted by rumours of a limited future within Menheniot then others were tempted to strike out as their work associates had done and responded directly to stories circulating within the Menheniot community itself.

Thomas Foote was mine agent and then manager at Treweatha Mine between 1861 and 1871 and was one of many who looked to news from Australia with a father's concern. His son John Foote found work in the Moonta Mines, South Australia, where he married a Cornish girl from St Ives and later moved on to mine in Hill End, New South Wales, where he was to tragically witness the death of his brother-in-law in a rock fall underground.[16] In 1865 John Prout resigned as an engineman at Wheal Trelawny to also seek his fortune at Moonta, where he became an underground miner for the first time in his life. He never returned but was to recall Menheniot affectionately as an old man in 1923, still in his adopted Moonta.[3] James Stephens of Crift Cottages eagerly awaited news of his son John's progress. He had sought his fortune in Inglewood, Victoria, and later Broken Hill, New South Wales. He too was never to return and died in Broken Hill in 1909.[17]

It was to be America which beckoned John Quintrell and his young wife Elizabeth. They left Menheniot for Wisconsin, USA, where John met an early death in 1867.[18] These personal sagas were to be repeated many times over as Menheniot's children tramped the world in a way never known before and never seen since.

By 1871 despite the continued availability of large numbers of mining jobs the signs that the social fabric of the parish was beginning to fray at the edges was evident. For the first time families consisting of wives with young families, but husbands strangely absent, were increasingly evident and money as well as news from distant mining fields was of prime concern to this group. With many experiencing similar unsettled times companionship amongst fellow mining families was for not the first time a source of necessary strength. At Merrymeet Mary Liddicoat, aged 30, a miner's wife was living with her children aged eleven, eight, three and one at her parents' home, seeking the family fold in what was for her uncertain times. At Sebastopol a totally female dominated group living together was Elizabeth Goldsworthy, a miner's widow, with her daughter-in-law Emma Goldsworthy, aged 29, with two young children as well as her married daughter Mary Lukey and her young child. Both the latter were described as lead miner's wives, with their husbands working away.

By the spring of 1871 the three major mines were still in production, although increasing costs, a difficult metal market and deep workings made the future doubtful and long term security out of the question. Fortunately for the working miner at least two, Wheal Mary Ann and Treweatha, were committed to keeping the levels of ore extraction high as their only hope of breaking even against a background of crippling fixed costs. However tribute and tutwork bargains would have been tightly controlled to the advantage of the mine during this difficult period. It was often the younger, fitter and best miners who voluntarily looked to distant lands first and at a time when it might have been supposed the pick of the best miners would have been available to the agents the signs were already evident that the numbers of inexperienced 15 to 19 year olds and older miners amongst the total workers was proportionately beginning to rise. Appendix G sets out miners' age profiles in detail and distinct changes clearly took place between 1851 and 1871.

In 1851 half the adult lead miners (defined as aged 15 and over) were aged 20 to 29 years; clearly the newly arrived and dominant single and young married western men. By the peak census year of 1861 the age groups were flattening out as the industry and its residents entered a more settled and mature period. By 1871 there were actually more miners aged 15 to 19 than 20 to 29 and the latter group were now barely a quarter of the total, whilst at the same time miners over forty had risen by a third. Finally, also in 1871 only 29 out of 264 miners could claim to be western men, whilst no less than 73% were of east Cornwall origin and almost half of the total had actually been born in Menheniot. This quite amazing turn round can only partly be explained by the original western immigrants' Menheniot born children becoming of working age and limited statistics available for typical copper mining parishes, such as St Cleer, do not produce the same heavy

The Square, Menheniot c1900. A deliveryman, postman, shopgirls and sixteen village children pose in this early view. Beyond the Post Office and Stores lies The White Hart, whilst Mine Hill leads past the inn and on up to the larger mines.

S. Bartlett collection

swing to the local labour market at a comparable stage in their development. It remains open to speculation whether Menheniot's particular trend was related to the peculiar characteristics of the lead mining industry or the historic presence of a higher non-mining population to be tapped in this rich agricultural parish, a feature clearly missing in the wilder moorland parishes of Caradon.

1872 and 1873 were to be the years of mass emigration from Menheniot and in this it was but one of many surrounding parishes which channelled migrants through Liskeard with a common but very different purpose to that experienced thirty years earlier. Many were to join the already established exodus to Australia. Amongst immigrants on the *Countess Russell* which sailed from Gravesend in March 1873 was R. Tailor of Menheniot, who was clearly a fiery lay preacher and was recorded on several occasions as preaching to the assembled ship's company. During the four month passage thirteen deaths were experienced, nine of them babies under one year old, whilst a further ten, mostly adults, died whilst the ship was in two weeks quarantine after anchoring in Keppel Bay, Australia. Conditions were clearly difficult and the voyage testing, a journey repeated by many Menheniot families bound for the mining fields on the far side of the world.[19] Another Menheniot man who left for Australia in the spring of 1873 was Charles Simmons. He sought his fortune in Peak Downs, Queensland, until the coppermining collapse there in 1876-77 when he made his way to Moonta Mines and later was to spend several years on the Rand, South Africa.[20] Moonta figures time and time again in quite separately gathered stories. Yet again in 1910 a long retired Menheniot man asked in the columns of his local Moonta newspaper whether others shared his recollection of celebrations that had taken place at Wheal Trelawny and how the old Cornish miners heartily sang with one voice.[21]

Other forces were however seeking to exploit the Menheniot and Liskeard districts' misfortunes. In September 1872 it was reported that for several months agents had been recruiting for the Lancashire cotton mills, boasting of the advantages for large families with much work on offer for children as well as wives at good rates. Transport was often paid or loans made for this by the agents and regular contingents left by train from Liskeard station.[22] The steady recruitment and exodus was still evident a year

later when in September 1873 fifty men were reported having left on the Monday whilst on the Tuesday ninety had assembled on the station only to find the cheque for their fares had failed to arrive. They were billeted overnight in local accommodation and continued their journey next day.[23]

A more sinister feature was however entering the recruitment drive. William Waddington, for the Burnley coal owners, was in September 1873 seeking to recruit 1,000 Cornish miners to break colliery strikes in the area and based himself in the White Horse Inn, Liskeard, for that purpose. He was at great pains to gloss over the real significance of what the Cornishmen would find on their arrival, suggesting it was more a question of the policy of employing union or non-union labour rather than strike breaking - a subtlety which was probably as incomprehensible then as it might seem now. It was stated that cottages, furniture and initially food would be provided and that it was intended to construct a Burnley village of Cornish miners. William

The Square, Menheniot 1912. Little has changed since 1900, except advertisements and metal signs are now prominent on the Post Office Stores. Oakleigh House has replaced the earlier residence in the left foreground. *S. Bartlett collection*

Post Office, Menheniot.

Copyright

Waddington successfully recruited over 600 men during this period, driven on by tempting offers which overcame what fear that may have existed of hostility and resentment at their ultimate destination. The vast majority were family men who made permanent homes in far off Lancashire. Not least amongst the attractions was the availability of mill work, a potentially valuable source of family income for wives and children.[24]

Clearly problems began to build up in Liskeard for William Waddington and he was to complain of a meeting organised in the Temperance Hall, Liskeard, by Miners Union agents urging men not to respond to what was clearly a strike breaking call. He urged the local men not to pay any attention to the paid delegates of the Miners Union, which he alleged had been the ruination of Cornish mining in the last few years. It would appear that as well as Cornish union men, representatives of the Burnley miners had also made the journey to Liskeard to appeal to the better natures of the local men. William Waddington also complained of notices being posted in the area warning men not to go to Lancashire and that the local mine managers were associating themselves with the call.[24] He chided that the local managers were fearful of losing their best men and whilst the bulk of recruitment would have been from the unemployed mine workforce, it does indeed suggest that local managers would not have associated themselves with the opposition if they had not been concerned about losing experienced workers. This strengthens the suggestion that at times despite high unemployment it was not any longer possible to find miners of the highest calibre for the area's mines. Despite the difficulties encountered in recruitment, the movement to the coal mining fields of the north-west played an important part in the steady exodus from Menheniot in 1873. James Watts, mine smith, left Menheniot for Burnley at this time as did William Barrett, lead miner, who became a coal miner and whose family worked in the cotton mills.[25] During the same period a further migration pattern emerged to the coalfields of north-east England and Durham was to become yet another distant outpost where Menheniot was to be remembered with affection in the years to come.

Another refuge for Menheniot's transient miners was to be the far northern outpost of Barrow-in-Furness where John Mallett, Thomas May and John Scarle and their families were to be found in 1881. The men were amongst a tight knit group of Cornish miners working in the iron mines near the town.

With this great mining exodus of the early 1870s the lights went out on Menheniot's mining fortunes for ever, despite flickering attempts at resuscitation at various times over the following ten years. A visitor to the quiet Menheniot of today may find it difficult to imagine that a century ago families in far flung corners of the world and in particular South Australia shared distant memories of this lush farming parish in far off eastern Cornwall. A memory that was shared elsewhere in this country too by many

forced to leave the industry for pastures new and in particular the coalfields of Lancashire and north-east England. By the census of 1881 increasing numbers of cottages had lain empty for many years and at Crift Cottages, the previous centre of so much life and vitality, over half the cottages lay derelict. In the ten years since 1871 the population had fallen by 38% from 2,205 to 1,373 and of 467 houses within the parish in 1871, 94 lay uninhabited and a further 67 had disappeared completely by 1881, a fall of some 35% in the occupied housing stock.

It is perhaps a good time to reflect on the relative fortunes of the three very different men who opened Menheniot's saga and whose names appeared from time to time throughout the thirty year story that has unfolded - William Bawden, immigrant western tin miner from Breage, William Bartlett, local farm boy who adopted the lead mining industry in his teenage years and Peter Clymo Jnr whose ingenuity, business drive and practical mining expertise set its stamp on Liskeard and Menheniot in a way unequalled by any other individual. The semi-derelict Crift Cottages of 1871 was still home to Breage born William Bawden. Once at the forefront of mining migration he was now 54 and clearly reluctant and in a poor position to consider new horizons. His only dependent was his wife Ann and it was over twenty years since he had marched into the parish with the western miners vanguard. One hopes that he found relative prosperity to see out the last decades of his life, no doubt reflecting with mixed feelings on the fortunes that the parish of Menheniot had brought him. He had settled prosperity for the second half of his working life, but his teenage son buried in Menheniot churchyard was a victim of a tough and uncompromising industry.

William Bartlett, brought up in the fields and with two generations of farm labouring tradition behind him had chosen the lead mining way as a teenager from that very first exciting year of 1843 and now in 1871 was bewilderingly considering his future as the industry crumbled and was abandoning him and his family along with many others of their kind. He was then aged 40 with a comfortable cottage at Treviddo Well, his third home in the area and was a well established mine worker. His eldest son John, aged 14, was already a mine labourer whilst twelve year old Edwin and ten year old William were still at school. His family too had not escaped child mortality with little Harriet aged eighteen months buried in Menheniot churchyard, a victim of pneumonia in 1868. The family future however was to be very different to the more traditional parish solution of following the mining trade to distant lands and with determined conviction and some versatility they sought options in other trades and in other places, but at the price of an inevitably divided family.

Both John and Edwin joined the railway and were to spend a lifetime working at local stations in Devon and Cornwall before retiring as country station masters at Doublebois, near Liskeard, and Staverton, near Totnes, respectively. William Jnr at age ten in 1871 too young to be part of the mining exodus, just disappeared completely for over half a century until a hidden corner of a local Devon newspaper obituary, recording the death of brother Edwin in 1933 contained the simple words; 'floral tribute from brother Will and family Australia'. Clearly at some stage he had seen greater opportunity lay abroad. William Snr left Menheniot too, severing generations of family tradition, but having demonstrated his versatility when next found in 1881 with wife Mary Ann, at Gunnislake on the Cornish/Devon border and described as a wall mason. A large pewter plate, ornamental now but once simple cottage ware and dated early 1800s, has been passed down in each family will since that time to the present day, a poignant reminder of

the Menheniot connection and all that goes with it for the author and his family.

Peter Clymo Jnr was spared the anguish of Wheal Mary Ann's closure in 1874 dying on 28 July 1870, aged 69, in Liskeard at his magnificent Dean House residence which had been built for him in 1855.[2] This is now known as Graylands. He had been purser at Wheal Mary Ann since its opening in 1845 and manager since 1846, brother James holding the position for the first year. He had opened up Wheal Trelawny in 1843 and was purser and manager until 1847 when London interests forced his resignation. All this had been made possible by the fortune he had already made in South Caradon, one of the great rags to riches success stories in Cornish mining. With the early death of his brother James in 1849 and the emigration of his cousin James Budge Clymo to Australia in 1848, to manage the Molong Mining Company, New South Wales, he took firm control of the management of South Caradon for the remainder of his lifetime.[26] He was

The White Hart, Menheniot, scene of many early Mine Adventurers meetings. Little changed from its appearance in 1900.

S. Bartlett 1990

also purser in 1854 and purser and manager from 1855 to 1861 of Wheal Wrey Consols, barely across the Menheniot parish boundary in adjacent St Ive and associated himself with numerous speculative mining concerns in the Liskeard area throughout his life. Whilst centred on Liskeard his mining interests spread to other parts of Cornwall.

His investments and managerial control extended way beyond mining, being a director and principal shareholder in the Liskeard & Looe Union Canal Company, the Liskeard & Caradon Railway, Webbs Hotel, the Liskeard Gas Company and a senior partner, with his old friend William West, in the Liskeard District Bank. He was a Justice of the Peace and member of the corporation for over twenty years and Mayor on three separate occasions.[27] All this from a man who had declared to the Kinnaird Inquiry into the condition of mines in 1864 that he had known no trade other than mining when a boy and had worked underground until the age of twenty three.[15] It was his astute managership of delicately poised ventures which made his name, for metal mining was not as simple as digging a hole in the ground and the right balance between cost and steady regular ore extraction at the right price was the key to a successful long term venture. His talents were clearly not confined to this catalogue of business success for it is recorded that there was no better brewer of punch in all Cornwall and he followed the Cornish adventurers' tradition that sumptuous eating and drinking was the only way to launch a new development or celebrate a generous dividend.[27]

The community could not forget the special place he had held both in Liskeard and the surrounding district and on the morning of his funeral a cortege of 1,100 mourners wound their way down from Dean House to the church with over 1,000 townspeople lining the way. Menheniot and St Cleer were well represented with 600 Wheal Mary Ann and South Caradon miners marching four deep leading the formal group, followed by the mayor Matthew Loam, another mining stalwart, magistrates and the full corporation. The hearse was drawn by four horses, twelve bearers walking by its side made up of ships' captains associated with the mining trade and mine agents. Following the hearse were family, friends and most tradesman in the town; shops having shutters drawn and normal trade suspended on this sad day.[27]

Clearly he was a leading figure in the commercial development of Liskeard and a major character in Cornish mining and industrial history in the nineteenth century. His name however now lies largely forgotten except by a few who have cared to probe the dusty cobwebs of long forgotten mining and civil records. To mention his name in Menheniot now would produce little recognition, yet well over a hundred years ago it would have been a household word, revered as the manager upon whom a parish's livelihood depended. His memorial now lies forgotten in a corner of Liskeard churchyard; perhaps a few more may now remember the part he played in the Menheniot and Liskeard mining story so long ago.

CHAPTER NINE
MINING ACCIDENTS AND MINERS' HEALTH

With heart so light he left his home, upon that fatal morn.
We little thought of his sad fate; His friends are left to mourn.
HENRY STEPHENS, KILLED TREWEATHA 1856.
MEMORIAL INSCRIPTION, MENHENIOT CHURCHYARD

By THE EARLY 1860s growing concern was being expressed nationally at standards of health and safety in mining, particularly in comparison with other industries and in Cornwall notably with the other dominant employer agriculture. Whilst personal bitterness surfaced in Menheniot from those whose health had suffered or whose loved ones had met untimely early death or disability, no organised voice emerged amongst the miners themselves for better conditions. It was left to well-meaning professional men, notably local doctors, to identify the underlying causes and lobby for change. In fact it was the large scale mining disasters of the coal industry, with repeated multiple deaths following explosions underground and serious tunnel collapses, which produced scenes of groups of distraught families gathering at the pithead. These made headline news and probably represents the most vivid picture coming forward into the twentieth century when mining safety is mentioned. In truth mining disasters were extremely rare in Cornwall, to the extent that none ever occurred throughout the history of mining in the Liskeard area nor specifically at all in Menheniot. Combustible gases were not a problem, bare candles fixed to the front of miners' hats by a ball of clay being standard and perfectly safe illumination whilst, in general terms, metal miners were driving through more stable ground than their coal mining counterparts. Cornish mines, nevertheless, were far from safe, and premature death and injury were features of mining life in Menheniot which were all too real. The majority of accidents were singular in nature and usually related to unsafe working practices, either by the miners themselves or relating to the general attitude of the mine manager towards maintaining a safe place of work. Premature or accidental blasting, localised rock falls, accidents with tools or equipment, falls from ladders and unsecured or unlit open shafts represented a typical catalogue of the hazards to be faced by the men of Menheniot.

The simple ladders, which were the only means of descent and ascent from depths of up to 250 fathoms (or 1,500 feet) in all Menheniot's mines, presented a very real accident hazard. Only Wheal Mary Ann installed a mechanical man engine and that not until 1868, within six years of closure. No Menheniot shafts were suitable for or ever were converted to accommodate the later and more familiar cages which revolutionised the time and effort spent in descent. A visitor to a Cornish mine in 1849 described what was for him a frightening descent to the bowels of the earth, a scene which could equally have applied to any Menheniot mine at this time.

As we approach the shaft we perceive steam rising from it. This, we are informed, is the breath of the men at work below. The very mine itself seems to breathe... The ladder is very narrow, with iron bars and is well nigh perpendicular. The bars are moist and greasy from the men passing up and down, which makes us cling all the more firmly, considering the unknown depth of the shaft and the almost perpendicular position of our means of descent. We reach 400 feet underground, a sufficient depth to bury St Pauls... We return again to the surface. We take about half an hour to do it, resting at the different levels as we ascend. We arrive at the top utterly exhausted and thankful that we have emerged again into daylight.[1]

Generally accepted rates of ascent were 100 fathoms in 20 to 30 minutes, which at Wheal Mary Ann's ultimate depth would have involved a difficult and tiring daily climb of 50 to 75 minutes for each miner.

One of Menheniot's first mining fatalities involved a fall in just such circumstances. In December 1846 David Higman was ascending the shaft after work in the then comparatively young and shallow Wheal Trelawny. He was reported as climbing with two picks in his hand, when he lost his footing falling 17 fathoms to the bottom of the shaft where he was killed instantly.[2] Then just two days after Christmas 1849 Philip Knuckey, aged 23, left home in Menheniot as usual to work at Wheal Trehane. Little did his wife Harriett know that she would be made a widow that day, for Philip was to be killed following an accident at the mine. Harriett, just 23 years of age, was left widowed with an infant son and six months after Philip's death she also gave birth to a daughter. We shall never know if Philip was aware that he was to become a father for the second time before his death. Patient research has traced Harriett some fifteen months later in March 1851, reduced with her children to lodging in the village and working as a labourer at the local mine, almost certainly dressing ore.

In October 1850 a further tragedy occurred when a miner named Lawry was killed by a rock fall in one of the levels at Wheal Mary Ann whilst a companion working with him was seriously injured.[3] Only ten months later in August 1851 Wheal Mary Ann claimed yet another victim when Robert Julyon, aged 25, met an untimely death. Robert was working deep underground when he too was caught in a roof collapse. His companions managed to stumble along the dust choked level to safety, but for Robert it was too late and his lifeless body was recovered and brought to the surface.[4] He was buried alongside his cousin John Hoar, who had died in December

Gravestone of Henry Stevens (sic), Menheniot. Henry Stephens died as the result of a fall down a shaft at Treweatha Mine in September 1856. The gravestone is inscribed with a poignant memorial that opened the chapter.

S. Bartlett 1991

1850 at the equally early age of 20. John Hoar's family was one of the many who had arrived in Menheniot from the St Austell area. Today's visitors will find a poignant memorial in the churchyard to Henry Stephens, who was killed in September 1856 as a result of a fall down a shaft at Treweatha Mine. The text is reproduced at the beginning of this chapter. He was just 18 years old and still lived with his parents at Crift Cottages, close to the mine. Members of the Stephens family later emigrated to Australia.

In January 1857 John Rowe of Quethiock suffered a serious accident whilst working in the northern part of Wheal Trelawny. A large stone fell away on him, smashing two of his toes, which with a part of the foot required amputation shortly afterwards. As with all such accidents, the journey back to the surface would have been agonising and slow, as John Rowe's pain racked body was eased along the long, dark and wet levels and helped upward to the surface.[5] At Wheal Trelawny Mine just two years later in March 1859, William Rowe was in the act of firming layers of tamping in a hole at the 130 fathoms level when the powder prematurely exploded. He suffered dreadful injuries to his left leg, head, face and arms but was brought to the surface still alive. He was carried to his home at Crift Cottages and given such attention as was possible but died about midnight. He was 27 years of age and left a young wife.[6] A somewhat different incident occurred in December 1869 when Thomas Wills and Thomas Kennedy were charged with killing William Greet at Wheal Mary Ann Mine. It was alleged that the three men, accompanied by a girl, had been playing on the man engine when the deceased ultimately got his head caught under the balance bob and was killed. The incident, whether horse-play or deliberate, was keenly felt in the close-knit village community and was subsequently the subject of much gossip.[7]

The catalogue of accidental injury and death continued as Saturday 15 April 1871 dawned, like many before, with the expectation of a well earned break after the morning shift was completed at the two principal mines. Fate however was to take a turn and in one of those inexplicable coincidences both mines were to experience serious accidents, the one at Wheal Mary Ann fatal, on that same Saturday. A group of miners were ascending in a good mood after the days shift at Wheal Mary Ann, riding in one of the trams normally used to raise ore from the levels far below to the surface. This in itself, whilst a tempting alternative to arduous ladder climbing, was a dangerous practice with little protection against potential accident. As they stepped out of the tram George Rowe, a 24 year old miner, slipped and was precipitated to the bottom of the shaft over 1,000 feet below, suffering dreadful injuries. His shattered body was retrieved by his colleagues and carried to the home of his grieving family. His father was sexton of the parish church at Menheniot.[8]

Meanwhile less than a mile up the road at Wheal Trelawny yet another drama was unfolding. A young miner lay trapped deep underground in a localised rock fall, his colleagues eventually freeing him and tending to his injuries. He was brought to the surface suffering from broken ribs and serious stomach injuries and was carried home, as was the only option at that time, to be tended by his family, supplemented by visits from the local surgeon contracted to the mine. Despite the odds stacked against him, a week later he was showing signs of making an eventual full recovery. This was the fourth serious mining injury this unnamed individual had suffered; in the first broken toes, the second a broken arm, the third a broken leg and now broken ribs and stomach injuries.[9] Clearly a man who was either dogged by bad luck or was a serious liability to his colleagues.

Andrew Kington was a Liskeard surgeon and in April 1862 described himself as mine Surgeon to West Caradon, St Cleer and ten or twelve other mines in the neighbourhood. When asked what were the most common causes of accidents which he was requested to attend, he responded that there had been rather a large number of gunpowder accidents lately. He had attended three in three months, two of the men having lost both eyes, another one eye and all had suffered from burnt hands. He had experienced a few accidents from machinery and two where youths had been caught between the rollers that ground up the ore and they each had lost a leg.[10]

In truth, despite the ever-present threat of accident, the real killer in Menheniot's mines, as elsewhere, was the shocking toll on the general health of miners working underground, notably with respiratory related diseases. Known in Cornwall simply as 'Miners' Disease', or the tell-tale 'Miners' Cough', every miner knew the signs and knew the penalty he was paying mining copper, tin and lead from the bowels of the earth. By 1862 the medical profession, mine owners and miners alike were beginning to understand the causes, but until practical remedies could be found, which in an industry with an uncertain future were also economically acceptable, the problem was half-heartedly tackled and progress was slow. The greatest threat at Menheniot was unquestionably gunpowder and stone dust choked tunnels after blasting, along with, according to the characteristics of the mine, extremes of cold, damp working conditions or high temperatures in confined locations causing severe perspiration. A miner described how prior to his coming to Menheniot he worked at Fowey Consols in overheated conditions driving into solid rock 'for ten years I worked naked but for my shoes and cap'. Long climbs after a hard day's work up perpendicular ladders, for cages or man engines did not exist at any Menheniot mine at this time, could take up to an exhausting hour of the miners' own time, from depths of up to 1,500 feet. After this exertion extreme changes of temperature would be experienced, particularly in the winter, on reaching the surface. Miners were very conscious of parts of the mine with 'bad air', as they called it, and ventilation in many mines was a serious problem when working at the ends of long levels well away from natural shaft ventilation, dramatically more so considering the physically exhausting nature of the work. Crippled miners would always point to periods of work in recent years where they had been exposed to long periods of bad air as the real accelerating point of their disability and in this the medical profession was unquestionably on their side.

There is no suggestion that Menheniot's mines were any worse than average in this respect, but nevertheless sad stories have come down to us from a medical survey carried out in the parish during July and August 1862 which deserve recording for posterity. One prematurely aged miner, just 36 years old, recounted

> I was a farm labourer until I was thirty with never a day's illness. I first worked at West Caradon, St Cleer for three years working in bad air, candles would not burn upright and other men were laid up after working there. I was ill as a consequence. I then went to Wheal Mary Ann, Menheniot for three years. Not much bad air, but a great deal of powder smoke in the 110 level. I worked there until sixteen months ago, when I was taken so ill that I could not work and I have not worked since.

Whilst at Wheal Mary Ann he complained of shivering, weakness in his limbs, a cough and severe pain on his left side. He now suffered from shivering fits, perspiration and occasionally spat blood; a man who had never had a day's sickness until he was thirty.[9]

Another 28 year old man, who first went underground at the age of eight, was described as of pale, sallow complexion with dark rings around his eyes. He had seen the world and now he was dying in Menheniot. When he first came to the parish he worked at Wheal Mary Ann for twelve months in the 90 level. The air was slight and there was cold damp. He then worked at Wheal Trelawny for two or three years in the 107 level. the air was warm and not good and sometimes the candles would not burn. He was already described as white and pale and sometimes suffered from shortness of breath. He then went abroad and worked in the Cobra Mines, Cuba, for three and a half years before moving on to America and working in the Rockland Mine for fourteen months. Because of increasing weakness and pain in the shoulders, heavy heart beat and shortness of breath he decided to return to Menheniot and was at home for a year before being able to work underground again. He was now back at work at Wheal Trelawny in the 140 level, but the previous week had suffered from a cough again with slight spots of blood. It was clear his working days were numbered.[9]

It has become a popular misconception that mining was an inevitably short term young man's employment and that older men were not to be seen underground. Despite these sad cases of early disability there is ample evidence of men working underground in their fifties, after a lifetime of underground exertions. Although the average age of deep miners at Wheal Mary Ann was twenty-eight at this time, within that average the experienced tributer, with a lifetime of skill at finding and following the ever-tenuous lode, was a valuable asset to complement the tough, younger men. Sadly crippling disabilities inevitably took their toll on this age group too and it is clear the working lives of these older men were nearing their close as we hear their experiences from Menheniot's past.

One miner suffering from chronic bronchitis and emphysema, aged 63, had worked underground since he was twelve. He had worked for many years in Gwennap, west Cornwall, and then Ashburton, Devon, for six years before arriving at the Liskeard area to work at West Caradon for five or six years. He had come to Menheniot thirteen years previous in 1849, when he was aged 50, during the area's great mining expansion and worked in Wheal Mary Ann for eight years, including a period of six months in very bad air in the 90 level. He was taken ill as a direct result of that and had not worked for five years. Despite his enforced absence, it has to be noted that he had succeeded in working underground until the age of 58. However, he was now suffering from shortness of breath, pain in the left breast and a bad cough. He was described as thin but not emaciated.[9]

Another miner, still working in Wheal Mary Ann, aged 54, had spent many years moving around western Cornwall between Gwinear, Marazion and St Ives before coming to Menheniot. He worked in Wheal Trelawny for eight years, including three or four months in bad air in the 108 level, although he did not lose any work despite suffering as a result. He now

Coldrenick Viaduct, scene of Menheniot's worst industrial accident when twelve men were killed during reconstruction in 1897. Witnesses described bodies scattered in all directions on the grassy slope below.

S. Bartlett collection

worked at Wheal Mary Ann and was currently experiencing no bad air. However, he suffered from a bad cough and black frothy spit, as if powder smoke was mixed with it.[9]

Yet another miner, aged 50, first went underground at eleven years of age and worked for many years in Gwennap, before moving up to central Cornwall and Fowey Consols prior to arriving in Menheniot. This route from the west via an intermediate working period in the central mining area surrounding St Austell, Fowey and Par was a well-trodden alternate path shared by many Menheniot miners as opposed to direct migration from west Cornwall. He worked at Wheal Trelawny for some years, before being forced to give up work ten months earlier. His condition had gradually worsened during the eight months before he gave up work and he complained of a pain in the right side and shortness of breath. He had also spat blood.[9]

Whilst moving around the Liskeard area building up his case histories the inspecting doctor was clearly an astute observer, for his descriptions of two other miners' physical appearances leaps out of the pages as vivid as any picture could have painted. He passed one man in the village described as of dark complexion but very sallow, looking weak, thin and worn with an 'anxious countenance'. The man he described was 39 years old. A second man was described as very aged looking, grey and somewhat bald. He was pale, thin and walked with a stooping gait. His age was 52.[9]

With somewhat predictable evasiveness, as soon as the finger of accusation pointed at a particular mine, the manager would, perhaps understandably, claim that with the continuous mobility of the mining community he would not accept responsibility for a condition which may have had its origins in a distant and quite different workplace.

Mining was however not to be the cause of Menheniot's largest single industrial accident, for in a now long forgotten incident in January 1897 twelve men were killed during the re-construction of the railway viaduct at Coldrenick. They had been manipulating a girder into place when a supporting platform collapsed and the men were hurled to the valley floor below. First witnesses on the scene, gazing down from the viaduct above, described seeing the bodies scattered in all directions on the grassy slope below. Twenty five children were orphaned as a result of the disaster, all the men being casual labourers employed by the contractors.[10] Later the same year, in November 1897, reconstruction of the adjacent Treviddo viaduct claimed a further two lives, men aged 19 and 32, in another fatal accident. The viaducts, which still dominate the valleys to the south of Menheniot village, take the main Cornish railway line sweeping through the parish and on to Plymouth and London. Originally they were of a wooden trestle design on stone piers, a design repeated throughout Cornwall. This however proved unsatisfactory in the long term and during this period the viaducts were progressively being replaced, each representing a major reconstruction project. Coldrenick and Treviddo viaducts not only claimed a heavy toll during reconstruction, but were not without incident during their original building. In April 1857, at Coldrenick, a stone fell and hit a man at the base of a pier whilst masons were working high on the piers above. The man was struck on the head and severely injured, incurring a suspected fractured skull.[11] During both periods the contractors would have brought a nucleus of their own men with them, supplemented by available local labour. In Menheniot this provided a valuable alternative source of work for temporarily unemployed mining labourers, several being referred to in 1857 as 'Railroad Labourers'.

Despite the harrowing cases described earlier, miners disabilities have to be taken in the context of over eight hundred men working in the parish successfully mining several thousand tons of lead ore every year. This, coupled with ample evidence of men commonly working twenty-five years underground and in cases up to forty years, suggests a nucleus of a workforce that was at least sufficiently fit to produce an economic return from their labours. In western Cornwall 42% of miners were typically described as healthy, 23% as pale and worn and 35% as delicate and ill. The first two categories totalling 65% were considered, within the standards of the day, to be fit for work.[9] This statistic rings true as a fairly accurate assessment of a workforce that was adequately performing, but with insight an enlightened management could have dramatically increased productivity by giving proper attention to their working conditions.

The true figures of those who died in mining accidents deep beneath the soil of Menheniot are lost in the mists of time, but we do know that by 1871 Wheal Mary Ann, which had been open 26 years by that time with three to go before closure, had claimed a total of 29 lives.[8] There is no suggestion that Wheal Mary Ann was regarded as more dangerous than its counterparts at that time and it is estimated that overall between 60 to 80 miners lost their lives in accidents during Menheniot's principal thirty-year mining period between the 1840s and 1870s, almost all being of a singular nature. A sad record which must never be forgotten, but quite different in composition to the more popular conception of occasional but large scale mining disasters. Nevertheless in cold statistical terms between two and three times a year, throughout the period, violent death visited the close knit mining community and yet another family mourned the passing of a father, son or daughter in a mining fatality.

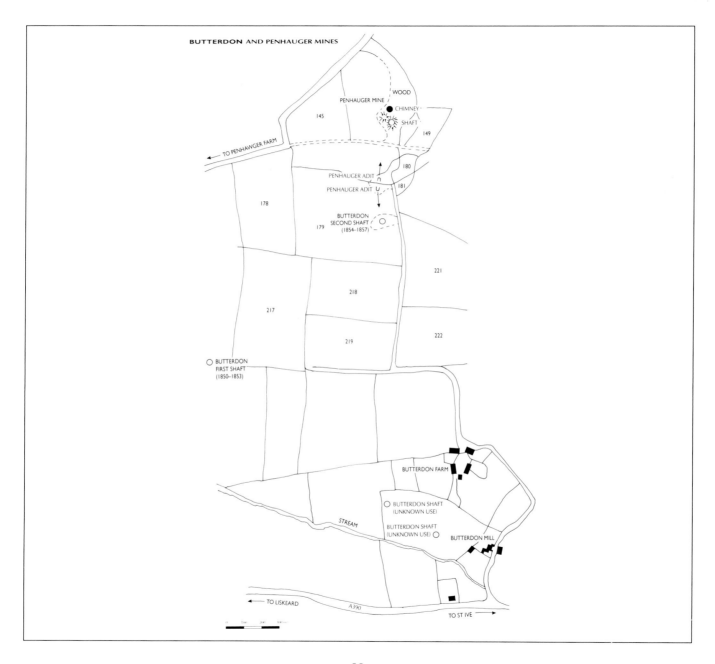

BUTTERDON AND PENHAUGER MINES

WOOD

PENHAUGER MINE

CHIMNEY
SHAFT

145

149

TO PENHAWGER FARM

180

PENHAUGER ADIT

181

PENHAUGER ADIT

178

BUTTERDON
SECOND SHAFT
(1854–1857)

179

221

218

217

219

222

BUTTERDON
FIRST SHAFT
(1850–1853)

BUTTERDON FARM

BUTTERDON SHAFT
(UNKNOWN USE)

BUTTERDON SHAFT
(UNKNOWN USE)

BUTTERDON MILL

STREAM

TO LISKEARD

A390

TO ST IVE

CHAPTER TEN
SMALLER MINING CONCERNS

*I pronounce this to be a first rate speculation
and well worthy of attention of capitalists.
(In reality a total failure)*
JAMES HOSKING 1854. EAST TRELAWNY

WHILST WHEAL MARY ANN, Wheal Trelawny, Treweatha and Wheal Trehane should rightly be remembered as the mines upon which Menheniot's fortunes were made, no story of the parish is complete without chronicling the small, long forgotten ventures which flanked these concerns during the principal mining period between 1843 and 1874. Few surface remains and no company records survive for any of the mines concerned. Their stories, and in some cases, even their existence is barely traceable in original records, but they too must take their rightful place in the chronicle of Menheniot's past. Later mining projects after 1875 are dealt with in the final chapter.

The history of the eight mines which follow tells without exception, if judged in purely financial terms, of abject failure without a single dividend being declared from any of them in any year of their existence. Some were clearly unwise speculations even to contemplate, whilst others in these early heady days showed enough promise from initial indications to conjure up hopes of major dividend paying mines of the future to the optimistic adventurers. Despite all the professional advice available, mining investment remained an unpredictable activity for all concerned and whilst sufficiently promising indications might be claimed, nature played many tricks on the unwary adventurer, with lodes unexpectedly improving or weakening in depth and length throughout initial explorations. These tricks were to be played here repeatedly, although many of the hardy investors showed exceptional strength and resolution keeping mines working, in many cases for years without profit in the hope of ultimate success. Even at their height none of the mines employed more than 20 or 30 persons and most of them only 10 to 20 miners. They provided supplementary work for the parish workforce, but when failure did occur the impact on Menheniot's economy was minimal when set against the workforce of over 800 at the nearby major concerns. Even so excitement and hope surrounded them all.

Without exception these smaller ventures sought to emulate the success of their larger neighbours, the latter lying immediately north of the village on rich parallel lead lodes coursing roughly on a north-south trajectory. Sweeping around the east side of these, along the Menheniot and St Ive/Quethiock parish boundary, were similar lodes which had been proved in Wheal Wrey, Wheal Ludcott and later North Trelawny on the St Ive/Quethiock side and this continuation was later also to be sought by Menheniot's speculative mines where the lodes crossed the parish boundary. From 1852 Treweatha Mine proved further separate lodes also coursing north-south and parallel to those heading towards Trelawny. In the northern part of the parish Wheal Venton, Butterdon and Penhauger sought the continuation of the Treweatha and Trelawny lodes north of those properties. To the south of the village, South Wheal Trelawny sought the Wheal Mary Ann and Wheal Trelawny lodes as they ran out of the southern limits of these setts. East Trelawny and Lambest Consols clung to the eastern side of the latter two mines, seeking parallel lodes. The western side of Wheal Mary Ann and Wheal Trelawny attracted the misnamed South Wheal Mary Ann, also hoping for parallel lodes on that side of the central area.

These then were the collection of small concerns clinging like limpets to all four sides of the rich central mining area of the parish, using names often containing the key words of 'Trelawny' or 'Mary Ann' to impress unwary distant investors, and desperately seeking a share of the riches which they knew existed tantalisingly just across the boundaries of the major established mines. With hindsight we know that their attempts to emulate the success of their larger neighbours was to end in failure, but at the time they had every reason to believe that the riches of Menheniot might spread further and with strength and enthusiasm embarked on their several projects.

SOUTH WHEAL TRELAWNY (1845-1854) was the only mine to be found within the village itself and was located immediately south of the church on the right hand side of the road leaving the village. A heavily overgrown raised piece of ground, immediately to the rear of a line of cottages, today marks the site of the former mine. Fields fall away behind these cottages and the parish burial ground to the valley floor below. It was from there that an adit was driven, both for drainage purposes and to explore the ground between there and the site of the mine, where a shaft was sunk. South Wheal Trelawny was to prove an expensive disaster, attracting harsh words from informed opinion during its short lifetime but somehow

The site of South Wheal Trelawny Mine 1845–1854. Located south of the church behind Minefield Cottages.

S. Bartlett 1991

sustaining the support of its loyal adventurers for longer than perhaps in hindsight was wise.

It was a very early speculation, commenced in the same year as the promising Wheal Mary Ann, with Trelawny started only two years before, whilst Wheal Trehane had yet to follow. The euphoria surrounding every speculation in the parish during this early period partly explains the over-estimation of South Wheal Trelawny's potential when almost immediately a lode was discovered within six feet of the surface. This coupled with the mine's important position immediately south of Wheal Mary Ann and Wheal Trelawny on the probable run of the lodes sealed for the unwary adventurers the potential strength of their investment.[1] The payment of a £2,000 premium to George Roby, the landlord, was an excess frowned upon from the start by shrewder outside opinion and did not endear this mine in certain professional quarters.[2] It was clearly thought this would become another successful and profitable concern although we now know that the rich lead lodes upon which Wheal Trelawny and Wheal Mary Ann were astride rapidly weakened as they passed southwards and no mineralised lode of any strength was ever to be found south of the village.

South Trelawny was held on a lease for 21 years at 1-15th dues and divided into 256 shares. The first year's working concentrated upon driving a lengthy adit from the adjacent valley to the west, across the property, towards the point where the engine shaft would be ultimately sunk. The steady progress was designed to prove the undertaking and from this adit, when Sobey's lode was identified, various drives were made and a winze sunk below the adit to establish if the lode improved with depth.[3] Meanwhile shallow work was done at the site where the shaft would be ultimately sunk.

An adventurers' meeting in November 1846, chaired by principal shareholder Charles Chippindale of Regents Park, London, heard that on their behalf the agents had decided upon the spot where the engine shaft would be sunk, to be known as Snell's shaft. William Lean had previously been appointed as manager and at this meeting William Jenkin was appointed resident agent. William Lean also took on the purser's duties temporarily whilst N. W. Tredinnick was contracted to supervise the erection of a 24-inch second hand pumping engine, which had been purchased from Hanson Mine, Breage, for £535.[4]

William Lean, addressing that November 1846 meeting, reported that the adit had taken on a new importance now that a shaft was to be sunk and it was to be driven with all speed to meet the shaft at depth in order to drain and ventilate the workings better. Snell's shaft was at that point a mere three fathoms deep but being sunk to a point where a communication with the adit could be made. Air was bad in the adit, now remote from the valley opening and only four men could be used for driving until communication with the shaft was made. A decision was also taken to sink a small ventilation shaft from surface to the adit to assist with the problems experienced. This was to be the second and only other shaft on the property. November 1846 had seen much rainfall and surface water was flooding the shaft as well as issuing from its walls, which was impeding progress and adding importance to achieving drainage by the adit which was concurrently being driven ever closer.[4]

Early 1847 saw work in the adit on Sobey's lode continuing, but the adventurers' attention turned to progress on the sinking of Snell's Shaft, which was the key to opening up the mine in depth. In June 1847 nine men were sinking the shaft at the rate of three fathoms per month and this work was to continue without intermission until 30 fathoms below adit was reached, where it was proposed to crosscut west to intersect the lode at depth. The shaft reached the level of the adit as planned and six men were then set to drive a crosscut west from the shaft with a view to communicating with the adit men coming towards them, in about two or three weeks time. When this communication was made a decision was taken to stop all exploratory work in the adit level, clearly an economy measure in the face of poor results and to concentrate on sinking the shaft with the intention of setting on more men again to probe the lode as levels were reached during the shaft's progression downwards.[5] It must already have been clear that the shallow lode cut at surface had not brought early riches and a long hard slog lay ahead for the adventurers at not inconsiderable expense.

By June 1847 the engine was complete and ready for use, but ironically after initially sinking to adit level in desperately wet, unpleasant and restrictive conditions the onset of drier summer weather rendered it initially unnecessary to start the engine.[6] January 1848 saw it coping well with the water, whilst the shaft had reached 21 fathoms below adit.[7] March produced a prediction that the intended depth of 30 fathoms below adit, along with a crosscut to cut the lode from there, would be completed by mid-June 1848. By the promised date the 30 fathom level below adit had been reached, but the crosscut had not been completed and William Lean, in apologising for this, pointed out this was due to the attention he had given to correctly and properly securing and dividing the shaft to ensure safe operation.[8] By September 1848 the promised 30 fathom crosscut west was being driven by eight men who had progressed 15 fathoms, but no claims of any finds were made.[9]

It had taken from November 1846 until September 1848 to sink Snell's Shaft to this point and reach what was still an inconclusive position in the crosscut. During that time no ore sales had been made. It was clearly time for a serious review of the mine's progress and the adventurers called for an independent inspection and joint report by John Bryant, manager of Wheal Trelawny and Robert Dunstan, manager of West Caradon, accompanied a little uneasily one suspects by William Lean, South Wheal Trelawny's manager, who clearly felt he had been diligent if not successful. In reviewing the property they described the adit as being 112 fathoms long driven horizontally from the valley outlet to intersect Snell's Shaft which had been sunk 30 fathoms below adit. They felt the adit had been driven towards a kindly lode intersected 19 fathoms west of the shaft with no doubt from its bearing that it was an extension of that discovered in Trelawny and Mary Ann. A crosscut had been driven west 19 fathoms from the bottom of Snell's Shaft to test that same lode 30 fathoms deeper. From that point the lode had been driven five fathoms north and four fathoms south. The lode in the north was currently small and the south disordered and split into branches, with killas between containing spots of lead. Having considered carefully they recommended that future prospects lay in sinking the engine shaft with all speed to the 50 fathom level below adit, from where a crosscut should be driven westwards, as at the 30 fathom level, to test the lode at the greater depth. In the meantime, recognising that this would take some time, the 30 fathom exploration north and south on the lode should continue to be driven by two men in each end to fully prove the lode.[10]

The independent assessment strictly confined itself to factually assessing the extent of the workings and to suggest the most likely way forward to seek elusive success. It did not offer any true financial assessment of the possible outcome of further explorations, neither did it seek to criticise the work which had already been done. All was obviously down to the adventurers to make their own decision and with brave resolution they elected to press on. Outside this tightly knit group the reputation of the mine was not high. John Watson commented drearily in the Mining Journal in January 1849 that unless operations improved he presumed the mine would soon be suspended. He considered little had been done and that which had at no profitable result. He had never held a high opinion of the undertaking and had earlier commented that the shares, like the shaft, were going downwards.[2] James Clymo, with his intimate knowledge of the Menheniot district, had similarly been critical of the mine's obsession with opening up the lodes west of the shaft and in an open letter to the Mining Journal in February 1849 stated,

In my opinion they may continue driving this level even as far as the town of Liskeard and never cut the lode in question and I am astonished at any one recommending such an insane proceeding.

The February 1849 shareholders' meeting confirmed that John Bryant, Robert Dunstan and William Lean's report would form the basis of the way forward for the mine, but the same meeting had to cope with a claim from mineral lord George Roby for £325.8s. for damage to land; a settlement of £128 being proposed. Clearly George Roby was disappointed he was not reaping the dues for ore sold that he had anticipated, but in truth he had risked nothing and had already benefited from the frowned-upon £2,000 premium. The same meeting ominously instructed the purser to take legal proceedings against all shareholders in arrears of the call to which a further call of 10s. per share was added at this meeting.[11]

Aerial view of Menheniot c1950. The church and square are prominent in the centre. Mine Hill leads to Wheal Mary Ann and Wheal Trelawny, centre top. The site of South Wheal Trelawny is clearly shown as the circular area of rough, tree covered ground to the south of the church, centre bottom of the picture. *S. Bartlett collection*

Despite these problems practical work continued and William Lean, through his resident agent William Jenkin, commenced deepening the shaft and driving the 30 fathoms crosscut. This continued steadily through 1849 and 1850. William Jenkin was Illogan born but by 1851 had still not brought his family east with him, lodging in Menheniot village with Richard Pugh, a mason, close to the mine. On South Wheal Trelawny's ultimate closure he was retained by Wheal Trelawny where he was one of the several agents at this large concern from 1854 to 1861, being used in 1854 to also oversee their secondary operations at Butterdon and Penhauger. By 1861 he had brought his family to live in Barn Street, Liskeard. There was a clear Wheal Trelawny influence in both agents employed and adventurers in South Wheal Trelawny, suggesting that although an independent concern, Wheal Trelawny was behind the speculation.

South Wheal Trelawny's shaft ultimately reached 50 fathoms below adit by January 1850 and was indeed pushed on to the 60 fathom level from which it was already crosscutting west by July 1850. In January 1850 a serious accident was only just averted when two joints failed and the engine's boiler could easily have burst with frightening consequences. Fortunately repairs were not expensive.[12] Work continued relentlessly until February 1852 when the adventurers' meeting again ominously instructed the purser to take legal steps against adventurers in arrears of calls, whilst Captain Dunstan had made a further report recommending that no more money be spent on the shallower levels, apart from one particular drive, due to the poor quality of the lode throughout the mine. However the very favourable change in the ground in the 60 fathom level led him to recommend sinking the shaft a further 20 fathoms.[13]

This rallying call for still further expenditure proved too much for the ailing adventurers and the next meeting in May 1852 recommended to suspend the sinking of the shaft, to take action against all shareholders in arrears of call and to make a £1 call per share to make good the losses of the company.[14] In August 1852 the mine was advertised for sale by private contract, complete with steam engine and materials.[15]

A short lived attempt was made to rework the mine between 1853 and 1854 and a meeting in October 1853 divided the new company into 240 shares, making a call of 7s.6d. per share.[16] No mention was made of the need to purchase a steam engine or equipment, suggesting the bulk was still lying idle on the site. A progress report, detailing crosscutting east and west of the shaft, was made in December 1853 by Joseph Kemp, manager of Wheal Trelawny, suggesting the latter company was again connected with the re-working. After this nothing more was heard and the short lived project was abandoned in 1854. In 1868 after the mine had been derelict for many years the South Trelawney Silver Lead Mining Company Ltd. was floated with an authorised capital of £6,000 in 300 shares of £20 each. Two-thirds of the shares were reported to have been taken up by seven subscribers, but nothing more was heard of the prospective venture and no work done.

WHEAL VENTON (1850-1858) was a well organised venture pursued with some vigour and purpose by investors who understood and were prepared, at least initially, to sink adequate financial resources in the undertaking knowing it might be several years before a return could be expected. Here was not to be the luxury of an instant shallow strike, but a well planned programme of exploration at depth was pursued with some optimism, in the genuine belief that a profitable outcome would ensue. In reality this was never to be and after an eight year struggle the mine was abandoned having never paid a single dividend. The mine was situated in the north of the parish on the Liskeard to St Ive and Callington turnpike (now the A390) at a point two and a half miles from Liskeard, adjacent to the roadside.[17]

The first meeting of adventurers was held at Lombard Street, London in May 1850, when an initial call of £1 per share was made, the company having been divided into 512 shares. The committee was entrusted by the adventurers with the task of identifying and acquiring a steam engine to work the mine.[18] Redruth born James Osborn took charge of the practical operations and by July 1850 he was able to report that the shaft had been sunk 10 fathoms in promising ground, the carpenter's shop finished and the smithy almost so. Construction of the engine house was progressing rapidly and several sections of the engine were on hand at the mine, awaiting assembly, as well as a capstan, whim and other equipment. James Osborn was clearly enthusiastic about what had quickly been achieved and invited two of the principal London investors, Charles Chippindale and W. Mount, who were expected to visit Menheniot for the Wheal Mary Ann and Wheal Trelawny meetings the following month, to visit Wheal Venton themselves to check progress.[19]

By the end of September the engine house was complete, the boiler house and stack progressing well and a whim, presumably horse powered, had been in use raising waste from the shaft bottom since the previous month. The engine shaft's depth had doubled to 21 fathoms, but a slight setback had been encountered with the secondhand engine, which had needed extensive repairs which were now well advanced.[21] Two months later James Osborn reported that the steam engine was complete and working well, although the shaft's progress at 25 fathoms was less advanced than had been hoped due to a five week delay caused by a great increase in water in the workings. This had proved a major stumbling block until the steam engine had been brought into use, which now more than adequately coped with the problem.[22] It was never the less a timely reminder of the need for expensive pumping arrangements, particularly so in the wet winter months, on even the most speculative of concerns below a token depth.

Meanwhile at the November adventurers' meeting progress was

acknowledged as satisfactory, a decision taken to subdivide the 512 shares into 1,024 and the third call of £1 per share made. Clearly stout hearts were called for, with long term returns the investors only realistic objective.[21] Nevertheless the London share market was happy with progress and by the end of December 1850 the price of Wheal Venton shares had risen from £1.10s. to £20 per share, a lofty position not to be maintained for long.[22]

1851 was to prove a steady but unspectacular year, with operations divided between the core task of deepening the main shaft and the equally essential work of driving exploratory levels at selected depths and indeed crosscuts from those levels, testing and probing according to the manager's judgement and the expertise of the working miner. This was slow demanding work through tough unrelenting ground at a pace which could only be understood by those who had witnessed the inch by inch progress, driving into solid uncompromising rock relieved only occasionally by patches of softer ground. At the end of the year the shaft depth had doubled to 49 fathoms and the various levels and crosscuts, whilst not producing a major breakthrough, exhibited promising signs at many points. Ore was being raised and dressed, but in small quantities and of moderate quality, no more than helping to offset exploration costs.[23]

As operations progressed into 1852 a certain tenseness could be detected in reports whilst signs were also evident of adventurers' impatience. February and March saw James Osborn concentrating on levels and crosscuts from the main shaft at 40 and 49 fathom depth with tolerable results, but nothing to suggest a major change in fortunes. It was clear a further year at the moderate level of success experienced in 1851 was not considered acceptable by the adventurers.[24] The May 1852 meeting instructed James Osborn to stop all operations in the 40 and 49 fathom levels and to concentrate all his energies in sinking the main shaft.[14] Clearly this was a determined effort to force elusive success from a mine producing tantalisingly good signs without actually delivering the success required. A target was set to reach a depth of 60 fathoms, within three months, where it was felt spirited exploration would uncover the valuable lode for so long sought.[25] By the end of 1852 the lode had indeed been cut at 60 fathoms but a level driven a bare three fathoms (or 18 feet) at that stage. The lode was cautiously described as better than that discovered at shallower levels, but was currently under water and there clearly were problems in maintaining drainage at this depth, certainly during a typically wet winter.

Despite the apparent importance attached to the 60 fathom level attention immediately and without explanation turned back to the shallower 30 fathom level and a crosscut was concentrated upon to intersect a lode thought to exist east of the shaft.[26] The likely explanation for this about turn was either temporary admission of defeat surrounding the drainage problem or, more likely, in response to known changing fortunes at the adjacent and recently commenced Treweatha Mine. Here a shallow but rich strike within months of commencement had attracted much attention and as Wheal Venton desperately sought a lead lode of reasonable quality it could now not only pin its hopes on a continuation of the Wheal Trelawny lode, proved so rich under that mine but of doubtful strength up to this date here, but also a fresh objective in seeking out the new Treweatha lode towards the eastern side of their property. The north-south course of the lead lodes through the district was now well understood, hence the excitement in the smaller mines to the north of their larger neighbours. The weakening of those lodes as soon as they left the centre of the parish however was yet to be fully appreciated and to be the ultimate downfall of these northern Menheniot speculations. Wheal Venton's trusty adventurers were not to know this at that time and we rejoin their spirited efforts as optimistic signs spurred them on to greater efforts.

Throughout the summer of 1853 claims were made that the engine was working well. However this disguised what had been clear from earlier reports that very little had been done at depth through the winter months until May due to the level of water in the workings[27]. Summer's respite enabled good progress to be made and by July 1853 James Osborn was reporting that the lode in the 60 fathom level continued to improve and was the best seen in the mine in the past two years.[28]

James Osborn was however not to see the outcome of this exploration, for he was taken ill and died, at the early age of 41, in October 1853 at his home in Castle Street, Liskeard, where he had lived with his wife Elizabeth and three young children. Typhus Fever was the cause of his early death. The services of William George Jnr as a replacement were quickly secured. He was barely 25 years of age but clearly a promising mine agent who had been born in St Mewan, near St Austell, in the central Cornish mining area which provided so much expertise for the mines of Liskeard and Menheniot. The remainder of 1853, 1854 and the bulk of 1855 could best be described as a steady, unspectacular period when little of note was heard of the mine, but it continued to be developed within the limitations of moderate investment and the similar limitations of an engine clearly working to its limits for the depth and extent of operations in hand. Towards the end of this period in December 1855 it was reported that little had been heard of the mine during the year, but that it now boasted a 30 fathom crosscut east which stretched the whole length of the sett. A commitment also existed to see the lode further at the troublesome but promising 60 fathom level, for which a new 50-inch steam engine, twice the size of the existing one, was now being assembled along with necessary buildings.[29]

The mine was stopped again in the winter of 1855/56 with drainage problems as the original engine struggled on, but in July 1856 the new 50-inch engine, manufactured by Nicholls, Williams and Co. of the Bedford Ironworks, Tavistock, was launched in spectacular fashion. Some parts may well have been manufactured locally, as the firm were also proprietors of the Roseland Iron Foundry, Menheniot. A large party of mine agents, gentlemen and landowners from the Liskeard area, assembled at the mine on the designated day and a substantial dinner was provided. Success to the mine, amongst many other toasts, were drunk by the assembled company. Celebrations broke up late that evening, with unanimous agreement from the by now florid faced guests that this spirited concern deserved to meet with success at a level which would repay the latest significant financial outlay.[30] Not long after this in December 1856 William George Jnr resigned his position and was replaced by Thomas Richards, manager of the adjacent Treweatha Mine, an experienced and respected individual. He was clearly a remote manager at Treweatha, resident agent William Rowe always presenting the detailed weekly reports, and Wheal Venton was now added to his list of managed concerns. He was clearly following the adventurers' wishes in maximising the benefits of the new pumping engine by continuing with driving at the 60 fathom level. By December 1856 he was able to report favourable indications in a crosscut west from that level, which had met the western lode, but that the favoured crosscut east designed to find the rich Treweatha lode was in hard ground, which he was convinced would become easier as it approached what he believed would prove to be the much sought after productive ground.[31] Throughout 1857 reports continued to be made of the 60 fathom crosscut steadily extending eastwards, with planned estimates now suggesting it would take until the autumn of that year to cut the Treweatha lode.

The last active report concerning the mine was made in January 1858, when Thomas Richards reported no doubt whatever that the branches of ore so far discovered would lead to something very good.[32] At some point in 1858 the adventurers finally abandoned all hope of achieving success and an auction of machinery and materials was held on the mine in December. The assets of the mine for disposal included the new 50-inch pumping engine, one 10 ton boiler, the original 25-inch pumping engine with whim cage, pumps, capstan and rope, a horse whim, shaft ladders, iron bucket rods, whim chain and ropes, two boring machines, smith's bellows, anvil, vice and tools, miners tools and chests, launders, two large sheds, wheel barrows and the account house furniture.[17] Today little remains to mark the efforts of a brave but unsuccessful company, two small areas of disturbed waste ground adjacent to the roadside marking the possible site.

BUTTERDON (1850-1857) was the second of the three principal northern trials, along with Wheal Venton and Penhauger, which were pursued concurrently and sought similar extensions of the main lead lodes as they ran northwards out of the parish. Unlike Wheal Venton, which was worked from a single shaft, the Butterdon adventurers carried out several trials in different parts of their sett. Two principal shafts were sunk. The first was worked between 1850 and 1853 and located 500 yards south-east of Penhawger Farm and 600 yards north-west of Butterdon Farm.[33] A prominently raised tree topped mound in the centre of a field in the position described still marks the site. An adit was then brought up from the River Tiddy into the centre of the sett, from a point below Butterdon Mill.[34] Two mysterious small shaft dumps exist 100 yards apart in a field immediately south of Butterdon Farm, commonly referred to as the site of Butterdon Mine, but in fact do not fit any of the extensive mine reports uncovered. They may mark shallow explorations which were never pursued in depth, ventilation shafts connected with work on the previously described adit or a crosscut from that adit to probe new ground. Work then moved 500 yards to the north-east and between 1854 and 1857 a second shaft was sunk on a parallel lode close to Butterdon's northern boundary with Penhauger. Adits were initially started from the valley floor between each mine into opposite hillsides; Butterdon's southwards and Penhauger's northwards. Butterdon's second shaft was then sunk on to the adit driven south, the site traceable as stony ground on the falling hillside.

The mine was leased in 1850 from R. S. Jago at 1-14th dues and divided into 812 shares. The purser throughout its life was John Philp of Wheal Trelawny, whilst progress reports were always made by Wheal Trelawny mine agents, supervising work at Butterdon in a part-time capacity. Joseph Kemp, Thomas Grenfell, William Bryant, William Jenkin and John Prince were all associated in this way and it was clear that although a separate cost book company, Butterdon was under the practical wing of the larger Wheal Trelawny.

July 1850 saw the engine shaft sunk seven fathoms from surface but not expected to be sunk much deeper, due to the influx of water, until the 22-inch pumping engine was operational. The engine had been ordered and stone was being acquired to build the engine house. Operations were at a very early stage, but an enthusiastic start had been made.[35] It was intended to sink to a depth of 40 fathoms, where the lode would be met and then to drive an exploratory level at that depth as well as a crosscut at the 30 above to meet it at a shallower level. By November 1850 the shaft had been sunk 19 fathoms and a call of 30s. per share was made to sustain operations.[36] By the end of December it was 26 fathoms deep and estimates made that the 30 fathom level would be reached within three weeks, when a crosscut would be started towards the lode.

A call of £1 per share was made in February 1851 and by April the lode at the 30 fathom level had been cut.[37] Sinking the main shaft below the 30 had however been temporarily suspended while the level at that depth was explored further. Sinking was resumed in May and significant progress made during the summer and autumn with the planned 40 fathoms depth passed and 50 fathoms reached by December 1851, where another exploratory

Butterdon Mine. The site of the mine's first shaft worked between 1850–1853, 600 yards north west of Butterdon Farm.

S. Bartlett 1991

crosscut was to be made. A further 15s. call was made at that time.[38] The wet winter of that year exposed the limitations of the engine when, despite being worked to its limits, the water began to rise in the bottom of the mine, first flooding the 50 then the 40 and almost reaching the 30 fathom level. Eventually the engine was stopped and it was only in mid-March that an attempt was made to recover the position.[24] It took almost a month to drain the mine below the 40 and mid-April to reach the deepest 50 fathom level.[39] During this time Wheal Venton had been suffering greatly and was much relieved when Butterdon rejoined the fray, assisting with the pumping in the immediate area. Four months had been lost and it was late April before the planned crosscut could be commenced at the 50.

During the summer of 1852 work progressed with the lode being extended steadily in both the 40 and 50 fathom levels.[40] Despite the appearance of progress, no rich lead deposits had been found and this must have been causing the adventurers some concern by this time, as calls continued to be made on their shares. At the September 1852 meeting a further call of 7s.6d. per share was made. John Philp registered concern that no less than £185 was in arrears of call and he was instructed to put the matter in the hands of Mr Stokes, their Solicitor, to pursue recovery of the various amounts.[41] Meanwhile practical work continued. In August it was stated with some optimism that in the 50 they were close to finding the slide in the south, clearly hoping for better things on the far side.[42] However when in September the lode was found beyond the slide it was to be no better and the decision was taken to suspend further work at that level. Operations on the lode were then confined to the 40 fathom level south, which was thought to be promising and less of a burden on the pumping engine. It was

also decided to restart the previously abandoned crosscut west in the shallower 30 fathom level.[43] John Watson, in his annual review of mining for 1852, simply stated Butterdon had so far disappointed expectations.[44] He chose few words to sum up what most adventurers must have felt keenly. Clearly operations were being strictly contained and some time in 1853 all working in the shaft was abandoned.

The mine then entered a secretive period, often a sure sign of poor progress and limited operations. Very few reports were published between early 1853 and summer 1854 and those that were said little of a detailed nature and were often joint with those of Penhauger Mine. Both were confined to work on new adits over the hill to the north-east which were driven into opposite hillsides on the course of the lode to prove the ground. About 70 fathoms had been laid open by December 1853, from an unknown start date.[45] Impetus increased in June 1854 when a decision was taken to sink a completely new shaft on to the adit in the position previously described high on the hill. By that date the walls of the new engine house were complete and the engineer was about to commence erection of the engine which was expected to be in operation within four or five weeks. The shaft was progressing well, with casing, dividing and footway ladders complete to the depth reached.[46] Sinking continued enthusiastically with a depth of 20 fathoms being attained by August, 27 fathoms by September and the 30 fathom level had been reached by October, and levels had started to be driven north and south on the course of the lode.[47] Four men contracted to drive the level north, whilst others extended what was considered to be a promising level south. About two tons of ore, which would have only contributed to offsetting costs, were ready for market.[48] A call of 15s. per

Butterdon Mine. Operations later moved over the hill, this second shaft located 500 yards north east of the former was worked between 1854–1857.

S. Bartlett 1991

share was made in October 1854.[49] At this time 20 miners were employed at Butterdon, which was as large a workforce as existed at any point in its life.

By November 1854 sinking had been resumed below the 30 fathom level, but progress was slow and by June 1855 a depth of only 42 fathoms had been reached.[50] The intervening winter may have contributed to this disappointing progress. In August Thomas Grenfell reported that the engine, having worked ceaselessly for the past fifteen months, had been temporarily stopped to lift the cylinder cover and cleanse the boiler.[51] In December 1855 he sadly reflected that although he had sufficient ore in small quantities for dressing, he had no machinery on the mine to reduce it to dressable size. In an interesting insight into the relative economics of a small mine, he stated that reducing it by hand with bucking hammers was hopelessly uneconomic, particularly in that area, where the average price was four small barrows for 1s. The latter an interesting reflection on the relatively higher wage rates paid in east Cornwall.[52]

During early 1856 work on extending the 43 fathom level north and south continued with guardedly optimistic reports continuing to be made by Thomas Grenfell. However the April 1856 meeting, held at Wheal Trelawny account house, was seeking something more dramatic and took the decision to discontinue the well exposed drivings north and south and concentrate all their resources on sinking the shaft.[53] By the end of July 1856 a depth of 50 fathoms had been reached where the lode southwards was found to be divided into eastern and western branches.[30] Exploration continued and the shaft bottom stabilised at 53 fathoms by February 1857.[54] The final routine report was made by Thomas Grenfell in March 1857 and this was followed by an adventurers' meeting in April. It was clearly felt that further expenditure could not be justified as increasing numbers of shares were in arrears of call and the inevitable decision to suspend all workings was taken. However the adventurers were not quite released from their former burden, for a final call of 8s. per share was made to cover existing liabilities.[55] An advertisement was placed in the *Mining Journal* in August 1857 with a view to selling the mine and its materials as a going concern. It was clearly hoped to attract another party to work it, great emphasis being placed on the fact that an engine was available on site. In fact our next mine, Penhauger, had been worked and abandoned by the Trelawny adventurers at the same time and was similarly advertised for disposal. Penhauger after several years dereliction was reworked by a new party, but for Butterdon it was to be the end of the road and another small mine slipped into the pages of history, having failed to deliver its early expectations despite seven long years of patient exploration.

PENHAUGER (1850-1861) was very much the smaller sister of Butterdon and during its first period of working, between 1850 and 1857, also came under the wing of the Wheal Trelawny adventurers. Whilst

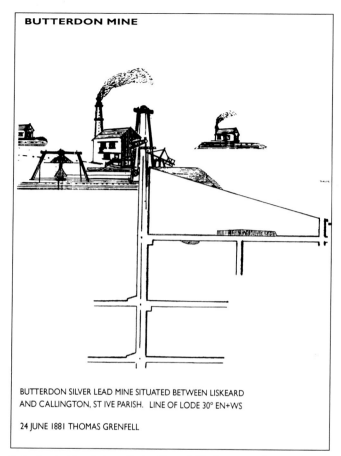

BUTTERDON MINE

BUTTERDON SILVER LEAD MINE SITUATED BETWEEN LISKEARD AND CALLINGTON, ST IVE PARISH. LINE OF LODE 30° EN+WS

24 JUNE 1881 THOMAS GRENFELL

Butterdon had hardly been flush with available finance, trials at Penhauger were even more tightly controlled and throughout its life it survived on meagre injections of capital. The results were clearly evident in the provision of only a small working steam engine, limited labour resources and a severely restricted ability to sink trials in depth. The willingness to pay only small calls and provide only moderate levels of equipment, to support the work in hand, led to inevitable accusation of inadequate trials having taken place before abandonment. Despite the moderate progress made, it has to be admitted Penhauger was one of the lengthiest trials within the parish, during two periods of working between 1850 and 1857 and between 1859 and 1861, and the undertaking rightly deserves its place in the Menheniot mining story.

The mine was worked under the name Penhauger, despite the adjacent farm always being spelt Penhawger. Penhauger, Butterdon and Wheal Venton are now firmly proven as located within the northern part of Menheniot parish, despite being often incorrectly listed under the mineral statistics for St Ive. Penhauger was the most northerly of the three, sharing all its mineral lodes with Butterdon to the south, the lodes lying as they did parallel in a north-south direction. The final shaft, worked between 1856 and 1857 and again between 1859 and 1861, was located 700 yards to the east of Penhawger Farm, now hidden within a wood on a steeply falling slope. It lay above the valley of the River Tiddy and two adits were brought up from a narrow valley floor at right angles to the river, one north and one south, their entrances located 60 yards apart. Dines incorrectly refers to both as belonging to Penhauger; in fact the northerly one was driven towards the previously described shaft but the southerly has now been identified as the site of Butterdon's final working described earlier. Other shallow trials were earlier made at unknown locations on the site, somewhat meagrely checking the several lodes which were believed to cross the sett.

A company was formed to work Penhauger in December 1850, but by June 1851 work was still of an exploratory nature at surface.[22] Having noted the improvement which had taken place at Butterdon, the agent had recommended against commencing the whim shaft at the point proposed at the previous meeting, but instead intended to trace the lode further north to the centre of the sett and there locate the engine shaft. At the same time shallow pits were being dug to probe the ground in the north of the sett.[56] Two weeks later the shaft had been started on the course of the lode and had reached five fathoms (or a mere 30 ft) and yet at that shallow depth they were already beginning to drive on the course of the lode to establish its true direction.[57] The agent had arranged for a horse whim to be erected by the end of August, after which it was intended to resume work on the engine shaft.[58] By the end of September it was being sunk by six men at the rate of four feet per week, but the water was ominously quick.[59] Work continued as best they could without steam power but by the end of December 1851, with the onset of winter, sinking had to be suspended due to the influx of water. The adventurers had however sensibly decided to purchase a small steam engine and the men contracted to sink the shaft were switched to assist with the raising of stone for the engine house and stack. At the December 1851 meeting a small call of 2s.6d. per share was made.[60]

After this very little was heard of Penhauger for some time, apart from Wheal Mary Ann's accounts showing a steam whim was bought from Penhauger for £200 in December 1852.[26] John Watson in his annual review of mining for 1852 stated that Penhauger had so far disappointed expectation, but inferred it was still being worked.[44] Regular reports resumed in August 1853, almost two years after they had last been made, with no mention of work any longer being carried out in connection with the original shaft or workings from it. Reports suggest activity was confined to an adit, driven on the course of the lode as a means to open it out over a reasonable length rather than simply for drainage. Joseph Kemp of Wheal Trelawny was responsible for ensuring work progressed satisfactorily during 1853 and 1854, as he also did for Butterdon and regular reports became once again a feature of Penhauger's working. Adventurers were reassured that indications remained promising, however by the end of November 1853 the onset of a wet winter had again caused an influx of water into the workings. Levels had by now been opened up below the adit and these had to be suspended. A horse-whim was in use at this time for raising water from the workings, but had proved totally inadequate.[61] Work had resumed in the spring and meanwhile the adit continued to be exploited, work being concentrated there and at fairly shallow levels below it throughout 1854. In June 1854 during successive weeks, a shaft was reported being sunk five and then six fathoms below surface, but its purpose and precise location is unclear.[62] No further reference was made to it. Two men were driving the adit end north on the course of the lode in November 1854.[63] John Watson, mining correspondent, sadly reflected at the end of 1854 that Penhauger had not yet answered expectations.[64]

Calls on the shares were still kept very low and in May 1855 were limited to 1s. per share.[65] 1855 was to be a year of cautious extension of operations around the adit, with few problems in following the lode, but with little to excite in terms of size and quality. Thomas Grenfell, agent at Wheal Trelawny, supervised detailed operations from 1855 until the end of the first period of working in 1857. He made detailed reports as progress was achieved, although this often was limited and could easily be contained within the briefest of descriptions.

In January 1856 Thomas Grenfell reported that operations were confined to surface work and again in February he reported that they had still not resumed working underground, water in the workings being the likely cause.[66] During April 1856 a significant adventurers' meeting took place at Webbs Hotel, Liskeard, when a far reaching decision was taken to sink a new shaft on the course of the lode, its location being 700 yards east of Penhawger farm, now hidden in the wood in the position described. It was intended to sink the shaft from surface to the already driven adit, then having made communication sink on downwards to prove the lode in depth. Within ten days of the meeting an enthusiastic Thomas Grenfell was reporting that the shaft was sunk nine feet and a month later it was complete down to adit level. Shaftmen were about to commence work on dividing and casing the shaft into two compartments, one for raising ore and rubbish, the other for the pumping gear and mens ladders.[67] This completed the first stage to adit level, but soon after the project began to encounter problems. Despite laying a wooden water course along the bottom of the adit to assist drainage, all efforts to sink below this level were frustrated by water problems, despite it being the usually favourable month of July. A horse-whim had been used to raise the water but it proved unable to cope and work was temporarily suspended.[30]

A decision had been taken at the adventurers' meeting to order a steam engine and preparatory work for this gained urgency in view of the emerging pumping difficulties. It must have been a wet summer that year for in July Thomas Grenfell reported that, weather permitting, he hoped the engine house would be ready for covering in by the next day. It was then intended to lift in and put the engine to work as soon as possible.[30] It had been intended to purchase a portable engine, shades of the adventurers' usual economy being evident here, but they were unable to find a suitable one and instead opted to dismantle and move the redundant engine from a previously abandoned shaft on the sett. This compelled them to incur the additional expense of building an engine house, boiler house and stack, but the manager reported that this more ambitious project would undoubtedly prove a wiser investment for the future. He added that he was adapting the engine to both draw the waste and any ore as well as pump the mine. The October 1856 meeting reported the engine was working well and a call of 7s. per share was made.[68] In fact by the end of September 1856 Thomas Grenfell had reported the shaft had been sunk six fathoms below adit.[69] No drainage problems were mentioned that winter, but sinking continued at what could best be described as Penhauger's usual pace, reaching barely 14 fathoms below adit by February and 15 fathoms by March 1857. The lode underlaid east and was described repeatedly as promising and of a kindly appearance. A call of 7s. per share, still moderate by any standards, was made in February 1857.[70]

With the apparent immediacy that was so often encountered with such concerns, the meeting held at Webbs Hotel in April 1857 decided that all workings should be suspended with immediate effect and that a call of 15s. per 1/808th share be made, to cover existing liabilities.[55] Workings were at last being a little more ambitiously pursued and it seemed an inappropriate time to suspend operations. There had been problems with payments of calls by adventurers, but a more likely reason lies in the fact that both Butterdon and Penhauger were abandoned at the same time. Shareholders in both were largely common with Wheal Trelawny and it is more likely that both mines were subjected to a common policy decision to cut losses and draw back interest to the principal undertaking, which continued to prove a safer investment.

Penhauger was offered for sale in August 1857, the shaft described as having been sunk 26 fathoms from surface or 17 fathoms below adit, with the lode in the adit having been opened up over a considerable length and being of a favourable appearance. 30 hundred-weight of ore were on the surface and included in the sale. Despite the willingness of the adventurers to abandon the sett, it was offered as a promising investment. No sale was however made.[71] The mine lay abandoned for almost two years until a party of Liskeard adventurers formed a new company to work the mine in July 1859. The local group were both influential and knowledgeable, with a list of principals prominent in the local mining community. Robert Knapp of Wheal Ludcott, St Ive, and located very close to Penhauger, was appointed manager, W. G. Nettle, purser, and Matthew Loam, engineer. The latter also took a substantial holding in the company and chaired the inaugural adventurers' meeting. A call of 2s. per share was made to raise £350 for the purchase of the engine and materials still on site, as well as to cover the first two months working expenses. The mine had been bought with a positive plan of development ready for implementation. It had been noted that whilst the adit had been probed over a considerable length with promising results and a shaft sunk 26 fathoms, no levels at any greater depth than the adit had been tried. The first priority was to drain the shaft and then to drive two new levels north and south on the course of the lode. They were particularly interested in reaching a point north, where lead had been found in the adit level above and was anticipated to have strengthened in depth. [72]

In the customary way the restarting of the mine was celebrated in July 1859 at The Bell Hotel, Liskeard, by a large party of influential gentlemen, under the presidency of Matthew Loam. The principal guests included Messrs Anstis, Caunter, Isaac, Hawke and Nettle of Liskeard and the chairman of West Caradon Mine, Richard Hallett, as well as its influential manager, Francis Pryor. After the dinner Captain Thomas Trevillion of Herodsfoot, William Johns and William Taylor of West Caradon and Robert Knapp of Wheal Ludcott, the future Penhauger manager, all rose and spoke encouragingly of the mine's prospects. They emphasised the fact that an engine was available, a shaft already sunk and that the adit level had been successfully exploited, marking the run and prospects of the lode. All this contributed to a great saving in time and money for the new adventurers.[72] What was not said was that although they had in truth acquired a bargain, which only required small periodic calls to sustain it, the engine was small with a limit to its pumping potential and if they were indeed serious, then a point would be reached where the expense of a new engine and higher pumping charges would have to be faced. How they then reacted would prove to be the real test to their commitment.

By March 1860 Robert Knapp was able to report that a 22 fathom level north had been started and was proceeding well with the possibility of ore to be taken away by good paying tribute, if its quality continued to improve. The 22 fathom south was showing signs of improvement. In the 11 fathom level, which had also been started, tribute ground was being opened up by a rise which was designed to meet a winze being sunk from the adit and this would also pay for working when communication was completed.[73] Barely one month later work near the shaft in the 22 fathom level and also in several other areas were all ready to be set. Ore was hoped to be raised and sold as soon as a small dressing floor could be provided. By May 1860, the 22 fathom level had been driven 10 fathoms north and eight fathoms south and men set to sink the shaft below that level. The small engine was still working well and Robert Knapp whilst not underestimating future potential pumping problems, assured the adventurers that the engine would cope with drainage from a further 10 to 15 fathoms deeper.[75] Whilst he had initially been very enthusiastic about the uncovering of ore, described as good saving work, future reports played down this aspect and concentrated on describing the development work being done to open out the mine. The mine was clearly to be developed with purpose, but lacked the major improvement in the ground which would herald a successful outcome. Despite this, promising signs abounded and explorations continued.

November 1860 found progress moderately successful in areas already being worked, whilst the shaft was now down 28 fathoms and Robert Knapp was already talking of the level he intended to drive at a depth of 32 or 34 fathoms, where favourable indications at the 22 fathom level would be resought at the greater depth. A new trial shaft was being sunk on the western lode discovered some time previously and this had reached a depth of only four fathoms, before being stopped through water. It was hoped it would eventually lead to something good. Dressing of ores had commenced, although the quantity was not great and it was expected to have a few tons ready for market within the next few months.[76] Calls throughout 1860 were limited to 1s. 6d. per share and it was stated that arrears of call were very light.[77]

It was therefore with some surprise that barely six months later the adventurers' meeting held in April 1861, with Matthew Loam in the chair, called for a special meeting to be held on 24 April to consider the question of abandoning the mine. Robert Knapp emphasised that he had no doubt of its ultimate success, but he could not recommend continuance with the present small engine.[78] Action was swift and as early as mid-May the mine and materials were offered for auction on site as a going concern. The materials consisted of one 10 horse-power steam engine, a five ton boiler, pitwork fixed in working order, horse whim, capstan and shears, smiths bellows and tools etc. The shaft was described as having reached 29 fathoms under adit or 38 fathoms from surface.[79] Webb and Geach, in their review of mining in the Liskeard area, published in 1863, stated that the mine was abandoned due to the lode underlying easterly at the eastern limit of the sett in such a way that it would have passed out of the mine in depth. An approach was made to the landlord for the rights to work the adjacent

ground, but the terms were too onerous and the mine abandoned after an inadequate trial.[80] This reason is however not corroborated in any of the final reports concerning the mine. The days of ready pursuit of speculative concerns were running out and Penhauger was never to be tried again. It is doubtful if it could ever have become another Wheal Trelawny, but with the right commitment of investment and resources it might just possibly have paid for a few short years.

SOUTH WHEAL MARY ANN (1853) was located adjacent to the western boundaries of Wheal Mary Ann, Wheal Trehane and Wheal Trelawny and west of Menheniot Village. A company was formed in Tavistock in April 1853 and Captain Henry Hodge was appointed as agent, Thomas Nicholls of Tavistock as purser and Thomas Fuller of Threadneedle Street, London, as secretary. The lease had been secured at 1-16th dues and the mine was described as having every prospect of becoming a lasting and profitable mine.[81] This was clearly a much overworked phrase and in reality activity on the ground hardly matched the grand conception. By August an adit had been driven a mere 26 feet into the hillside parallel with the village. The ground was said to be moderate for driving and would probably have been set to no more than two men.[82] By September 1853 there had been little change and Henry Hodge, who was only a part-time agent, reported that he currently had no men at work, but had set the adit end that day to two men.[83] That report was to be the last recorded evidence of the mine's existence and as with many other minor concerns it disappeared without trace; an unsuccessful venture which was quickly proved to have little prospect of success.

EAST TRELAWNY (1854-1856) was to be found immediately to the east of Wheal Trelawny and Wheal Trehane and south of Treweatha Mine. It also lay immediately to the south of Wheal Wrey and North Trelawny, both located just across the parish boundary in St Ive/Quethiock and hope was held that the lodes of those mines would run through this new property. By September 1854 two lodes had been traced by costeaning and a third by November 1854 using similar means, but it remained far too early to determine whether lead in payable quantities would be found. An adit had been driven to the most promising, named the Champion Lode, and had cut it at a point 12 to 14 feet deep, where small deposits of silver lead ore had been found.[84] Whilst spirited, these trials would have been accomplished with minimum financial outlay, without machinery and involving limited labour resources, until the full character of the lodes could be established and more ambitious exploration in depth justified. Several noteworthy mining principals visited the property at this time and pronounced the signs as promising, the mine a first rate speculation and well worthy of the attention of investors; support that was essential for any lengthy and proper trials. A year later calls were still being made, when at a meeting in the

Queens Head, Tavistock, in September 1855 the accounts for the past quarter were presented. Appointments and salaries for the principals were confirmed, without doubt of a part time nature, with P. Harvey confirmed as agent at £4.4s. per month and Ponsford Fisher as purser at £2.2s. per month, the latter the chairman of the meeting. A committee of three shareholders, all mine captains but none Liskeard men, suggesting this was very much an outside funded project, were appointed to visit the mine and with Captain Harvey decide what work should be prosecuted to ensure the mine's successful development. One ominous sign was that 1,685 of the 6,000 shares had been relinquished and transferred to the purser to be offered for sale.[85] Clearly all was not well at this time. Although the shares continued to be listed in the *Mining Journal* until September 1856 little more was heard of East Trelawny and it slid into obscurity along with the other unsuccessful speculations.

LAMBEST CONSOLS (1856-1858) was formed in Plymouth in September 1856 and divided into 6,000 shares with an initial call of 6d. per share.[86] It was described as a valuable piece of mineral ground when first proposed and was an impressive sized sett measuring one mile from north to south and half a mile from east to west. It ran parallel to the eastern boundaries of Wheal Trelawny, Wheal Mary Ann and to Menheniot village. The lodes of Wheal Wrey, Wheal Ludcott and North Trelawny were considered to pass through the sett as did the eastern lode of Treweatha Mine. Lambest Consols clearly took a similar position and was considered to repeat the characteristics of the previously described East Trelawny, taking a position immediately south of that mine. A quite separate set of adventurers were behind this speculation and it was but a coincidence that Lambest Consols emerged on the scene just as the trials at East Trelawny were finally abandoned.

The existence of two or three lodes was easily established at a shallow depth of only 10 to 12 feet in which stones of lead ore were found.[69] The elation which this produced was clearly an essential and, dare it be said, a well stage managed part of ensuring initial optimism amongst potential investors. Yet again the identification of the run of a lode, with some evidence of lead being present, was a long way from confirmation of a rich deposit of marketable proportions, but eternal optimism ruled the day and glazed expressions prevailed as success to rival the adjacent Wheal Trelawny and Wheal Mary Ann was as ever believed possible.

By February 1857 initial trials without machinery or mechanical pumping had gone well, an adit had been brought up from the valley and a shaft started. It was recommended that more ambitious development should now commence with the shaft being sunk to 20 fathoms and a small engine erected.[87] This decision was confirmed in Plymouth that week and a further call of 6d. per share was made on the then revised capital of 4,474 shares.[88] The adventurers were fortunate to have secured the part-time services of Robert Dunstan, a much sought after name for fronting mining projects in the Liskeard area. He had managed West Caradon for some years and up to six speculative mines on a part time basis in the previous five years. By May 1857 work on the mine was progressing well, the walls of the engine house were up and the 16-inch engine, calculated to put the mine down to a depth of 50 fathoms, was in the course of being moved from Plymouth. It was scheduled to reach the mine early the following week.[89] A further call of 6d. per share was made to defray the cost of the engine and to cover the next two months working. In December 1857 Robert Dunstan reported the ground in the shaft was much improved and his men were making good progress in sinking.[90] After the December 1857 meeting no further reports were issued and at some point during 1858 optimism and funds became exhausted and yet another minor concern slipped into the pages of history. Typical of these minor ventures, no obvious remains are apparent today, no plans have survived and the precise location of the shafts cannot be traced with certainty.

HENDRA CONSOLS (1866) might easily have slipped into the mists of time without record, but for a single item of correspondence submitted to the *Mining Journal* in March 1866. It recorded that operations had been commenced driving an adit on the course of the lode into a hillside in Menheniot. The lode was described as four feet wide and interspersed throughout with silver lead. The mine was stated to adjoin Wheal Trelawny and Wheal Mary Ann mines and to have parallel lodes with them. It was said to be worked by a few private individuals together with the mineral lords who had taken one quarter part as an investment. Vigorous prosecution was promised, but nothing more was heard of this small undertaking that promised much and produced little. So with Hendra Consols, the least important and last of these minor ventures bit the dust, leaving only the three surviving major concerns of Wheal Mary Ann, Wheal Trelawny (which had by then absorbed Trehane) and Treweatha to battle out the last years of Menheniot's major mining period, which was brought to a close in 1874. Such ventures as were to follow from 1875 were of a very different nature, being born into an already despondent and economically broken community, they attempted unsuccessfully to rediscover past glories which in truth were never there to be found.

CHAPTER ELEVEN
LATER MINING VENTURES

It is not the mine that is exhausted;
it is the patience, pluck and perserverence of the Adventureres
MATTHEW LOAM, LISKEARD 1880.

A S AUTUMN 1874 turned to the chill winds of winter and Menheniot braced itself for the difficult months ahead, it was time to reflect upon the state of the mining industry on which the parish had so heavily depended to support the greatly increased population of the last thirty years. The winter of 1874 was truly the worst the beleaguered mining community had faced, with for the first time all the mine engine houses throughout the parish standing silent, cold and gaunt. At the end of September 1874 operations had been entirely suspended at Wheal Mary Ann, with materials being drawn to the surface ready for auctioning.[1] On that last day, as the once familiar sound of a working steam engine and clanking machinery from across the hill died away, a silence fell over Menheniot unheard since the far off days before the mining era. A walk through Menheniot's lanes in that long cold winter revealed not only Wheal Mary Ann standing silent, but Wheal Trelawny, that other parish stalwart, temporarily taken over by the former for its last three years, equally silent, having effectively collapsed as anindependent concern in 1871.[2] Continuing northwards through the narrow lanes, Treweatha emerged from behind winter hedgerows, crows circling its cold and smokeless stacks, abandoned in 1872 unable after many struggling years to support further heavy losses.[3]

The speculative concerns which briefly gleamed brightly in prospective developers' eyes, but left little behind for future generations to reflect, were but fading memories belonging to the heady years of the 1840s and 1850s and already names like South Wheal Trelawny, Penhauger, Butterdon and Wheal Venton belonged to the past. As groups of disconsolate miners shook their heads and wondered disbelievingly whether the good times had gone for ever, it was difficult to believe that less than five short years ago there had been 355 underground and surface workers at Wheal Trelawny, 300 at Wheal Mary Ann and 174 at Treweatha.[4] Some 829 working opportunities had been lost, hitting families hard where not only the head of the house, but sons, daughters and certainly younger wives had similarly found employment. Only one question that really mattered remained unanswered; was this really the end of Menheniot mining?

In short the answer was no, but in truth those who were now leaving the area by the hundred for pastures new, including to coal mining in the north-west and north-east of England as well as migration to Australia and other far flung lands, were making the more realistic and accurate assessment of the true prospects. But our story must continue and new mining names were shortly to emerge, a few on genuinely virgin ground, others on old setts re-packaged with renewed if slightly tarnished enthusiasm and sporting the old dusted off superlatives, 'this project just cannot fail'. With London money harder to come by and the reputation of Cornish mining remaining at a low ebb, there was increased reliance on the Cornish investors for some of these latter projects, limited in extent as they were to be. The genuine determination amongst Liskeard businessmen, merchants and professional men to resort to self help should not be underestimated. The better chronicled deprivations of Cornish mining families produced the greatest sympathy, but in truth the very fabric and prosperity of the business community that supported and serviced local mining had suffered similarly at their own level and in their own way. One suspects however a few were not quite sure whether to believe in their own enthusiasm, but not to do so meant admission of defeat and recognition of impending financial ruin.

It is perhaps sad that the saga of Menheniot's mining era cannot be brought to a close with the story of Wheal Mary Ann and Wheal Trelawny's triumphant development, yielding steady and not insignificant financial returns to the lucky adventurers and steadier and more reliable rewards for the working miner than common beliefs on miners' general conditions might suggest. These were the heady days of fortunes made, settling back into no less than twenty-five years of secure employment and steady wages for the miners' families, until the last few years of decline. But, for the sake of historical accuracy, we must continue to factually record the death throes of an industry which had outlived its ability to economically survive and for which the richest pickings had long since gone.

WEST MARY ANN (1875-1884) was situated three quarters of a mile west of Wheal Mary Ann and its shaft was sunk high on the side of a hill at a point 500 yards north by east of Roseland, which itself is located about a mile along the lane leading westwards from Menheniot church towards

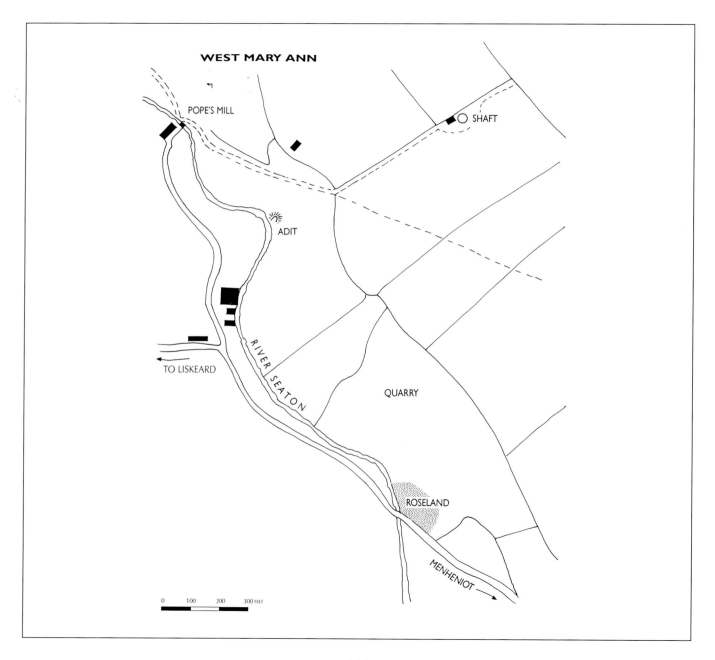

WEST MARY ANN

POPE'S MILL

SHAFT

ADIT

RIVER SEATON

TO LISKEARD

QUARRY

ROSELAND

MENHENIOT

0   100   200   300 FEET

Liskeard. An adit was brought up near the River Seaton from a point 450 yards north-north-west of Roseland.[5] The site and adit entrance can still be traced by following the footpath from Popes Mill (see mine plan). The mine was worked for lead in two separate stages between 1875 and 1884 but there are no records of any output. W. G. Nettle of Liskeard, nephew of the late Peter Clymo Jnr, was the purser and consistent influence throughout the mine's nine-year period of working.[6] He had been purser at Wheal Mary Ann for its last four years up to closure in 1874 and throughout 1875 was responsible for winding up the affairs of the mine, coincidental with forming the company to work West Mary Ann.[7] Likewise James Stevens, who had been made redundant as mine agent at Wheal Mary Ann in 1874, reappeared here the next year controlling the practical affairs of the new mine.[8] All of this clearly points to former local shareholders in Wheal Mary Ann being associated with this new young company, that sought to emulate the lost youth and vibrancy of its once great neighbour.

Reports that the new mine would carry all the positive features inherited from Wheal Mary Ann were misleading to say the least and typical of loose claims often made to boost speculative developments adjacent to previous well known concerns. In fact lying as it did to the west of Wheal Mary Ann, this mine was located on a parallel lead lode rather than a continuation of the proven Wheal Mary Ann one. The parallel lodes were understood to traverse the parish in a general north to south direction, but only the central lode had delivered the real riches for both Wheal Mary Ann and Wheal Trelawny. This most westerly of Menheniot's speculations was located on a previously undiscovered minor lode which, if in hindsight offered little, at the time fuelled the hopes of a new rich find and sustained intermittent, moderate scale exploration over nine long years.

The mine was divided into 3,000 shares mostly sold locally and during the first year of operation costs were described as under £30 monthly. Sinking of the shaft commenced on the hillside overlooking the River Seaton in May 1875 and had reached a depth of 13 fathoms by that December. James Stevens reported that after initial easy and promising progress, sinking had proved to be both slow and expensive through hard ground, although long term prospects were promising.[8] No mention of the luxury of a steam engine accompanied this first working and by December high winter rainfall had caused further sinking to be suspended until the spring. Miners worked knee deep in freezing water gushing from the shaft walls and frustrating valiant efforts to make further progress.

A reflective James Stevens re-directed his men towards driving the adit from the bank of the River Seaton, far below, deep into the side of the hill towards a point where it would intersect the temporarily suspended shaft. The adit aided natural drainage from the surrounding area into the river, whilst the driving also improved James Steven's understanding of the nature

West Mary Ann. A small concern worked between 1875–1884. The site marked today by a small dump on the side of a working field.

S. Bartlett 1991

of the ground beneath the property. By December 1875 it had reached a point 38 fathoms into the hillside and was continuing in an east-north-east direction.[8]

January 1876 saw the adventurers registering disappointment that the lode had still not been found, despite efforts made at exploratory sinking and driving. However, it was agreed that work should continue in the hope of reaching their objective.[9] Two weeks later the nature of the ground was reported to have changed and to be showing a favourable indication.[10] By the end of March it was claimed that the Wheal Mary Ann lode had been met, although in reality this must have been a parallel lode, but despite these reassurances by October 1876 the property was described as recently suspended.[11]

Inactivity was brief and a new lease was taken out in September 1877 at 1-18th dues, with W. G. Nettle still in charge of financial affairs and chairing most adventurers' meetings; clearly the driving force behind the company's operations. By August 1878 he was able to report a winze being sunk from the adit level with promising indications.[12]

By July 1879 a 22-inch engine had been bought for the mine and a year later W. G. Nettle was to comment that, 'our little steam engine is answering remarkably well, drawing water and stuff without inconvenience or delay'. Shares were recorded as being mostly locally held and not dealt with on the London market.[13] This supports the conjecture that by this time a small concern such as this only tended to carry the confidence of local

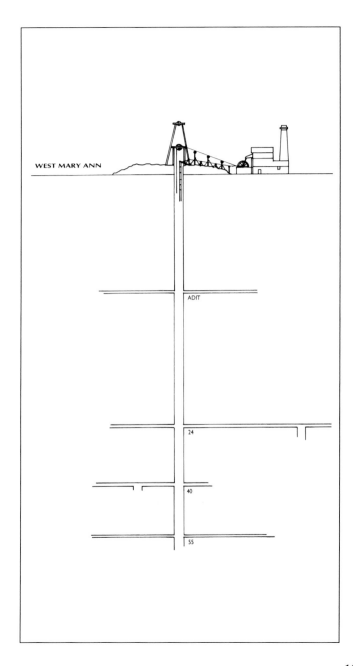

WEST MARY ANN

ADIT

24

40

55

adventurers. In 1879 nine men were employed underground with four surface workers and the total numbers remained at 13 throughout 1880 and 1881, only slightly fluctuating to 10 in 1882, 20 in 1883 and 16 in 1884. This indicated the tight financial constraints which only permitted steady but restrained development, providing hope but only meagre employment opportunity to the large number of unemployed miners in the village.

Work continued throughout 1880, noticeably kept away from the public gaze, whilst correspondents made a plea for more frequent reports from this unassuming concern.[14] Again that August the mine was described as a promising little known concern, overshadowed by the then current flood of publicity associated with the re-opening of Wheal Hony and Trelawny United. The engine shaft was reported as slowly but steadily being sunk and had reached 20 fathoms below adit by August.[15]

In December 1880 W. G. Nettle reported that a proposal some months previously to change the existing 3,000 share holding to a limited company of 5,000 shares had been dropped. Recent improvements in the mine had led the committee to recommend that current developments were best suited to benefit the existing small number of shareholders.[16] During 1881 exploration continued both north and south, following the lode at a depth of 24 fathoms under adit.[17] Steady if cautious exploration continued throughout succeeding years, with investors' impatience tried at times, then calmed with reassurances of positive signs of success. Calls of 3s. to 5s. a quarter per share continued through 1881 and similar expenses fell on the adventurers during the following few years.[18]

During 1883 whilst W. G. Nettle continued to manage the finances of the operation, Captain T. F. Tremellon emerged directing practical operations. In February he insisted a better engine was necessary to support further sinking of the shaft; the present one now experiencing difficulty in maintaining drainage.[19] By June the erection of the engine house, boiler house and chimney was almost complete, whilst it was reported that the replacement engine was in process of removal from the former Wheal Mary Ann site. It was hoped the engine would soon be started. It was inferred the bottom level of the mine was currently suspended due to flooding.[20] The source for the second hand engine was surprising; Wheal Mary Ann having been closed nine years previously, with exhaustive attempts made at the time to sell surplus engines and materials.

A flurry of such positive activity sometimes proved too much for a delicately balanced concern and despite thinly veneered reassurances, it was not entirely without surprise that in October 1884 it was resolved to suspend all operations and offer the mine for sale as a going concern.[21] An auction was quickly arranged in November but no new purchaser could be found, in consequence it was somewhat quaintly reported of the 'non-attendance of bidders'.[22] The mine was described as having reached a depth of 55 fathoms and that surface machinery consisted of a 24-inch pumping and winding engine with associated pitwork.[23] It was proposed to auction all saleable materials and this took place in March 1885 with the assets slightly differently described as a 22-inch winding engine, four horse-power portable vertical winding and pumping engine with associated boilers, pitwork, rope, pipes and tools.[24]

W. G. Nettle, the purser, superintended the task of winding up the company and must have reflected on the fact that he was performing the same task for the very much larger Wheal Mary Ann in 1875 when West Mary Ann was launched with all the hopes and expectations associated with the former successful mining ventures in the area.

A small locally funded concern, West Mary Ann had lacked the large scale investment associated with other larger projects. For nine long years it had unsuccessfully sought to demonstrate that Menheniot's mining potential was not yet exhausted until eventually its loyal local shareholders had to accept inevitable defeat.

Meanwhile a venture of quite different proportions WHEAL HONY & TRELAWNY UNITED (1880-1884) had been launched. Doubters questioned the judgement of considering such a high cost venture at a difficult time for Cornish mining, but equally forceful and well reasoned argument was put forward by the promoters, who pointed to a unique opportunity which presented itself to explore previously untried and potentially rich mineral ground denied to earlier speculations. The argument was tempting. It was known that both Wheal Trelawny in 1871 and Wheal Mary Ann (by then incorporating Trelawny) in 1874 had succumbed due to their inability to extend their virtually exhausted sett beyond its northern boundary. At every level Wheal Trelawny had worked the strong central lead lode, which had run first through Wheal Mary Ann and then the latter, right up to this boundary and on occasions illegally beyond. Mineral lord Dr Honey had repeatedly refused permission to work his ground. Now after his death his executors were at long last prepared to grant a lease to the new company.

The proposed property consisted of the recently released land coupled with the former Trelawny workings. This gave the mine ready made shaft access to a depth of 210 fathoms via the old mine, with new levels only needing to be driven into the untried ground across the boundary. This represented a significant saving in initial development costs and was seen as an important point in favour of the proposal. Furthermore the availability of modern powered rock drills and more sophisticated dressing equipment added to the boast that a modern mine could operate significantly more efficiently than its predecessors. Against this, as the only working mine in the immediate area, doubters pointed to the potentially massive pumping task facing the mine which needed careful assessment and provision. This latter feature was in fairness never underestimated, although the cost proved substantial. Finally the greatest unknown, upon which the whole project rested, was whether the potentially glittering prizes would be valuable enough to produce a successful return, given the scale of the outlay which would be needed and the state of the lead market.[25]

The proposers however were confident and The Wheal Hony & Trelawny United Silver Lead Mining Company Ltd. was launched in July 1880 with a capital of £50,000 in 25,000 £2 shares. William Derry and mining engineer Matthew Loam were the inspirations behind the development, the former said to hold 10% of the company's shares. Nevertheless, heavy dependence on the London investment market was reflected in the choice of chairman George Brockelbank and directors S. Burney-Walker, John Romanes and Edward Palmer. H. R. Lewis was appointed the London based company secretary. Practical mining direction was as ever Cornish with Matthew Loam confirmed as engineer and William Hancock as manager, both Liskeard based. The latter had experience of Wheal Trelawny as a young man and had been mine agent under Peter Clymo Jnr at nearby Wheal Wrey, St Ive some years earlier.[26]

The derelict Trelawny surface workings were examined and a decision taken to locate the 90-inch pumping engine, specified by Matthew Loam, on the former Smith's shaft within Trelawny's northern surface site.[27] This area is identified today by the surviving single tall chimney, a landmark for many miles north of the village and surrounded by a large area of still disturbed ground. Trelawny's former Vivian's shaft, 120 yards south of Smith's and connected by an existing level underground, was stipulated for whim haulage.[28] On the new sett additional shafts would be sunk over the next few years, as levels were extended north; these being Derry's 150 yards and Lewis's 480 yards north-east of Chippindale's shaft. The latter, although not mentioned in initial plans, was also to be returned to active use for whim haulage whilst Vivian's in reality is much more likely to have been confined to use as miners access to the levels leading to the new mine.

The original Trelawny south site and Wheal Mary Ann's surface workings saw no such renewed activity, although the former Trelawny account house was the location for celebrations to mark the laying of the foundation stone for the new engine house in December 1880.[25] Practical work had commenced that October, supervised by William Hancock, and by the end of 1880 a small workforce of five underground and forty surface workers were employed. The total increased to eighty five by the end of 1881; all involved in development tasks with full scale production mining still a distant aspiration.

The ceremony to lay the foundation stone of the new engine house took place on Saturday 4 December 1880, creating considerable excitement in the district and attracting a large crowd of guests and onlookers. Matthew Loam stated that they were gathered to inaugurate what he believed would become a great and valuable mine. He well remembered Menheniot's mines in their glory, a great source of pride to all concerned. Whilst enthusiasm could not have been greater amongst the principals, a more suspicious mining market looked on with interest and a little concern at the renewed activity in far off Menheniot.[25]

The 90-inch engine was claimed to be the largest still working in Cornwall and had been located at Crenver & Abraham mine where it had lain idle since 1876. The illustrious Harvey & Co. of Hayle had been agents for the sale; Matthew Loam personally examining the engine before

recommending purchase. The securing of this second-hand giant, described as in excellent condition, had saved almost four months in terms of time and £2,000 in cost over a new engine for the undertaking. Dismantling and subsequent transport across the county was a challenging exercise and an awesome sight; the visible evidence of a new and important commitment in an uncertain industry.

In June 1881 it left Crenver & Abraham in parts by waggon to Camborne station from where it travelled east to Liskeard by rail. From there the parts were hauled to the mine, notably the massive cylinder by a team of 26 horses. The journey along the narrow, ill-kept and steeply graded lanes to Menheniot was traumatic, with the waggon wheels becoming totally embedded in the rutted track, and after unsuccessful efforts was abandoned

Wheal Hony and Trelawny United used the old Smith's and Chippindale's shafts and levels to drive into the new ground. Later Derry's and the Lewis's were sunk, too late to rescue the ailing concern.

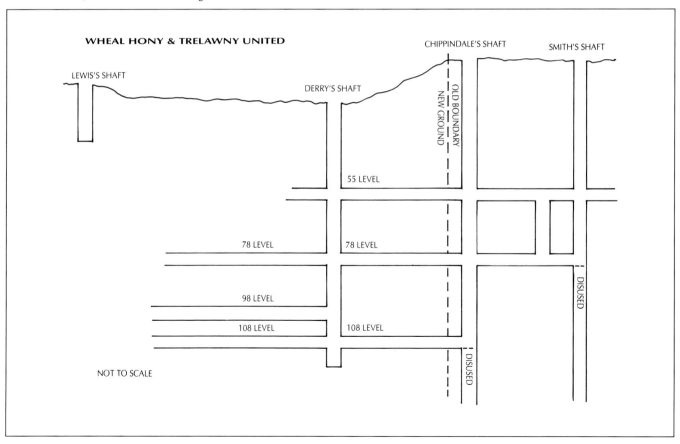

WHEAL HONY & TRELAWNY UNITED

LEWIS'S SHAFT

DERRY'S SHAFT

CHIPPINDALE'S SHAFT

SMITH'S SHAFT

OLD BOUNDARY
NEW GROUND

55 LEVEL

78 LEVEL

78 LEVEL

98 LEVEL

108 LEVEL

108 LEVEL

DISUSED

DISUSED

NOT TO SCALE

overnight where it lay. The final mile or so to the mine was completed the following day after the waggon wheels had been jacked free.[45]

By July 1881, the extensive preparatory surface work was nearing completion. Most buildings were finished and these included the engine and boiler houses, smiths' and carpenters' shops, offices and stores. The erection of the engine itself was scheduled to be completed by early August and plans were being laid for pumping to commence the following month. At least at surface the undertaking gave the appearance of confidence, order and scale to reassure prospective investors.[28]

Elsewhere William Hancock had not been idle. An adit had been opened up from the former Wheal Mary Ann workings, which had immediately dropped the water level in Smith's shaft to 30 fathoms. The old shaft itself had been cleared and timbered to that depth and the shallow level communicating Smith's with Vivian's opened up again. Costeaning had taken place right across the property and shallow pits were to be seen at many points in surrounding fields where the ground was being probed for evidence to confirm the lie and potential value of the lodes. As well as the expected Trelawny main lode, three lesser ones were encountered, including one to be called the Brockelbank lode which was considered to hold much promise. A separate company was to be formed in 1882 to work this new lode, its separate identity being more for financial than practical reasons. We shall return to look closer at East Hony (1882-1884) a little later.[28]

Saturday 17 September 1881 was an important day long remembered in Menheniot as large crowds gathered to witness the starting of the new 90-inch engine. Principal guests from London and Liskeard included George Brockelbank, H. R. Lewis, Matthew Loam, William Paynter Jnr, John Martyn, E. G. Hamley and William Derry, and an impressive account house lunch followed. Matthew Loam, amidst resounding cheers, described it as a great day for Menheniot and as the massive engine swung into life he raised his glass to 'confounding the doubters'. In this he was a little premature and subsequent events proved the realities of mining speculation presented massive hurdles, both financial and practical, to be overcome.[29]

The mine plan illustrates the somewhat unusual method adopted to open out the workings, accepted as most cost effective at the time but criticised later as contributing to the long and costly development period which was still under way when the undertaking finally collapsed. The location chosen for the huge 90-inch pumping engine, the work clearing the former Smith's, Chippindale's and Vivian's shafts and the reopening of the long silent levels leading northwards towards the former Trelawny boundary, where the new drivings would commence, all concentrated initial efforts at the extreme edge of the new sett far from where ultimately the most promising signs would be found.

By February 1882 William Hancock was able to report that Smith's shaft

8 Dean Terrace, Liskeard, home in 1861 of Matthew Loam, Mine Engineer, the inspiration behind Wheal Hony and Trelawny United.

S. Bartlett 1989

was cleared and secured to a depth of 65 fathoms, Chippindale's similarly to the 55 and Vivian's cleared and secured with footway access provided. This indeed suggested the latter had adopted its former role as principal access point for the miners. Even at this late stage, when modern equipment was boasted in other areas, conventional ladders remained the miners lot as they descended at the beginning of each shift to the dark depths below. By that February the previously abandoned 55 fathom level had been cleared the 170 yards to the former boundary and six men had been set to drive the level into the new sett.[30]

During 1882 steady if unspectacular progress was made driving 55, 78 and 108 fathom levels from the old boundary deep into the new sett. Soon the 108 became the centre of activity and by December 1882 this level was being enthusiastically pressed forward; modern rock boring machinery being reported in use.[31] The mine's inventory on closure included one Barrow and three Eclipse rock drills, unheard of equipment in the former Wheal Trelawny and Wheal Mary Ann workings.[32] Whilst clearly a revolution for the management of the mine, their advantages were less obvious to the working miner as deafening noise and choking stone dust became an additional hazard faced at the cramped, ill lit and poorly ventilated rock face.

Meanwhile favourable probing in the centre of the sett had led to the commencement of Derry's shaft late in 1881 and this had reached a depth of

THE
Wheal Hony and Trelawny United Silver-Lead Mining Company, Limited.

Registered under the Limited Liability Acts of 1862 and 1867, by which the liability of the shareholder is limited to the amount of his shares.

CAPITAL £50,000, IN 25,000 SHARES OF £2 EACH.

ISSUE OF 17,750 SHARES AT PAR OF £2 EACH.

PAYABLE:—10s. per share on application; 10s. per share on allotment; 10s. per share on 1st August, 1880; and 10s. per share on 1st September, 1880.
In cases where no allotment is made the money paid on application will be returned in full.

DIRECTORS.

G. BROCKELBANK, Esq., Thornsett Road, Anerley.
S. BURNEY WARNER, Esq., B.A., 23, Stanhope Gardens, South Kensington.

J. ROMANES, Esq., Heene Terrace, West Worthing.
E. PALMER, Esq., 7, Tresillean Crescent, St. John's, S.E.; and Folkestone.

SOLICITOR—F. ROMER, Esq., 13, Warwick-court, Holborn.
BANKERS—Messrs. ROBARTS, LUBBOCK, and CO., Lombard-street, London.
Messrs. CLYMO, TREFFRY, HAWKE, WEST, POLKINGHORNE, and CO., Liskeard.
AUDITORS—Messrs. COOPER, WINTLE, and CO., Coleman Street Buildings, E.C.
ENGINEERS—Messrs. LOAM AND SONS, Liskeard.
SECRETARY—Mr. H. R. LEWIS.

OFFICES,—BARTHOLOMEW HOUSE, BARTHOLOMEW LANE, LONDON.

PROSPECTUS.

This company is formed for puchasing and working a property rich in silver-lead, known as Hony Estate, situate near Liskeard, Cornwall, together with the celebrated Wheal Trelawny Silver-Lead Mine immediately adjoining on the south.

The Hony property comprises the mineral riches of the great silver-lead bearing lode in Cornwall, intact from the very surface to a depth already proved of 300 fathoms, extending nearly half a mile in length from the boundaries of the Wheal Trelawny on the south to the celebrated Treweatha on the north.

The estate was the property of the late Dr. Hony, who had firmly resolved never to sell or let it, notwithstanding the repeated solicitations of capitalists and the most tempting offers.

The offers were made owing to the extraordinary richness of the silver-lead bearing lode in the celebrated Wheal Mary Ann and Trelawny on the south, Treweatha on the north, and the continuance of the lode without variation right through Hony property from boundary to boundary. During the lifetime of Dr. Hony the Trelawny miners encroached beyond their boundary on the Hony estate, and extracted some silver-lead ore, for which the Wheal Trelawny Company had to pay large sum of money by way of compensation.

The rich mineral deposit consists of a strongly compressed and concentrated silver-lead bearing lode from 3 to 6 ft. wide, which may be considered proved from the surface to a depth of 300 fathoms, extending the whole length of the property, and containing the richest ore in large paying quantities. It averages about 1 ton of silver-lead ore per fathom, and as the ore contains from 50 to 60 ozs. of silver per ton the value per fathom is estimated at over £2C.

The mine having been so proved to a depth of 300 fms. on a run of 330 fms., it is calculated that the quantity of workable silver-lead ore is of the value of about

ONE MILLION SIX HUNDRED THOUSAND POUNDS STERLING.

The adjoining mines, Wheal Mary Ann, Wheal Trelawny, and Treweatha, re-turned silver-lead ore worth over £1,500,000 sterling from the same lode, and paid very large dividends to shareholders.

Capt. Hancock, Grenfell, Pearce, Willcocks, Hodge, and Metherell, who have known the property from 20 to 30 years, verify the above statements, and give full details in their reports, copies of which may be had at the offices of the company.

Capt. HANCOCK says:—" I have known the ground for 30 years, and worked in the Trelawny Mine, near Hony, about 24 years ago; since then was agent in the district under the late Mr. Peter Clymo. It is one of the best (if not the best) pieces of mining ground for silver-lead in the county, and cannot, in my opinion, fail to make a good dividend property."

Capt. WILLCOCKS writes:—" Whoever is fortunate enough to secure this property will have the most profitable mine in the county and a certain fortune."

Capt. METHERELL says:—" The lode may be considered proved to 300 fms., so that there is no speculation or risk. I will merely add that I know of no other property with such certainty of success."

Capt. HODGE writes:—" I have not the slightest hesitation in saying that there is not another mining property in the kingdom with such prospects and such a certainty of immense profit, and having such advantages for economical and speedy development."

Mr. Matthew Loam (the company's engineer) writes: " If there is any confidence in Cornish mines, this scheme is worthy of it."

Estimated cost of raising and dressing 1 ton of ore, and expenses of management £8 0 0

	£	s	d
Yield one cubic fathom — one ton value	20	0	0
Cost, as above	8	0	0
Profit per ton	£12	0	0

150 tons per month at £12, or a net profit of £21,600 per annum, being 43 per cent, per annum on the entire share capital of the company.

This estimate does not include profits that may arise from the deeper working of the Wheal Trelawny. In the opinion of the best captains, the Wheal Trelawny will help to swell the dividends of the company.

The shafts sunk in the Wheal Trelawny are available for pumping and winding the ore, thus saving an immense amount of time, and enabling the silver-lead ore to be speedily raised and made marketable.

High-roads pass through the property, and the Liskeard and Menheniot Stations of the Cornwall Railway are each within about two miles of the property, rendering the carriage of silver-lead and materials very convenient and inexpensive.

The following are the names and dates of the agreements and leases for acquisition of the property:—1st June, 1880, Messrs. Hony, Iliffe, and Russell and Messrs. Hamley and Derry; 28th May, 1880, C. Trelawny and Messrs. Hamley and Derry; 31st June, 1880, W. K. Milborne and Messrs. Hamley and Derry.

Prospectuses, with forms of application for shares, can be obtained at the Offices of the Company, solicitor, bankers, and auditors. The reports, plans, and agreements above referred to may be inspected at the Company's offices.

The vendors provide all expenses necessary to the formation of the Company up to allotment. £5 per cent. per annum discount will be allowed for prepayments. Priority of application will be considered.

Wheal Hony and Trelawny United was launched with maximum publicity, this large advertisement being placed in the London published *Mining Journal* on 3 July 1880.

21 fathoms by February 1882. The centre of the sett was now recognised as the most likely point for the lode to strengthen and the 55, 78 and 108 levels were being driven steadily northwards towards that point. Whilst the 90-inch at Smith's remained controlling pumping operations, at Derry's preparations for whim haulage and ore dressing were in hand. Dressing floors were completed and excavations dug for a wheel pit and crusher house by the end of 1882. By that date the shaft had reached a depth of 55 fathoms and basic dressing had commenced, in advance of installation of more sophisticated equipment. A good parcel of ore had been built up for sale early in the new year. All of this had come as a by-product of the development work and was still small recompense when set against the significant outlay.

As 1883 dawned it had to be admitted that a year of hard driving had produced promising indications but no spectacular break through. However January 1883 saw excitement rising as the 108 steadily improved and men were set to break away the moderate ore-ground so far opened up. Increasing criticism was being voiced by distant investors at the lack of dividends, linked to dissatisfaction with the lengthy development phase. At the end of 1882 a change in local management took place when William Hancock left the mine. We do not know if he resigned or whether dissatisfaction forced him out. By June 1885 he was dead, at the age of 57, and buried in Liskeard churchyard.

William Derry immediately took over as manager. The locally based businessman, with a significant 10% shareholding, had been with Matthew Loam the driving force behind the speculation from conception to development. He once light heartedly told a shareholders' meeting he had been, 'Almost constantly on the mine and when he was absent in body he was there in spirit'. Until that time he had not held a formal position in the company, although his name had always been associated with progress reports. Now his role at the heart of the development was formalised and he would remain in charge at the mine until closure.[30]

As understanding of the improved strength of the lode in the centre of the sett increased, another new shaft, Lewis's, was started 330 yards north of Derry's. By May 1883 this had been sunk 10 fathoms from surface in extremely promising ground and evidence that this was the area of greatest promise increased.[33] With hindsight a growing body of opinion now expressed the view that following the lode at depth from the former Trelawny mine had proved both costly and slow and was the root cause of gathering financial storm clouds. Why, they echoed, if the previously described new shaft at Lewis's was seen to be at the centre of promising ore ground had not a new shaft in the centre of the sett been pursued from inception. In reality if a strong lode had been found as the boundary had been crossed the story would have been very different, but the fact the argument was taking place at all was indicative of collapsing confidence in this extensive project. Meanwhile whilst methodology was being criticised, far more significantly the price of lead on the market was falling.

Clear signs were there to be seen of an underfunded company sinking into deep trouble. At an early stage Brenton Symons felt the company was over ambitious and recommended that, 'Operations be confined to the main lode, because in truth the property is so extensive that the present capital is only sufficient to attack it in detail'.[34] The setting up of East Hony mine as a separate company directly stemmed from this, driven by the need to raise extra capital for this second project. At the June 1883 meeting it was admitted that the whole of the original capital of £50,000 was now spent plus a further £10,000 raised from debentures, although acting chairman Keppel Garnier was at great pains to justify that a great deal had been achieved for that money. Indeed his passionate commitment from the chair, in the face of rising criticism, secured support to raise a further £25,000 to fund an extension of the project.[35] Time however was running out for Wheal Hony & Trelawny United and whether investors were prepared to commit a further £25,000 to the project was another question.

Meanwhile in the relative tranquillity of Menheniot practical operations continued. Signs were beginning to emerge that the property was at last coming right. By July 1883 William Derry was able to report the temporarily disordered lode had been recut in the 108 and was of the finest possible

Wheal Hony and Trelawny United. Mine offices and weighbridge still standing over 100 years after closure. *S. Bartlett 1989*

character.[36] Three months later it was reported that the 78 and 108 levels were being driven north at the rate of 30 yards per month by a committed workforce.[37] William Derry continued to speak highly of their prospects, but real progress was starkly revealed by the 1883 annual production return of only 58 tons of lead ore. This has to be compared with over 1,000 tons per year from each of Wheal Mary Ann and Wheal Trelawny many years before.

Like so many concerns before, whilst the manager in far off Menheniot continued to talk encouragingly of minor successes and long term plans, an announcement broke from the company's registered office in London at the beginning of January 1884 that the concern was to be wound up.[38] Clearly attempts to raise the additional £25,000 in capital had failed. This coupled

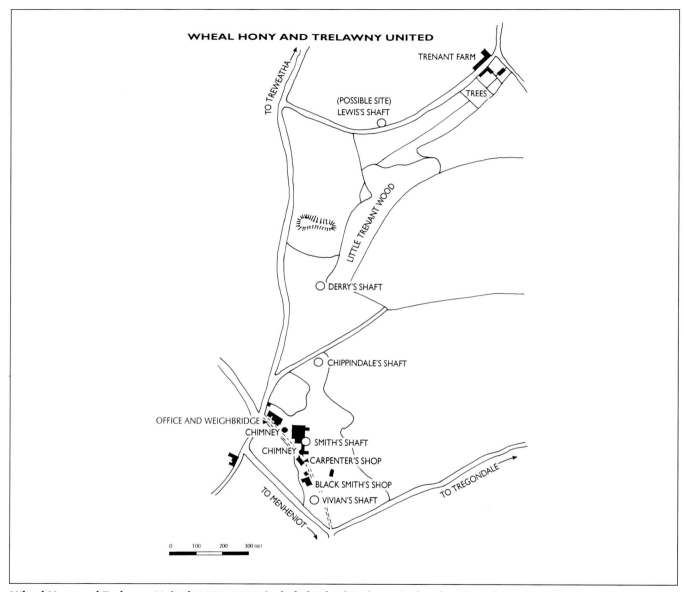

WHEAL HONY AND TRELAWNY UNITED

TO TREWEATHA

TRENANT FARM

(POSSIBLE SITE)
LEWIS'S SHAFT

TREES

LITTLE TRENANT WOOD

○ DERRY'S SHAFT

○ CHIPPINDALE'S SHAFT

OFFICE AND WEIGHBRIDGE
CHIMNEY
○ SMITH'S SHAFT
CHIMNEY
CARPENTER'S SHOP
BLACK SMITH'S SHOP
○ VIVIAN'S SHAFT

TO MENHENIOT

TO TREGONDALE

0   100   200   300 FEET

Wheal Hony and Trelawny United (1880–1884) included Wheal Trelawny's abandoned northern site as the centre of its surface operations and new shafts at Derry's and Lewis's

Derry's Shaft, Wheal Hony and Trelawny United. Sunk in 1881 and abandoned upon closure in 1884, located in the centre of this large sett. The site is marked by the light area, centre left. *S. Bartlett 1991*

Lewis's Shaft, Wheal Hony and Trelawny United. Probable shaft site the scrubby ground immediately behind the lane hedge in the foreground. Started early in 1883 and abandoned in 1884. *S. Bartlett 1991*

with the depressed state of the lead market hastened the inevitable end to an ambitious and some would have said reckless project. It had bravely sought to revitalise Menheniot's mining heritage in genuine virgin ground, despite mining expert J. Y. Watson's repeated claims to the contrary - a strange lapse from a man who earlier knew Menheniot well. The venture is best described as a genuine, if naive attempt given the state of the industry, to launch a project which unquestionably would have yielded reasonable success had the mineral rights been released thirty years earlier in a strong market. At the same time it would then have been supported by other mines sharing pumping operations on all sides - Treweatha to the north and Wheal Trelawny and Wheal Mary Ann to the south.

Winding up procedures were initiated in January 1884 and the first task was the merging of the separate companies Hony & Trelawny United and East Hony, as a legal move to ease winding up arrangements. The merger had no visible effect in distant Menheniot.[39] George Brockelbank and John Romanes, chairman and director at inception, were formally established as liquidators.[40]

A public auction was held on the mine in August 1885, some twenty months after winding up was first announced. In fact thirty tons of lead ore was brought to surface during 1884 and it is clear operations continued on a limited scale for some time, ensuring withdrawal was made in an orderly fashion. The August 1885 auction included the 90-inch pumping engine with six 11 ton boilers, a steam whim engine with two boilers, a Phoenix compound pumping engine, a pair of horizontal engines with capstan and winding cage, an air compressor, two donkey engines and one 40 feet

waterwheel. Also included were the one Barrow and three Eclipse rock drills, as well as modern dressing machinery.[32]

The sale proved depressing in the extreme. None of the heavy pitwork was said to have been sold and about 300 miscellaneous lots went at low prices.[41] Only £950 was bid for the 90-inch engine, which was withdrawn from sale to gather rust awaiting a serious bidder. Eventually in 1888 the 90-inch engine was bought by the Whicham Mining Company for their iron mine near Millom, Cumberland. The long journey was made by sea that November aboard the steamer *Wansfell* to Barrow in Furness for onward transit by rail to Millom. Storms and bad stowage caused damage to various parts on the arduous voyage, but the engine was to be found at work at its new location a year later.[45] So ended Menheniot's last major mining venture and with it the hopes of those miners who remained in the parish.

EAST HONY (1882-1884) formed the north-eastern corner of Wheal Hony & Trelawny United's ground and was structured as a separate company for financial reasons to enable additional capital to be raised. By June 1881 Hony & Trelawny United, through the digging of shallow pits over a wide area across its extensive property, had uncovered three new lodes of varying quality; one attracting particular attention and this became known as the Brockelbank lode. A crosscut adit was immediately brought up from the valley south of Trenant Farm and had intersected the lode by the end of June. Manager William Hancock then turned attention to driving on the course of the lode and word soon spread that a secondary area of major exploration was emerging in northern Menheniot.[28]

By February 1882 instructions had been given to sink a shaft on to the

Wheal Hony and Trelawny United. Menheniot's most prominent remaining mine landmark, a memorial to a singularly unsuccessful venture.

S. Bartlett 1991

St Mary's Lead Works (1902). Built to process lead waste from the former Wheal Mary Ann site, photographed soon after operations commenced.

adit, with the intention of sinking on the course of the lode below that point to a depth of 50 to 80 fathoms. This had already reached three fathoms below adit level by this time and was timbered throughout. William Hancock also reported that a second-hand 24-inch engine had been purchased at a moderate price for drainage and that the engine house and necessary buildings, presumably of fairly limited extent, were in a forward state.[30]

By this time negotiations were well advanced to form an independent company to be called The East Hony Mining Co. Ltd. with a capital of £50,000 in £1 shares. Present shareholders were offered first option at purchasing shares in the new company. To secure a proper run on the lode it was necessary to negotiate a lease for an adjacent piece of ground, owned by Archdeacon Woollcombe, and this was secured at a premium of £300.[30]

It was therefore with the company's customary enthusiasm that

development work was put in hand. It appears that the agents of the parent mine directed the practical affairs at East Hony throughout its short existence. In 1882 eight surface workers were reported as employed. From that point development suffered the same ups and downs as the parent mine and as funds became exhausted the joint decision to commence winding up proceedings, taken in January 1884, saw first the merging of the two companies and then the rundown of practical operations.[39] Mine materials were auctioned in the joint sale in August 1885, some twenty months after winding up was first announced.[32]

Sole reference to TREGONDALE MINE was found amongst a list of properties managed by H. R. Lewis & Co. of Bartholomew Lane, London, in the City's *Post Office Directory* of 1887. H. R. Lewis had by coincidence been the company secretary of both Wheal Hony & Trelawny United and East Hony mines. No records exist of any work ever being done on site, or of the precise location of the mine. Tregondale Farm is to be found three quarters of a mile east of Wheal Hony & Trelawny United's original surface works and about the same distance south of Trenant farm, near the former East Hony mine. The area carries some logic as a latterday small scale operation re-visiting these once tried lodes.

During the 1890s pesticides were in great demand due to the bol-weevil epidemic in the United States then ravaging the southern cotton crop and arsenic remained the prime source for dealing with this problem until artificial pesticides killed the trade. The Tamar Valley mines gained great prominence in arsenic production during this period, particularly the famed Devon Great Consols, and it was claimed that the Liskeard area played its own part in this trade. Previous general works on Cornish mining have incorrectly claimed that Wheal Trelawny was again reworked in connection with this activity under the title ANGLO PENINSULA MINING & CHEMICAL COMPANY (1896-1902) for Arsenic Pyrite.

By returning to original newspaper sources it has been possible to establish that this operation in fact took place at New Trelawny (sometimes known as Gang Mine) in the parish of St Ive and not in Menheniot at all. The misquoted previous references all appear to lead back to one common source; an incorrect entry in the official annual mining statistics of the day. A sobering reminder of the potential pitfalls which await latter day mining chroniclers. No doubt the present residents of Menheniot will not be too upset to hear that arsenic production does not appear to have been a feature of their recent past.

Despite the end of deep mining, Menheniot's story was still not finished as successive companies reworked the remaining tips. Today their much reduced remains have largely blended into the natural surroundings. In 1900 however these still stood bare and gaunt, tumbling down the steep slopes west and north of Wheal Mary Ann, rising again within yards on to the former Wheal Trehane site. Much of this area in turn was buried under

Wheal Trelawny waste, brought across the lane from the latter's southern site, the location of the present Trelawny residence, probably by a system of overhead buckets. A little further north and in front of the surviving chimney, lay the substantial tips of Wheal Trelawny's northern site whilst further north still lay Treweatha's remains. All have been worked to varying degrees by companies who moved thousands of tons before the first world war, again between the wars and in varying degrees up to recent times.

ST MARYS LEAD WORKS was built to process lead waste, principally from the Wheal Mary Ann site and was located to the left of the lane beyond the mine, hidden behind the steep slope which forms the mine's northern boundary. Preparatory work commenced in mid-1900 and by December a small engine house and boiler house had been completed and tram lines laid around the tips. At the same time a Wilfley concentrator and other equipment were in an advanced state of installation and practical operations were scheduled to commence in mid-December.[42] By September 1901 the works was in full production, with 21 tons of silver lead sold to Sheldon, Bush and Co. in the previous six weeks and a further 80 tons of middlings waiting treatment by the jigs. 50 ounces of silver to each ton of lead was being separated, a valuable secondary source of income well known to those mining men who had gone before.[43]

The company's fortunes seem to have fluctuated according to market conditions and it is likely this small operation closed and re-opened on a number of occasions before and after the first world war. The original company was shown in voluntary liquidation in 1908, whilst in March 1913 it was reported that operations were about to restart following the then rising price of lead.[44] One suspects the first world war would have had some influence, but despite the difficult economic years which followed the company, then formally titled St Mary's Lead Works Ltd., was shown to have been taken over by Menheniot Lead Works Ltd. in March 1926. Operations continued into recent living memory and undoubtedly older members of the Menheniot community may recall the works still in operation.

CHAPTER TWELVE
CONCLUSION

AS THE STORY of Menheniot's mines draws to a close it is worth reflecting upon the long road we have travelled since 1843 and in particular the kaleidoscope of change that embraced the parish between the 1840s and 1870s, the latter period marking the end of large scale mining in Menheniot. The long ago census of 1841 had contained no clues as to what might emerge, revealing a sleepy agricultural community little changed over the previous centuries. Yet not far away in Liskeard an important business centre for the rapidly expanding Caradon copper mines was growing, providing a nucleus of mining expertise ready to speculate should new areas of mining promise emerge. Critically, as towns and cities were expanding, the demand by the Victorian building trade for lead was growing rapidly too and the scene was set for speculators to descend on unsuspecting Menheniot once the presence of previously undiscovered lead deposits was established.

The richest mines we now know were north of the village strung out in a line from north to south, starting with Treweatha, then Wheal Trelawny, Wheal Trehane and lastly near the village Wheal Mary Ann. These were as we have seen joined by smaller speculative concerns which clustered around the edges of the rich central lead lode like bees around a honeypot, none ever to find the fortune they so enthusiastically sought and tending to survive but a few short years before disappearing as quickly as they had arrived on the scene.

Expansion in those early years saw each mine grow from small beginnings until by 1851 Wheal Trelawny employed 408, Wheal Mary Ann 422, Wheal Trehane 100 and by 1854 Treweatha was also in full production with 125. It is worth remembering more than a third of those employed at each mine were in fact women and children, supplementing family income on the dressing floors, with some of the young mine boys additionally working underground. Initially some Menheniot farm labourers, along with tradesmen such as carpenters and masons, were recruited by the new companies. However, experienced miners were essential in those early days and what is best described as an army of migrant workers steadily poured into the parish, followed closely by wives and young families. Western Cornwall, the St Austell area and the Devon border around Tavistock dominated the influx; the latter categories in the main western men too who were now moving on to more promising horizons.

Despite this kaleidoscope of change, within ten years a settled community had emerged, growing mining families beginning to blend with their farm labouring neighbours. Despite the hardships and deprivations of a tough industry steady and, for the best tributers, well paid employment by the standards of the day were experienced. It is well recorded that higher wage rates were paid in east Cornwall than in the western mines. As time moved on the second decade saw the proportion of Menheniot born miners rapidly increasing to a degree that took them beyond a role of labouring support to their experienced western colleagues. Likewise mine boys and girls were often by then recruited from farm labouring households, where ten years before it was the immigrant workforce which had almost exclusively provided the young mine boys and girls for the mines. It is worth remembering Menheniot would have been characterised at this time by the relative youth of its population, initially a large group of single men balanced by an equally large proportion of young married miners with small children. In 1851 Crift Cottages typified the start of this period, where behind the sixteen miners' cottage doors were eleven children aged one year or less, only two of whom had actually been born in Menheniot.

The good times were however not to last and the third decade saw the process of first the large mines experiencing financial problems, followed by the long struggle that led to ultimate closure. As the 1860s progressed and the black years of 1871 to 1874 approached, more Menheniot men followed the earlier road taken by their western counterparts, finding work in distant lands wherever the mining calling took them. South Australia figured prominently amongst the chosen destinations and it is known that here at least Menheniot exiles were in sufficient quantities to gravitate together in the distant communities of that state, notably around Moonta; a common bond and memory of far off Menheniot sustaining them as they established new lives in a new land. Never had Menheniot's postman been so eagerly awaited as aged parents or temporarily separated families waited for news from the far corners of the world.

We should not forget either the Victorian businessmen and practical management teams who were the driving force behind the investment and development of the group of mines central to our story. Deep mining involved a long, expensive and unpredictable development period requiring stout hearts and flexible bank balances which, given luck and sound judgement, could for a few produce significant returns. For some it could even make fortunes. Mining histories can become a protracted list of dates and impersonal events; it is hoped that here these Victorian men of industry and practical expertise, names now long forgotten in the mists of time, have been rightly placed at the centre of each mine's story where they so correctly belong.

Lastly we should not forget Menheniot itself, a rich agricultural parish by nature, characterised by deeply undulating hills and valleys. Here wherever nature is allowed to run riot high hedgerows and a dense lush coverage of bushes and thickly wooded areas dominate. Set amongst it are a network of sunken winding lanes leading to the central village square, dominated by the large parish church. This combination of rich agricultural land and lush natural cover has today conspired to hide Menheniot's past and to the casual observer it is probably only the surviving chimney of Wheal Hony & Trelawny United, now lonely and unsupported by an adjacent engine house, which gives any clue to Menheniot's mining past. No spectacular engine houses remain here to tempt the visitor, unlike those which dominate Caradon Hill and the cliffs of western Cornwall, although less spectacular secrets lie hidden for the more persistent searcher to find.

Indeed, when the quest to uncover the full story of Menheniot's mines and the community they supported was embarked upon, many facts proved as elusive to uncover as those hidden remains. With persistence much has now become clearer and it is hoped that in doing so a greatly improved knowledge of the locality's past has been gained and rightfully set down.

Perhaps the last word belongs to the miners themselves who wherever possible have been given equal prominence with the mines, although their stories have often proved even more elusive to uncover than that of the structures themselves. A great deal of space has been given wherever possible to the make up, origins and movement of the ordinary working miner. Their stories too have hopefully enhanced our understanding of the life and the times of a Cornish mining village, typical in many ways but unique in others.

ADIT Horizontal tunnel for naturally draining the mine, usually commenced from an adjacent valley.

ADVENTURER Partner or shareholder in a Cornish mine.

ATTLE Rubbish containing little or no ore.

BACK That part of the lode nearest the surface.

BAL Cornish term for a mine.

BEARERS Supports to the pumps in the engine shaft.

BOB The engine beam.

BRANCH A small vein which separates from the lode.

BURROW A heap of deads, attle, rubbish.

CALL Payment owed by Adventurers to balance mine debts and provide for next period of working.

CASING Wooden planks dividing a shaft into separate compartments.

CAUNTER LODE A lode which inclines at a considerable angle to the other lodes in the area.

COLLAR The timber by which the upper parts of a shaft are kept from falling together.

CONNECTING RODS The large rods attached to the engine beam.

CORE Miners' shift, usually of six hours.

COST BOOK System of mine book-keeping regulated by the Stannary Laws of Cornwall.

COSTEANING Sinking of shallow pits in the exploratory search for lodes.

CROP The best ore.

CROSS-COURSE A lode or vein which crosses or intersects the main lode at an angle.

CROSS-CUT A level driven at right angles to the direction of the lode.

DEADS Rubbish containing little or no ore.

DEAD-GROUND A portion of the lode in which there is no ore.

DIALLING Surveying a mine.

DRESSING Cleaning and preparing the ore.

DRIVING Extending a level horizontally.

END The furthest extent of a level.

ENGINEMAN Man who attends to and works the mine engine.

ENGINE SHAFT Shaft for pumping water to drain the mine

FATHOM Measurement of mine depth, equal to six feet.

FLAT RODS Rods for horizontally transmitting motion from the engine to a remote location.

FOOTWAY The ladders used by miners to descend into the mine.

FORK A shaft or mine 'in-fork' is one which has been pumped clear of water.

GOSSAN Oxide of iron and quartz.

GRASS The surface of a mine.

HALVANS Ores not sufficiently rich to be offered for sale without further removal of impurities.

HORSE The dead ground between two branches of a lode at the point of their separation.

JUNCTION Point at which veins unite.

KIBBLE A bucket for drawing ore to the surface.

KILLAS Clay slate.

LAUNDERS Gutters for the drainage of water, usually made of wood.

LEAT A watercourse.

LEAVINGS The ores which are left after the best is taken out.

LEVELS Galleries driven horizontally on the lode, usually at ten-fathom intervals.

LODE The regular vein containing ore.

PARCEL A heap of ore dressed and ready for sale.

PARE (or **PAIR**) Gang of mining men of indeterminate number.

PITCH Piece of ground let to tributers.

PITMAN One employed to look after the lifts of pumps and the drainage.

PITWORK The pumps and other apparatus of the engine shaft.

PLAT Ground taken away underground to store ores or deads, usually adjacent to the shaft.

PURSER The cashier or mine paymaster.

RISING Digging upwards towards the surface.

RUN When excavations fall together.

RUN OF A LODE Its direction.

SETTING DAY Day on which tribute pitches in a mine are auctioned.

SLIDE Vertical dislocation of the lode.

SOLLAR A small platform at the base of a ladder.

STAMPS Machinery for crushing ores using water.

STOPE Level from which ore is taken.

STRING A small vein.

STUFF Deads or rubbish.

SUMP Bottom of the engine shaft.

SUMP SHAFT The engine shaft.

SUMPMEN Men who attend the machinery in the engine shaft.

TAMPING Material, usually soft stone, for packing a gunpowder charge.

TICKETING The sale of ores.

TRIBUTER Miner paid by proportion of the ore raised.

TUTWORKER Miner paid for driving at a certain price per fathom.

UNDERLAY SHAFT Shaft sunk at a slight angle, on the course of the lode, as opposed to vertical.

WHIM Apparatus worked by horse, steam or water for raising ore.

WINZE An underground shaft sunk between two levels, but not upwards to the surface.

Edited from the *Mining Journal* 1848

APPENDIX B
MENHENIOT'S PRINCIPAL MINES LEAD ORE AND SILVER PRODUCTION

YEAR	WHEAL TRELAWNY ORE (tons)	SILVER (ozs)	WHEAL MARY ANN ORE (tons)	SILVER (ozs)	WHEAL TREHANE ORE (tons)	SILVER (ozs)	TREWEATHA ORE (tons)	SILVER (ozs)
1843	–	–	–	–	–	–	–	–
1844	–	–	–	–	–	–	–	–
1845	280	–	–	–	–	–	–	–
1846	529	–	166	–	–	–	–	–
1847	883	–	192	–	312	–	–	–
1848	413	–	334	–	422	–	–	–
1849	1296	–	873	–	460	–	–	–
1850	1496	–	1186	–	430	–	–	–
1851	1112	–	1265	–	414	–	–	–
1852	972	33906	995	38600	506	22000	–	–
1853	979	29797	1005	40160	473	14574	78	4866
1854	783	26174	1100	44470	570	14580	331	19320
1855	837	26235	1111	46530	459	14996	316	13884
1856	1029	34093	1314	52638	313	12876	351	5598
1857	1108	39075	1597	61625	172	623	336	14190
1858	1307	49000	1428	59796	–	–	215	8694
1859	1333	49950	1418	59400	–	–	133	5383
1860	1251	47000	1194	49632	–	–	154	585
1861	798	31150	1135	42761	–	–	10	112
1862	1005	42080	911	44060	–	–	39	432
1863	1074	45990	845	42402	–	–	105	1044
1864	800	38034	752	35464	–	–	89	858
1865	833	37770	730	33120	–	–	36	726
1866	879	30464	830	38000	–	–	142	2980
1867	1272	51516	1049	56199	–	–	314	9938
1868	756	30618	1140	61061	–		184	5754
1869	875	35964	1006	53911	–	–	340	10704
1870	390	15768	942	50610	–	–	356	11214
1871	363	14688	1048	56199	–	–	687	21630
1872	–	–	1254	67210	–	–	155	7464
1873	–	–	760	40399	–	–	–	–
1874	–	–	538	28850	–	–	–	–
1875	–	–	6	–	–	–	–	–
TOTAL	24653	709272	28124	1103097	4531	79649	4371	145376

Source: Mineral Statistics from *Cornish Mines*, University of Exeter Press 1987

APPENDIX C
MENHENIOT'S MINES - NUMBERS EMPLOYED

MINE	WORKED	1846	1849	1851	1853	1854	1856	1862	1863	1867	1868	1870
Wheal Trelawny	1843-71	130	360	408	N/A	N/A	300	450	N/A	N/A	363	355
Wheal Mary Ann	1845-74	15	125	422	N/A	N/A	310	350	N/A	300	N/A	300
Wheal Trehane	1846-57	N/A	100	100	N/A	N/A	N/A	–	–	–	–	–
Treweatha	1852-72	–	–	–	N/A	125	125	20	37	N/A	N/A	174
South Wheal Trelawny	1845-54	N/A	N/A	12	N/A	N/A	–	–	–	–	–	–
Butterdon	1850-57	–	–	N/A	N/A	N/A	20	–	–	–	–	–
Wheal Venton	1850-58	–	–	N/A	N/A	N/A	N/A	–	–	–	–	–
Penhauger	1850-61	–	–	N/A	N/A	N/A	N/A	–	–	–	–	–
South Wheal Mary Ann	1853	–	–	–	2	–	–	–	–	–	–	–
East Trelawny	1854-56	–	–	–	–	N/A	N/A	–	–	–	–	–
Lambest Consols	1856-58	–	–	–	–	–	N/A	–	–	–	–	–
Hendra Consols	1866	–	–	–	–	–	–	–	–	–	–	–

NOTE: (N/A) Figures not available

(–) Mine not open

ADDITIONAL INFORMATION

1851	Wheal Mary Ann	Total 422 comprising:	280 men, 68 women, 74 children
1851	Wheal Trelawny	Total 408 comprising:	258 men, 72 women, 78 children
1856	Wheal Mary Ann	Total 310 comprising:	200 men, 110 women and children
1856	Wheal Trelawny	Total 300 comprising:	200 men, 100 women and children
1856	Treweatha	Total 125 comprising:	75 men, 50 women and children
1868	Wheal Trelawny	Total 363 comprising:	206 men tutwork/tribute, 25 trammen and fillers underground, 132 men/boys/girls at surface

MINE	WORKED	1875	1876	1877	1878	1879	1880	1881	1882	1883	1884
West Mary Ann	1875-84	N/A	N/A	N/A	17	13	13	13	10	20	16
Wheal Hony +Trelawny Ltd	1880-84	–	–	–	–	–	45	85	94	87	50
East Hony	1882-84	–	–	–	–	–	–	–	8	N/A	N/A
Tregondale	1887	–	–	–	–	–	–	–	–	–	–

NOTE: (N/A) Figures not available

APPENDIX D
POPULATION STATISTICS FOR THE PARISH OF MENHENIOT.

YEAR	POPULATION	HOUSES INHABITED	HOUSES UNINHABITED	HOUSES BEING BUILT
1801	918	150	11	–
1811	1024	171	10	1
1821	1170	N/A	N/A	N/A
1831	1253	200	3	1
1841	1221	237	10	–
1851	1944	315	6	10
1861	2423	433	13	2
1871	2205	434	33	1
1881	1373	306	94	4
1891	1191	277	71	–
1901	1183	288	N/A	N/A

NOTE: (N/A) Information not available

APPENDIX E
1851 MENHENIOT POPULATION BY OCCUPATION AND AGE PROFILE

OCCUPATION		TOTAL	UNDER 15	15-19	20-29	30-39	40-49	50-59	OVER 60
Lead Miner		226	–	37	114	42	18	13	2
Mine Labourer		55	38	12	3	2	–	–	–
Mine Girl		57	14	27	14	1	1	–	–
Copper Miner		5	–	1	1	1	2	–	–
Mine Agent		6	–	–	1	1	3	1	–
Mine Engineer/Engineman		10	–	1	4	2	3	–	–
Mine Clerk/Cook		2	–	–	1	1	–	–	–
TOTAL MINING		361	52	78	138	50	27	14	2
Farm Labourer		205	25	34	42	35	26	18	25
Farm Servant		35	15	11	7	1	–	1	–
Farmer		50	–	–	3	12	11	12	12
TOTAL FARMING		290	40	45	52	48	37	31	37
House Servant		86	10	33	31	5	3	2	2
Blacksmith		25	4	7	7	3	2	–	2
Carpenter		25	–	3	9	6	1	4	2
Miller		16	–	3	2	6	3	1	1
Shoemaker		16	1	4	4	2	2	1	2
Dressmaker		10	–	5	3	2	–	–	–
Mason		9	–	1	2	–	1	3	2
Tailor		5	–	–	1	2	2	–	–
Housekeeper		3	–	–	1	–	1	–	–
Woodman		3	–	1	–	–	2	–	–
Cook		2	–	–	1	–	–	1	–
Governess/Nurse		4	–	–	1	–	–	1	2
Postman		2	–	–	–	1	–	–	1
Schoolmaster		2	–	–	2	–	–	–	–
Vicar/Curate		2	–	–	–	1	1	–	–
Waggoner		2	–	1	1	–	–	–	–
Others Working (*)		25	1	5	3	4	6	2	4
TOTAL GENERAL		237	16	63	68	32	24	15	19
Scholars	M.	117	113	4	–	–	–	–	–
	F.	115	114	1	–	–	–	–	–
Parish Relief		38	–	–	–	–	1	2	35
No Occupation (!)	M.	194	182	7	1	–	2	1	1
	F.	569	186	36	98	98	70	45	36
GRAND TOTAL		1921	703	234	357	228	161	108	130

NOTES

(*)   Comprises one groom, errand boy, highway labourer, parish sexton, private means, solicitors clerk, tollgate keeper, brassfounder, butcher, confectioner, cooper, corn merchant, draper and grocer, iron foundry labourer, iron moulder, leatherworker, printer, potato merchant, saddler and harness maker, innkeeper, house proprietor, washerwomen (2) and drapers assistant (2).

(!)   Mostly children (other than scholars) and housewives.

(M)   Male   (F)   Female

APPENDIX F
MENHENIOT CHILD OCCUPATION AND AGE PROFILE

1841 – CHILDS AGES

OCCUPATION		TOTAL	14	13	12	11	10	9	8 AND UNDER
No Status	M.	196	3	7	8	11	17	12	138
	F.	202	13	9	10	10	17	7	136
Farm Servant	M.	39	9	7	7	1	12	1	2
	F.	16	2	4	6	1	2	–	1
Farm Labourer		4	–	2	1	–	–	1	–
House Servant		2	1	–	–	–	1	–	–
Servant Miller		2	1	1	–	–	–	–	–
TOTAL		461	29	30	32	23	49	21	277

1851 - CHILDS AGES

OCCUPATION		TOTAL	14	13	12	11	10	9	8 AND UNDER
Scholar	M.	113	1	3	6	7	10	19	67
	F.	114	4	3	14	13	10	13	57
No Status	M.	182	3	2	2	4	4	3	164
	F.	186	6	2	4	7	6	7	154
Mine Boy	M.	38	10	5	8	8	3	2	2
Mine Girl	F.	14	4	3	3	2	1	–	1
Farm Servant		15	5	1	4	4	1	–	–
Farm Labourer		25	6	7	7	2	2	1	–
House Servant		10	3	2	2	3	–	–	–
Millers Labourer		1	1	–	–	–	–	–	–
Blacksmith		4	1	1	2	–	–	–	–
Errand Boy		1	–	–	–	1	–	–	–
TOTAL		703	44	29	52	51	37	45	445

1861 - CHILDS AGES

OCCUPATION		TOTAL	14	13	12	11	10	9	8 AND UNDER
Scholar	M.	202	1	5	8	12	23	28	125
	F.	198	5	4	18	8	23	23	117
No Status	M.	204	–	2	2	6	1	7	186
	F.	208	2	6	3	5	10	3	179
Mine Boy	M.	66	16	24	9	12	3	2	–
Mine Girl	F.	34	8	10	7	6	3	–	–
Farm Servant		7	–	–	4	–	1	2	–
Farm Labourer		7	–	1	3	2	–	1	–
House Servant		13	4	3	3	1	1	1	–
Carpenter		1	1	–	–	–	–	–	–
Carter		18	6	3	2	3	3	1	–
Errand Boy		1	–	–	–	–	–	1	–
Cow/Ox/Plough Boy		7	–	2	1	2	1	1	–
Cordwainer		1	1	–	–	–	–	–	–
Mine Smith		1	–	1	–	–	–	–	–
TOTAL		968	44	61	60	57	69	70	607

NOTE: (M) Male, (F) Female

APPENDIX G
MENHENIOT MINERS BY OCCUPATION AND AGE PROFILE

1851	TOTAL	UNDER 15	15-19	20-29	30-39	40-49	50-59	OVER 60
Lead Miner	226	–	37	114	42	18	13	2
Mine Labourer	55	38	12	3	2	–	–	–
Mine Girl	57	14	27	14	1	1	–	–
Copper Miner	5	–	1	1	1	2	–	–
Mine Agent	6	–	–	1	1	3	1	–
Mine Engineer	9	–	1	4	1	3	–	–
Mine Engineman	1	–	–	–	1	–	–	–
Mine Clerk	1	–	–	–	1	–	–	–
Mine Cook	1	–	–	1	–	–	–	–
TOTAL	361	52	78	138	50	27	14	2

1861	TOTAL	UNDER 15	15-19	20-29	30-39	40-49	50-59	OVER 60
Lead Miner	280	–	69	111	55	28	12	5
Mine Labourer	120	66	19	10	4	8	9	4
Mine Girl	74	34	24	·15	1	–	–	–
Mine Agent	3	–	–	–	–	2	1	–
Mine Engineer	10	–	1	1	2	4	2	–
Mine Engineman	6	–	1	2	3	–	–	–
Mine Blacksmith	5	1	2	1	1	–	–	–
TOTAL	498	101	116	140	66	42	24	9

1871	TOTAL	UNDER 15	15-19	20-29	30-39	40-49	50-59	OVER 60
Lead Miner *	264	40	62	54	41	36	29	2
Mine Girl	36	6	17	12	1	–	–	–
Copper Miner	2	–	–	1	–	1	–	–
Mine Agent	7	–	–	–	2	2	3	–
Mine Engineer	4	–	–	1	1	2	–	–
Mine Engineman	7	–	–	–	3	2	1	1
TOTAL	320	46	79	68	48	43	33	3

NOTE * : Including Mine Labourers.

APPENDIX H

Menheniot's resident mining population had arrived from all over Cornwall during the boom years prior to the 1851 census. As an indicator of area of origin, all resident miners are grouped below by parish of birth adjusted, in the case of those with children, to birthplace of youngest child prior to their arrival in Menheniot or Liskeard. Menheniot born men predominated the mine labourers ranks, western/central men the fully fledged lead miner group. (See also map on page 70)

Western Men	Number	Eastern Men	Number
Kenwyn	22	Menheniot	66
Kea	18	Liskeard	7
Breage	16	Quethiock	6
Wendron	10	St Ive	5
Ludgvan	9	St Neot	5
St Agnes	8	St Cleer	4
St Erth	8	Bodmin	2
Crowan	5	St Keyne	2
St Hilary	5	St Winnow	2
Gwennap	4	St Germans	2
Perranuthnoe	3	St Teath	1
Camborne	1	Egloshayle	1
Gwinear	1	Duloe	1
Sithney	1	Antony	1
Redruth	1	South Hill	1
Grampound	1	Callington	1
Lelant	1	Millbrook	1
St Just	1	Pelynt	1
Phillack	1	St Minver	1
	116		110

Central Men	Number	Summary of Total	Number
St Austell	13	Western Men	116
Tywardreath	9	Eastern Men	110
St Mewan	6	Central Men	42
Roche	2	Not Known	11
St Stephan	2	Outside Cornwall	2
St Blazey	2		
Lanivet	2		281
Lanlivery	2		
St Ender	1		
St Ewe	1		
Luxulyan	1		
Cornelly	1		
	42		

APPENDIX I
MENHENIOT MINE MANAGEMENT TEAMS

WHEAL MARY ANN – Worked 1845-74

MANAGERS		MINE AGENTS	
1845	James Clymo	1847-65	Henry Hodge
1846-70	Peter Clymo Jnr	1849	Henry Vivian
1870-73	Joseph Harris	1853-54	P.P. Roskilly
1873-74	No Manager	1855-58	Robert Knapp
		1859-70	Joseph Harris *
		1860-74	James Stevens
PURSERS		1867-74	James Skeat
1845-70	Peter Clymo Jnr		
1870-74	William Nettle		* Became Manager

WHEAL TRELAWNY – Worked 1843-71

MANAGERS		MINE AGENTS	
1843-47	Peter Clymo Jnr	1844-49	Henry Vivian
1847-49	John Bryant	1847-49	Joseph Kemp *
1849-54	Joseph Kemp	1849-51	Thomas Ellery
1854-61	William Bryant #	1854-61	William Jenkin
1856-58	John Prince	1854-70	Thomas Grenfell *
1861-64	Francis Pryor	1862-64	Richard Pryor *
1864	Richard Pryor	1864-71	John Pryor
1864-70	William Johns	1865	Mr Trathan
1870-71	Thomas Grenfell		
		PURSERS	
# Managing Agent under		1843-47	Peter Clymo Jnr
John Prince 1856-58		1847-49	John Bryant $
* Became Manager			John Philp $
$ Joint Pursers		1849-61	John Philp
		1862-64	James Cock
		1864-70	Thomas Pryor
		1871	Not Known

WHEAL TREHANE – Worked 1846-57

MANAGERS		MINE AGENT	
1846-47	N. Faull	1846-47	John Bryant
1847-55	Samuel Richards		
1855-56	Thomas Woolcock	PURSER	
1856-57	M. Edwards	1846-57	John Philp

TREWEATHA – Worked 1852-72

MANAGERS		PURSERS	
1852	Not Known	1852	Not Known
1853	James Osborn	1853-55	J. A. Joseph
1853	William George Jnr (Temp)	1855-57	Mr Hambly
1854-60	Thomas Richards	1858-60	Not Known
1860-63	James Wolferstan	1861-63	James Wolferstan
1864-71	Thomas Foote	1864-67	Not Known
1872	Not Known	1868-70	Thomas Horswill
		1871-72	Not Known

MINE AGENTS	
1853-60	William Rowe
1861-63	Thomas Foote *
1861-71	John Scoble

* Became Manager

SOUTH WHEAL TRELAWNY – Worked 1845-54

MANAGERS		PURSERS	
1845-51	William Lean	1845-46	John Harvey
1851	William Jenkin	1847-50	William Lean
1853	Joseph Kemp	1852	Edward Crouch

MINE AGENT	
1845-50	William Jenkin *

* Became Manager

BUTTERDON Worked – 1850-57

MANAGER/AGENT		PURSER	
1851-54	Joseph Kemp	1851-57	John Philp
1854	William Bryant		
1854	William Jenkin		
1855-57	Thomas Grenfell		
1856-57	John Prince		

NOTE: All were Wheal Trelawny Agents administering Butterdon in a part time capacity.

WHEAL VENTON – Worked 1850-58

MANAGERS		PURSERS	
1850-53	James Osborn	1850	John Watson
1853-56	William George Jnr	1851	R. and S. Davey
1856-58	Thomas Richards		

PENHAUGER – Worked 1850-57/1859-61

MANAGER/AGENT		PURSER	
1853-54	Joseph Kemp	1857	John Philp
1854	William Bryant	1859-61	William Nettle
1854	William Jenkin		
1855-57	Thomas Greenfell		
1856-57	John Prince		
1859-61	Robert Knapp		

NOTE: Until 1857 all were Wheal Trelawny Agents administering Penhauger in a part time capacity. A separate Company worked the mine 1859-61.

SOUTH WEAL MARY ANN – Worked 1853

MINE AGENT		PURSER	
1853	Henry Hodge	1853	Thomas Nicholls

EAST TRELAWNY – Worked 1854-56

MANAGER		PURSER	
1855	P. Harvey	1855	Ponsford Fisher

LAMBEST CONSOLS – Worked 1856-58

MANAGER	
1856-57	Robert Dunstan

WEST MARY ANN – Worked 1875-84

MANAGER		PURSER	
1875	James Stevens	1875-84	William Nettle
1883	T. F. Tremellon		

WHEAL HONY & TRELAWNY UNITED LTD. – Worked 1880-84

MANAGER		CHAIRMAN	
1880-82	William Hancock	1880-84	George Brockelbank
1883-84	William Derry		
MINE AGENTS		SECRETARY	
1882-83	John Pearce	1880-83	H. R. Lewis
1882-83	Hubert Lanyon		

APPENDIX J
MINE PRINCIPALS AT HOME IN 1851/61/71

The majority of Menheniot mine agents lived either in the village or in nearby Liskeard. The Population Census for both places, taken every ten years, reveal many personal details about those who helped to build Menheniot's mines. Similarly their birthplace or those of their wives and children, gives vital clues to the families movements prior to arrival in the area. The absence of Liskeard or Menheniot born men becomes immediately apparent, confirming the mobility which existed. The following extracts are typical of the families of mining principals to be found in Menheniot and Liskeard at the time:

1851 Census – 30 March 1851
MENHENIOT VILLAGE

Henry Vivian	Head	Married	Aged 59	Lead Mine Agent	Born Camborne
Elizabeth Vivian	Wife	Married	Aged 50		Born St Austell
Ann Vivian	Daughter	Unmarried	Aged 23		Born St Austell
William Jenkin	Lodger	Married	Aged 49	Mine Agent	Born Illogan
Lodger at house of Richard and Catharine Pugh, Mason					
Henry Hodge	Head	Married	Aged 39	Lead Mine Agent	Born Sithney
Elizabeth Hodge	Wife	Married	Aged 30		Born Tregony
Ruth Snell	Visitor	Unmarried	Aged 14		Born Tregony
Mary Pollard	Head	Unmarried	Aged 87	Farmer of 41 Acres	Born Menheniot
Ann Tythe	Sister	Widow	Aged 86	Annuitant	Born Menheniot
Mary P. Hawkes	Niece	Widow	Aged 62	Annuitant	Born Altarnun
Mary L. Hawkes	Grand Niece	Unmarried	Aged 17	Scholar	Born Plymouth, Devon
John L. Hawkes	Grand Nephew	Unmarried	Aged 16	Scholar	Born Plymouth, Devon
Richard Coombe	Servant	Married	Aged 55	Agricultural Labourer	Born Linkinhorne
Mary Coombe	Servant	Married	Aged 56	House Servant	Born Lezant
Mary Haddy	Servant	Unmarried	Aged 32	House Servant	Born Liskeard
John A. Sommers	Servant	Unmarried	Aged 17	Agricultural Labourer	Born Halberton, Devon
NOTE Mary Pollard – Mineral Lord Wheal Mary Ann					

TREVARTHA, MENHENIOT

Joseph Richards	Head	Married	Aged 32	Lead Mine Captain	Born Mary Tavy, Devon
Mary Ann Richards	Wife	Married	Aged 20		Born Brazil, Sth America

QUARRY, MENHENIOT

Joseph Kemp Snr	Head	Married	Aged 41	Mine Agent	Born Gwinear
Grace Kemp	Wife	Married	Aged 42		Born Phillack
Joseph Kemp Jnr	Son	Unmarried	Aged 22	Mine Agent	Born St Erth
John Kemp	Son	Unmarried	Aged 17	Lead Miner	Born St Erth
Thomas Kemp	Son	Unmarried	Aged 14	Lead Miner	Born St Erth
Grace Kemp	Daughter		Aged 12	Scholar	Born St Erth
William Kemp	Son		Aged 9	Scholar	Born St Erth
Ann Kemp	Daughter		Aged 7	Scholar	Born St Erth
Henry Kemp	Son		Aged 5	Scholar	Born Menheniot
Lewis Kemp	Son		Aged 4		Born Menheniot
Mary James	Sister-in-law	Unmarried	Aged 50		Born Phillack

1851 Census – 30 March 1851 (cont.)

BARRAS STREET, LISKEARD

Peter Clymo Jnr	Head	Married	Aged 49	Mine Agent	Born Camborne
Mary Clymo	Wife	Married	Aged 41		Born Devonport, Devon

BARN STREET, LISKEARD

Thomas Ellery	Head	Married	Aged 56	Mine Agent	Born Redruth
Mary Ellery	Wife	Married	Aged 55		Born Camborne
Julia Ellery	Daughter	Unmarried	Aged 23		Born Camborne
Henry Ellery	Son	Unmarried	Aged 17	Lead Miner	Born Redruth
John Ellery	Son	Unmarried	Aged 15	Lead Miner	Born Redruth
Johnson Ellery	Son	Unmarried	Aged 19	Lead Miner	Born Falmouth

CASTLE STREET, LISKEARD

James Osborn	Head	Married	Aged 39	Mine Agent	Born Redruth
Elizabeth Osborn	Wife	Married	Aged 39		Born St Austell
Mary Osborn	Daughter		Aged 3		Born Liskeard
James Osborn	Son		Aged 2		Born Liskeard
Ann Osborn	Daughter		Aged 1 month		Born Liskeard
Jane Light	Servant	Unmarried	Aged 14	House Servant	Born Lanreath

TREVECCO COTTAGES, LISKEARD

Robert Dunstan	Head	Married	Aged 43	Mine Agent	Born Modbury, Devon
Ann Dunstan	Wife	Married	Aged 41		Born Tywardreath
Martha Dunstan	Daughter	Unmarried	Aged 18		Born Lanlivery
Elizabeth Dunstan	Daughter	Unmarried	Aged 17	Dressmaker	Born St Blazey
Ann Dunstan	Daughter	Unmarried	Aged 15	Scholar	Born Tywardreath
Sarah Dunstan	Daughter		Aged 12	Scholar	Born Tywardreath
John Dunstan	Son		Aged 10	Scholar	Born Lanreath
William Dunstan	Son		Aged 6	Scholar	Born Bodmin
Joanna Dunstan	Daughter		Aged 4	Scholar	Born Liskeard
Robert Dunstan	Son		Aged 2		Born Liskeard
Eliza Dunstan	Visitor	Widow	Aged 59		Born St Neot

1861 Census - 8 April 1861

MERRYMEET, MENHENIOT

James Stevens	Head	Married	Aged 40	Lead Mine Agent	Born St Agnes
Eliza Stevens	Wife	Married	Aged 39		Born Redruth
John Stevens	Son	Unmarried	Aged 19	Lead Miner	Born Kenwyn
Eliza Stevens	Daughter	Unmarried	Aged 17	Scholar	Born Menheniot
David Stevens	Son	Unmarried	Aged 15	Lead Miner	Born Menheniot
Katherine Stevens	Daughter		Aged 8	Scholar	Born Menheniot
James Stevens	Son		Aged 6	Scholar	Born Menheniot
Alma Stevens	Daughter		Aged 4	Scholar	Born Menheniot
Jessie Stevens	Daughter		Aged 1	Scholar	Born Menheniot

1861 Census – 8 April 1861 (cont.)

MENHENIOT VILLAGE

Henry Hodge	Head	Married	Aged 49	Mine Agent	Born Sithney
Elizabeth Hodge	Wife	Married	Aged 40		Born Tregony
Ruth Snell	Visitor	Unmarried	Aged 24	Dressmaker	Born Tregony

BARN STREET, LISKEARD

John Philp	Head	Unmarried	Aged 78	Mine Purser	Born Liskeard
Ellen Philp	Niece	Unmarried	Aged 31	Housekeeper	Born Okehampton, Devon
Eliza Barnecutt	Servant	Unmarried	Aged 20	House Servant	Born Liskeard
William Jenkin	Head	Married	Aged 59	Mine Agent	Born Illogan
Ann Jenkin	Wife	Married	Aged 54		Born Cubest
John Jenkin	Son	Unmarried	Aged 20	Miner	Born Camborne
Alfred Jenkin	Son	Unmarried	Aged 16	Miner	Born Camborne
Emily Pascoe	Servant	Unmarried	Aged 16	House Servant	Born Breage
Elizabeth Mutton	Grand Daughter		Aged 8	Scholar	Born Camborne

BARREL STREET, LISKEARD

William George Jnr	Head	Married	Aged 33	Mine Agent & Draper	Born St Mewan
Ann George	Wife	Married	Aged 33		Born Camborne
Ellen George	Daughter		Aged 8	Scholar	Born Liskeard
Charles George	Son		Aged 5	Scholar	Born Liskeard
Mary George	Daughter		Aged 3		Born Liskeard
Emily George	Daughter		Aged 2 months		Born Liskeard
Elizabeth Walters	Assistant	Unmarried	Aged 24	Draper	Born East Looe
Elizabeth Paull	Servant	Unmarried	Aged 19	General Servant	Born St Mewan

DEAN HOUSE, LISKEARD

Peter Clymo Jnr	Head	Married	Aged 59	Mine Agent	Born Camborne
Mary Clymo	Wife	Married	Aged 50		Born Devonport, Devon
Agnes Williams	Visitor	Widow	Aged 39		Born Redruth
Amelia Blaney	Servant	Unmarried	Aged 27	Cook	Born Gwennap
Charlotte Bowden	Servant	Unmarried	Aged 21	Housemaid	Born Looe

8 DEAN TERRACE, LISKEARD

Mathew Loam	Head	Married	Aged 42	Mining & Mechanical Engineer	Born Crowan
Patience Loam	Wife	Married	Aged 44		Born Gwennap
Michael Loam	Son	Unmarried	Aged 20	Pupil	Born Gwennap
Thomas Hannay	Art Pupil	Unmarried	Aged 19	Pupil	Born Gatehouse, Scotland
Sophia Husband	Servant	Unmarried	Aged 20	House Servant	Born St Blazey
Mary A. Buzza	Servant	Unmarried	Aged 16	House Servant	Born Gwennap

1861 Census – 8 April 1861 (cont.)

LOWER DEAN, LISKEARD

Robert Dunstan	Head	Married	Aged 53	Surveyor of Mines	Born Modbury, Devon
Anne Dunstan	Wife	Married	Aged 51		Born Tywardreath
Martha Dunstan	Daughter	Unmarried	Aged 29		Born Lanlivery
Elizabeth Dunston	Daughter	Unmarried	Aged 27		Born St Blazey
Anne Dunston	Daughter	Unmarried	Aged 25		Born Tywardreath
Sarah Dunston	Daughter	Unmarried	Aged 22		Born Tywardreath
John Dunston	Son	Unmarried	Aged 20	Chemist & Drugist	Born Lanreath
William Dunston	Son	Unmarried	Aged 16	Scholar	Born Bodmin
Robert Dunston	Son		Aged 12	Scholar	Born Liskeard
Mary G. Dunston	Daughter		Aged 9		Born Liskeard
Mary Sweat	Servant	Unmarried	Aged 18		Born St Neot

ADDINGTON PLACE, LISKEARD

Joseph Harris	Head	Married	Aged 44	Mine Agent	Born Camborne
Ann Harris	Wife	Married	Aged 49		Born St Blazey
James Harris	Son		Aged 7	Scholar	Born St Blazey
Ann Tomblyn	Servant	Unmarried	Aged 17	House Servant	Not Known

Thomas Grenfell	Head	Married	Aged 42	Mine Agent	Born Crowan
Elizabeth Grenfell	Wife	Married	Aged 49		Born Lanreath
Margaret Genfell	Daughter	Unmarried	Aged 19		Born St Just
Martha Wilcock	Aunt	Widow	Aged 76		Born Lanreath

CASTLE GARDENS, LISKEARD

William Bryant	Head	Married	Aged 54	Mine Agent	Born Perranuthnoe
Phyllis Bryant	Wife	Married	Aged 56		Born Perranuthnoe
James Bryant	Son	Unmarried	Aged 31	Lead Miner	Born Perranuthnoe
Elizabeth Bryant	Daughter	Unmarried	Aged 27		Born Perranuthnoe
Grace Bryant	Daughter	Unmarried	Aged 25		Born Perranuthnoe
Benjamin Bryant	Son	Unmarried	Aged 22	Lead Miner	Born Perranuthnoe
John Bryant	Son	Unmarried	Aged 19	Lead Miner	Born Perranuthnoe
Walter Bryant	Son	Unmarried	Aged 17	Scholar	Born Perranuthnoe
Alfred Bryant	Son		Aged 14	Scholar	Born Perranuthnoe

WEST CARADON, ST CLEER

William Johns	Head	Married	Aged 44	Mine Agent	Born Redruth
Mary Johns	Wife	Married	Aged 38		Born Tywardreath
Mary Johns	Daughter	Unmarried	Aged 16		Born Redruth
James Johns	Son		Aged 14	Accountant	Born Redruth
Andrew Johns	Son		Aged 10	Scholar	Born Redruth
Samuel Johns	Son		Aged 9	Scholar	Born Redruth
Johanna Johns	Daughter		Aged 5	Scholar	Born Gwennap
William Johns	Son		Aged 3	Scholar	Born Gwennap
John Johns	Son		Aged 2		Born Gwennap
Charles Johns	Son		Aged 10 months		Born St Cleer

1871 Census - 2 April 1871
MENHENIOT VILLAGE

James Skeat	Head	Married	Aged 31	Lead Mine Agent	Born St Blazey
Grace Skeat	Wife	Married	Aged 30		Born Tywardreath
John H. Skeat	Son		Aged 9		Born St Blazey
Joseph Skeat	Son		Aged 7		Born St Blazey
Elizabeth H. Skeat	Daughter		Aged 6		Born St Blazey
James W. H. Skeat	Son		Aged 5		Born St Blazey
Florence M. Skeat	Daughter		Aged 11 months		Born Menheniot
James Stephens	Head	Married	Aged 50	Mine Agent	Born St Agnes
Eliza Stephens	Wife	Married	Aged 49		Born Redruth
Kate Stephens	Daughter		Aged 17	Milliner	Born Menheniot
James Stephens	Son		Aged 16	Miner	Born Menheniot
Alma Stephens	Daughter		Aged 14		Born Menheniot
Jessie Stephen	Daughter		Aged 11	Scholar	Born Menheniot
Eddy Stephens	Son		Aged 9	Scholar	Born Liskeard

NOTE Spelt Stevens in 1861 Census and in most mining reports

John Pryor	Head	Married	Aged 34	Mine Agent	Born Camborne
Emma Pryor	Wife	Married	Aged 19		Born Sheriock
Richard Pryor	Son		Aged 1		Born Menheniot

TREGONDALE, MENHENIOT

Thomas Grenfell	Head	Married	Aged 50	Lead Mine Agent	Born Crowan
Elizabeth Grenfell	Wife	Married	Aged 57		Born Lanreath
Jessey Ford	Servant	Unmarried	Aged 27	General Servant	Born St Germans

TREWEATHA, MENHENIOT (appears to be Treweatha Farm House)

Thomas Foote	Head	Married	Aged 49	Lead Mine Agent	Born Berr Ferris, Devon
Jane Foote	Wife	Married	Aged 48		Born Berr Ferris, Devon
– Foote	Daughter	Unmarried	Aged 23	Draperist	Born Berr Ferris, Devon
Alfred Foote	Son	Unmarried	Aged 20	Carpenter	Born Berr Ferris, Devon
Henry Foote	Son	Unmarried	Aged 18	Blacksmith	Born Berr Ferris, Devon
Selina Foote	Daughter	Unmarried	Aged 16	Scholar	Born Berr Ferris, Devon
Ellen Foote	Daughter	Unmarried	Aged 14	Scholar	Born Berr Ferris, Devon
Lucy Foote	Daughter		Aged 13	Scholar	Born Berr Ferris, Devon
James Foote	Son		Aged 11	Scholar	Born Berr Ferris, Devon
Charles Foote	Son		Aged 9	Scholar	Born Berr Ferris, Devon
John Scoble	Head	Married	Aged 53	Lead Miner (*sic*)	Born Kea
Martha Scoble	Wife	Married	Aged 54		Born Kea
Ann Hill	Daughter	Married	Aged 23		Born Lanivet
James Scoble	Son	Unmarried	Aged 19	Lead Miner	Born Menheniot
William Scoble	Son	Unmarried	Aged 15	Blacksmith	Born Menheniot

ACKNOWLEDGMENTS

THROUGHOUT THE YEARS of research and then development of the book itself, numerous individuals have encouraged, contributed or suggested areas of new research; sometimes providing that final clue when a particular aspect was in danger of grinding to an inconclusive halt. I can only mention a few, but to the remainder offer my thanks for contributions large and small.

Acknowledgment goes to the staff of Birmingham City Library (where much of the *Mining Journal* research took place), the Public Record Office, Kew and London, the British Library Newspaper Library, Colindale, London, the Cornwall Record Office, Truro, the Local Studies Library, Redruth, and to the members of the Cornwall Family History Society, who freely corresponded and contributed to the stories of mining families. Specific contributions are acknowledged from the Rev. Gordon Moyle of South Australia, Mary Shipp of Tennessee, Brian Slee of Australia, Jim Barrett of Sheffield, George Bishop of Pensilva, Geoffrey Watts of Torpoint, Cyril Symons, Geoff Crocker, Henry Sneyd and Katie Collins, all of Menheniot, Philip Payton of St Cleer and Bernard Deacon of Redruth.

Photographs, memorabilia and postcard collections are all individually credited, with specific acknowledgements made to contributions from Henry Sneyd, Geoff Crocker, Justin Brooke and Alan Kittridge.

Roy Shambrook deserves special thanks for early support and suggesting useful research sources, whilst particular acknowledgement must go to Justin Brooke who kept me on the straight and narrow and provided constant support throughout the project, on to reading of drafts as the mining history chapters took shape. Lastly thanks to Deanna and Doreen who helped with the unenviable task of typing the draft, and to my wife Lin and family, who put up with a great deal as a minor interest became a major obsession. They, I know, will breathe a particular sigh of relief as publication becomes a reality.

BIBLIOGRAPHY

Allen, J. *History of the Borough of Liskeard*, 1856.

Barton, D. B. *The Mines & Mineral Railways of East Cornwall & West Devon*, 1964.

Barton, D. B. *The Cornish Beam Engine*, 1969.

Bolitho, P. *The Story of Methodism in the Liskeard District*, 1967.

Brooke, J. *Stannary Tales; the Shady Side of Mining*, 1980.

Burt, R. *Cornish Mines*, 1987.

Burt, R. *Lead Mining In Britain*, 1984.

Carkeet, J. *The Diary of John Carkeet*, 1873.

Collins, J.H. *Observations on the West of England Mining Region*, 1912.

Deacon, B. *Liskeard and Its People*, 1989.

Dines, H. G. *Metalliferous Mining Region of South West England*, 1956.

Foster, C. Le Neve, *The Lode at Wheal Mary Ann*, TRGSC Vol. 9, 1874.

Henwood, W. J. *The Mines of Menheniot, Lanreath & St.Pinnock*, TRGSC Vol. 8, 1871.

Jenkin A. K. H. *Mines and Miners of Cornwall, Part XII Around Liskeard*, 1966.

The Kinnaird Report. Sessional Papers, House of Commons 1864, XXIV Part II. (Public Record Office: ZHC BPP)

Liefchild, J. R. *Cornwall: Its Mines & Miners*, 1857.

Marshall, W. *Rural Economy of the West of England*, 1806.

Ormerod, I. *The 1873 Coal Strike in Burnley*, 1980.

Payton, P. *The Cornish Miner in Australia*, 1984.

Postal Directory for Cornwall, 1856 and 1862.

Spargo, T. *The Mines of Cornwall*, 1865.

Tredinnick, R. *Review of Cornish & Devon Mining Enterprise*, 1857.

Watson, J. *Compendium of British Mining*, 1843.

Webb & Geach *History and Progress of Mining in the Caradon & Liskeard District*, 1863.

Williams, J. *The Cornish & Devon Mining Directory*, 1862 and 1870.

NEWSPAPERS AND PERIODICALS

The Cornish Times [CT], Liskeard.

The Cornish Telegraph, Penzance.

The Liskeard Gazette & East Cornwall Advertiser [LGECA], Liskeard.

The Mining & Smelting Magazine (Volume 2, 1862) [MSM], London.

The Mining Journal [MJ], London.

The Mining World [MW], London.

The Peoples Weekly [PW], Moonta, South Australia.

The Royal Cornwall Gazette [RCG], Truro.

The West Briton [WB], Truro.

OTHER SOURCES

Cornwall Police Records. Cornwall Record Office: CC/POL/41.

Mines and Mining Maps and Records. Cornwall Record Office.

REFERENCES

Attention is drawn to these detailed references for those wishing to pursue research sources. Full titles of books, newspapers and journals are to be found in the Bibliography.

CHAPTER 1 - THE SCENE IS SET.

1. Allen, 1856.
2. MJ, 27 January 1849, 13 July 1872.
3. MJ, 27 January 1849, 6 January 1866; Watson, 1843.

CHAPTER 2 - MINING ORGANISATION & PRACTICE.

1. MJ, 5 July 1879.
2. Liefchild, 1857; MJ, 8 December 1849.
3. Kinnaird, 1864.
4. MJ, 8 December 1849.
5. MSM, 1862.

CHAPTER 3 - WHEAL TRELAWNY.

1. Cornwall Record Office R.4921.
2. MJ, 5 January 1856.
3. MJ, 10 November 1846.
4. MJ, 17 September 1859.
5. MJ, 25 May 1844.
6. MJ, 28 December 1844.
7. MJ, 26 July 1845.
8. MJ, 2 August 1845.
9. MJ, 14 February 1846.
10. MJ, 11 July 1846.
11. MJ, 31 October 1846.
12. MJ, 23 January 1847.
13. MJ, 9 January 1847.
14. MJ, 3 July 1847, 25 March 1848, 23 September 1848, 11 August 1849.
15. MJ, 27 November 1847, 27 Jan. 1849, 11 Aug. 1849.
16. MJ, 16 November 1850.
17. MJ, 6 September 1851.
18. MJ, 10 February 1849.
19. MJ, 17 February 1849.
20. MJ, 19 June 1849.
21. MJ, 22 May 1847, 29 May 1847.
22. MJ, 24 July 1847.
23. MJ, 27 November 1847.
24. MJ, 12 May 1849.

25. MJ, 20 December 1851.
26. Dines, 1956.
27. MJ, 3 April 1847.
28. MJ, 3 July 1847, 24 July 1847, 25 September 1847.
29. MJ, 27 May 1848.
30. MJ, 17 November 1849.
31. MJ, 6 January 1849.
32. MJ, 27 July 1850.
33. MJ, 26 April 1851.
34. MJ, 20 August 1853.
35. MJ, 15 October 1853, 17 June 1854.
36. MJ, 2 February 1861.
37. MJ, 16 February 1861.
38. RCG, 31 December 1870.
39. MJ, 6 April 1861.
40. MJ, 25 May 1861.
41. MJ, 3 August 1861.
42. MJ, 14 May 1864.
43. MJ, 19 November 1864, 17 December 1864.
44. Kinnaird, 1864.
45. Spargo, 1865.
46. Williams, 1862.
47. MJ, 21 March 1868; Williams, 1870.
48. MJ, 20 February 1864.
49. MJ, 18 March 1865.
50. MJ, 17 June 1865.
51. MJ, 16 September 1865, 23 December 1865, 23 June 1866, 29 September 1866.
52. Cornwall Record Office MRO R31E/J22.
53. MJ, 23 March 1867, 21 March 1868.
54. MJ, 22 June 1867, 21 December 1867.
55. MJ, 21 March 1868.
56. MJ, 20 June 1868.
57. MJ, 5 September 1868.
58. MJ, 19 September 1868.
59. MJ, 19 December 1868.
60. MJ, 25 September 1869.
61. MJ, 25 December 1869.
62. Williams, 1870.
63. MJ, 26 March 1870.
64. LGECA, 9 July 1870.
65. MJ, 22 October 1870.
66. MJ, 21 January 1871.
67. MJ, 15 April 1871.
68. MJ, 29 April 1871.
69. MJ, 20 May 1871.

70. MJ, 31 January 1873.
71. MJ, 8 July 1871.
72. PW, 23 July 1910.

CHAPTER 4 - WHEAL MARY ANN.

1. Kinnaird, 1864.
2. Webb & Geach, 1863.
3. Cornwall Record Office MRO/4196/BOX.
4. MJ, 26 July 1845, 28 March 1846, 31 October 1846.
5. MJ, 17 September 1859.
6. Brooke, 1980.
7. MJ, 6 June 1846.
8. MJ, 11 July 1846.
9. MJ, 10 October 1846.
10. MJ, 30 January 1847.
11. MJ, 10 April 1847.
12. MJ, 29 May 1847.
13. MJ, 25 September 1847.
14. MJ, 27 November 1847.
15. MJ, 25 March 1848.
16. MJ, 3 June 1848.
17. MJ, 22 July 1848.
18. MJ, 25 November 1848.
19. MJ, 19 May 1849.
20. MJ, 28 September 1850.
21. MJ, 17 November 1849.
22. MJ, 18 August 1849.
23. MJ, 27 January 1866, 2 November 1872.
24. MJ, 28 December 1850.
25. MJ, 15 February 1851.
26. MJ, 23 August 1851, 10 April 1852, 18 Sept.1852.
27. MJ, 18 December 1852.
28. MJ, 18 June 1853.
29. MJ, 24 September 1853, 15 October 1853.
30. MJ, 18 March 1854, 17 June 1854.
31. MJ, 23 September 1854.
32. MJ, 14 February 1857, 22 August 1857.
33. MJ, 19 December 1857.
34. MJ, 14 February 1857, 3 July 1858.
35. MSM, 1862.
36. MJ, 30 November 1861.
37. MJ, 29 September 1860.
38. MJ, 29 December 1860, 9 March 1861.
39. MJ, 13 June 1863.
40. MJ, 12 December 1863, 18 June 1864.

41. MJ, 17 September 1864.
42. MJ, 17 March 1866.
43. MJ, 18 June 1864, 10 June 1865, 15 December 1866, 13 June 1868, 26 March 1870; MSM, 1862.
44. MJ, 15 June 1867, 23 March 1870, 23 July 1870.
45. MJ, 13 June 1868.
46. MJ, 12 September 1868, 12 December 1868.
47. MJ, 13 March 1869.
48. MJ, 12 June 1869.
49. LGECA, 6 August 1870.
50. MJ, 20 August 1870.
51. MJ, 12 August 1871.
52. MJ, 9 September 1871, 9 December 1871.
53. MJ, 30 December 1871.
54. MJ, 9 March 1872, 8 June 1872, 7 September 1872, 7 December 1872.
55. MJ, 2 November 1872.
56. MJ, 7 December 1872, 15 March 1873.
57. MW, 19 April 1873, 30 August 1873.
58. MJ, 4 October 1873, 3 January 1874.
59. MJ, 4 April 1874.
60. MJ, 3 October 1874.
61. MJ, 14 November 1874.
62. MJ, 6 February 1875.
63. MJ, 6 March 1875, 19 June 1875.
64. MJ, 1 May 1875.
65. MJ, 6 March 1875.
66. Barton, 1969.

CHAPTER 5 - WHEAL TREHANE.

1. Collins, 1912.
2. Dines, 1956.
3. MJ, 20 January 1849.
4. MJ, 28 March 1846, 11 July 1846.
5. MJ, 13 June 1846.
6. MJ, 22 August 1846.
7. MJ, 24 October 1846.
8. MJ, 2 January 1847.
9. MJ, 29 May 1847.
10. MJ, 1 May 1847.
11. MJ, 1 May 1847, 12 June 1847.
12. MJ, 15 August 1846.
13. MJ, 25 December 1847.
14. MJ, 3 June 1848, 20 January 1849.
15. MJ, 29 December 1849.
16. Tredinnick, 1857.
17. MJ, 12 January 1850.
18. MJ, 23 February 1850.
19. MJ, 12 April 1851.
20. MJ, 29 July 1854.
21. MJ, 9 September 1854.
22. MJ, 26 July 1856.

23. MJ, 10 October 1857.
24. MJ, 16 July 1859.

CHAPTER 6 - TREWEATHA MINE.

1. Tredinnick, 1857.
2. Dines, 1956.
3. Tredinnick, 1857; Kinnaird, 1864; MJ, 14 April 1866.
4. MJ, 4 September 1852.
5. MJ, 9 April 1853.
6. MJ, 20 August 1853.
7. MJ, 15 October 1853.
8. MJ, 10 December 1853.
9. MJ, 24 June 1854.
10. MJ, 16 September 1854.
11. MJ, 18 November 1854.
12. MJ, 25 November 1854.
13. MJ, 5 May 1855.
14. MJ, 8 September 1855, 15 September 1855.
15. MJ, 8 December 1855.
16. MJ, 16 February 1856, 27 Dec. 1856, 8 Aug. 1857.
17. Tredinnick, 1857; MJ, 22 August 1857.
18. MJ, 7 November 1857.
19. MJ, 30 January 1858.
20. MJ, 26 September 1857.
21. MJ, 30 January 1858, 26 February 1859, 31 December 1859.
22. MJ, 21 January 1860.
23. MJ, 12 February 1859.
24. MJ, 9 April 1859.
25. MJ, 30 April 1859.
26. MJ, 24 September 1859.
27. MJ, 2 June 1860.
28. MJ, 28 July 1860.
29. MJ, 20 October 1860.
30. MJ, 5 January 1861.
31. Williams, 1862; Kinnaird, 1864.
32. MJ, 13 April 1861, 18 May 1861, 31 May 1862; Webb & Geach, 1863.
33. MJ, 5 September 1863.
34. MJ, 30 January 1864.
35. Kinnaird, 1864.
36. MJ, 20 February 1864.
37. MJ, 7 January 1865.
38. MJ, 18 February 1865.
39. MJ, 12 August 1865.
40. MJ, 23 September 1865.
41. MJ, 14 April 1866.
42. MJ, 19 May 1866.
43. MJ, 27 January 1866.
44. MJ, 20 July 1867.
45. MJ, 19 October 1867.
46. MJ, 23 November 1867.

47. MJ, 30 May 1868.
48. MJ, 21 November 1868.
49. MJ, 4 September 1869.
50. MJ, 18 December 1869, 11 June 1870, 30 July 1870, 11 February 1871, 18 March 1871.
51. MJ, 11 June 1870.
52. MJ, 11 February 1871.
53. MJ, 18 March 1871.
54. MJ, 10 December 1870.
55. MJ, 10 August 1872.
56. MJ, 7 September 1872, 14 September 1872.
57. Barton, 1969.

CHAPTER 7 - TRANSPORT COMMUNICATIONS.

1. MJ, 15 October 1853; Allen, 1856.
2. Webb & Geach, 1863.
3. Messenger, M. J. Paper on St Germans Quay Tramway.

CHAPTER 8 - MENHENIOT FAMILY LIFE.

1. Marshall, 1806.
2. Allen, 1856.
3. PW, 16 June 1923.
4. WB, 13 May 1842.
5. Cornwall Record Office CC/POL/41.
6. LGECA, 4 April 1857.
7. LGECA, 18 April 1857.
8. LGECA, 30 May 1857.
9. WB, 24 July 1857.
10. CT, 16 June 1860.
11. LGECA, 23 November 1861.
12. Bolitho, 1967.
13. Menheniot Parish Guide.
14. Postal Directory for Cornwall, 1856 and 1862.
15. Kinnaird, 1864.
16. Papers: Rev. Gordon Moyle, South Australia.
17. Papers: Brian Slee, Manuka, Australia.
18. Papers: Mary Shipp, Memphis, Tennessee.
19. The diary of John Carkeet 1873.
20. Payton, 1984.
21. PW, 23 July 1910.
22. WB, 19 September 1872.
23. WB, 18 September 1873.
24. Ormerod.
25. Papers G. Watts, Torpoint, J. Barrett, Sheffield.
26. MJ, 4 November 1848.
27. LGECA, 6 August 1870.
28. The Cornish Telegraph, 7 July 1880.

CHAPTER 9 - MINING ACCIDENTS AND MINERS HEALTH.

1. MJ, 1 December 1849.
2. MJ, , 5 December 1846.
3. MJ, 19 October 1850.
4. MJ, 23 August 1851.
5. LGECA, 31 January 1857.
6. WB, 25 March 1859.
7. MJ, 18 December 1869.
8. CT, 22 April 1871.
9. Kinnaird, 1864.
10. WB, 1 February 1897.
11. LGECA, 25 April 1857.

CHAPTER 10 - SMALLER MINING CONCERNS.

1. MJ, 6 December 1845.
2. MJ, 22 August 1846.
3. MJ, 25 April 1846.
4. MJ, 5 December 1846; Henwood, 1871.
5. MJ, 26 June 1847.
6. MJ, 3 July 1847.
7. MJ, 1 January 1848.
8. MJ, 10 June 1848.
9. MJ, 9 September 1848.
10. MJ, 4 November 1848.
11. MJ, 17 February 1849.
12. MJ, 19 January 1850, 13 July 1850.
13. MJ, 7 February 1852.
14. MJ, 5 June 1852.
15. MJ, 7 August 1852.
16. MJ, 22 October 1853.
17. MJ, 4 December 1858.
18. MJ, 25 May 1850.
19. MJ, 27 July 1850.
20. MJ, 28 September 1850.
21. MJ, 30 November 1850.
22. MJ, 28 December 1850.
23. MJ, 31 January 1852.
24. MJ, 7 February 1852, 13 March 1852.
25. MJ, 31 July 1852.
26. MJ, , 18 December 1852.
27. MJ, 28 May 1853, 4 June 1853.
28. MJ, 9 July 1853.
29. MJ, 29 December 1855.
30. MJ, 26 July 1856.
31. MJ, 27 December 1856.
32. MJ, 30 January 1858.
33. Dines, 1956.
34. Jenkin, 1966.
35. MJ, 13 July 1850.
36. MJ, 16 November 1850.
37. MJ, 10 February 1851, 8 April 1851.
38. MJ, 7 June 1851, 20 December 1851.
39. MJ, 3 April 1852.
40. MJ, 24 July 1852, 21 August 1852.
41. MJ, 18 September 1852.
42. MJ, 21 August 1852.
43. MJ, 25 September 1852.
44. MJ, 25 December 1852.
45. MJ, 10 December 1853.
46. MJ, 17 June 1854.
47. MJ, 5 August 1854, 9 September 1854, 7 Oct. 1854.
48. MJ, 14 October 1854.
49. MJ, 21 October 1854.
50. MJ, 2 June 1855.
51. MJ, 8 September 1855.
52. MJ, 5 January 1856.
53. MJ, 10 May 1856.
54. MJ, 14 February 1857.
55. LGECA, 2 May 1857.
56. MJ, 21 June 1851.
57. MJ, 5 July 1851.
58. MJ, 30 August 1851.
59. MJ, 27 September 1851.
60. MJ, 20 December 1851.
61. MJ, 26 November 1853.
62. MJ, 17 June 1854. 24 June 1854.
63. MJ, 18 November 1854.
64. MJ, 23 December 1854.
65. MJ, 5 May 1855.
66. MJ, 12 January 1856, 16 February 1856.
67. MJ, 10 May 1856, 14 June 1856.
68. MJ, 1 November 1856.
69. MJ, 27 September 1856.
70. MJ, 14 February 1857, 14 March 1857.
71. MJ, 8 August 1857.
72. MJ, 23 July 1859.
73. MJ, 10 March 1860.
74. MJ, 7 April 1860.
75. MJ, 12 May 1860.
76. MJ, 17 November 1860.
77. MJ, 12 May 1860, 17 November 1860; CT, 18 August 1860.
78. MJ, 13 April 1861.
79. MJ, 4 May 1861.
80. Webb & Geach, 1863.
81. MJ, 9 April 1853, 30 April 1853.
82. MJ, 13 August 1853.
83. MJ, 17 September 1853.
84. MJ, 23 September 1854, 18 November 1854, 25 November 1854.
85. MJ, 15 September 1855.
86. RCG, 3 October 1856.
87. MJ, 21 February 1857.
88. LGECA, 28 February 1857.
89. MJ, 6 June 1857.
90. MJ, 5 December 1857.

CHAPTER 11 - LATER MINING VENTURES.

1. MJ, 3 October 1874.
2. MJ, 2 May 1871, 12 August 1871.
3. MJ, 10 August 1872, 7 September 1872.
4. Williams, 1870.
5. Dines, 1956.
6. MJ, 25 October 1884.
7. MJ, 1 May 1875, 13 May 1876.
8. MJ, 11 December 1875.
9. MJ, 15 January 1876.
10. MJ, 29 January 1876.
11. MJ, 1 April 1876, 14 October 1876.
12. MJ, 24 August 1878.
13. MJ, 5 July 1879, 18 December 1880.
14. MJ, 31 July 1880.
15. MJ, 21 August 1880.
16. MJ, 25 December 1880.
17. MJ, 12 February 1881.
18. MJ, 16 April 1881; MW, 27 August 1881.
19. MJ, 3 February 1883.
20. MJ, 9 June 1883.
21. MJ, 18 October 1884.
22. MW, 15 November 1884.
23. MJ, 25 October 1884.
24. MJ, 21 February 1885.
25. MJ, 11 December 1880.
26. MJ, 3 July 1880.
27. MJ, 6 November 1880.
28. MJ, 2 July 1881.
29. MJ, 24 September 1881.
30. MJ, 25 February 1882.
31. MJ, 16 December 1882.
32. MJ, 11 July 1885.
33. MJ, 2 June 1883.
34. MJ, 3 December 1881.
35. MJ, 23 June 1883.
36. MJ, 28 July 1883.
37. MJ, 27 October 1883.
38. MJ, 3 January 1884.
39. MJ, 21 January 1884.
40. MJ, 24 April 1884.
41. MJ, 15 August 1885.
42. MJ, 17 November 1900, 1 December 1900.
43. MJ, 7 September 1901.
44. MJ, 15 March 1913.
45. Barton, 1969.

GENERAL INDEX

NAME INDEX